SAINTS
OF
VALOR

SAINTS
OF
VALOR

MORMON MEDAL OF HONOR RECIPIENTS

Sherman L. Fleek

Jim Gonyo

Good Bless!

Sherman L. Fleek

SALT LAKE CITY, UTAH
GREG KOFFORD BOOKS
2011

Greg Kofford Books
P.O. Box 1362
Draper, UT 84020
www. koffordbooks.com

2015	14	13	12	11	5	4	3	2	1

Library of Congress Cataloging-in-Publication Data

Fleek, Sherman L., author.
    Saints of valor : LDS medal of honor recipients / Sherman L. Fleek.
    pages cm
    Includes bibliographical references and index.
    ISBN 978-1-58958-171-5
    1. Mormon men—Biography. 2. Medal of Honor—Biography. 3. Soldiers—United States—Biography. I. Title.
    BX8693.F64 2011
    355.0092'8893—dc23
                            2011035698

Dedicated to all Americans
who served in the Armed Forces,
during war and peace,
and especially to those who
returned home scarred or who
"gave the last full measure of devotion."

CONTENTS

Part 3
The Cold War

FOREWORD

Robert C. Freeman

This book is expressly dedicated to telling the stories of Latter-day Saints who have received this nation's highest honor: the Medal of Honor. While surprisingly few in number, the individual stories of these heroes are anything but insignificant. These accounts are powerful and poignant, producing a keener appreciation for the notion of noble and selfless service. The scriptural ideal, "Greater love hath no man than this, that he lay down his life for his friends" (John 15:13), has no apter fulfillment than in the context of war. In the case of the nine Latter-day Saints whose heroic actions are vividly recounted by the accomplished military historian Sherman L. Fleek, five survived to return home and four did not. All were nonetheless prepared to give their lives for friends both known and unknown.

There is an obvious and understandable question that must be asked in connection with a volume such as this. It is simply this, "What of the countless others who have deserved such attention but who, through the vicissitudes of history, never had their day of fame?" It is true that many other fallen warriors and others merited this decoration. Likely some were Latter-day Saints. Of course, for various reasons the valor of some is not given its due attention. There are always issues of race, religion, and a variety of other cultural or political issues that are obstacles for what otherwise ought to be. In the end, we are left to embrace the eternal perspective that, in the case of the unnamed hero, like the fallen and unidentified soldier, daily remembered in our nation's best-known military cemetery, Arlington, they are surely known to God.

On the topic of Latter-day Saints in the military, the stories recounted in this volume represent a distinctive pinnacle; but the pattern of Latter-day Saints' service in wartime has been remarkable, from the experience of the Mormon Battalion down to the present day. Sherman Fleek tells the stories of five Medal of Honor recipients from World War II, two from Vietnam, and one each from World War I and Korea. Each story is unique. Each is worthy of preserving for Latter-day Saints both old and young and of telling again and again through the generations that follow.

The reality is that some of these individuals were not strong in the gospel at the time of their youthful service. One recipient didn't join the LDS Church until well after his service in the military concluded. Wisely, the determination was made to commemorate in this volume all soldiers who were Latter-day Saints by any definition and at any point in their lives who received this decoration. As a military historian, Sherman Fleek is not primarily focused on the spiritual qualities of these individuals. Instead, their achievement was valor in combat. Little in war is inspiring, but even with war's horrors, these gripping combat accounts can indeed inspire. As a Latter-day Saint himself, he wants to preserve the legacy of other Latter-day Saints in the military for us today and for those yet unborn.

The author has exerted great efforts to discover relevant government, military, and family records from which to reconstruct the stories of these men. The main focus has been to emphasize the circumstances and events for which their gallantry received the nation's highest military award. As we consider these heroes, we should think also of the families they left behind. Only three were married at the time of their service in the military. Most were young and single with bright hopes and futures ahead of them. Given their exhibition of courage and valor, they would have led full and contributing lives in society. But destiny willed it otherwise. We are simply left to be grateful for their gift of courage.

One of those who returned home, and the first Latter-day Saint to be a Medal of Honor recipient was Thomas Neibaur. Private Neibaur's story is particularly notable because through it we see that sometimes heroes are forgotten. On his return home from World War I, he was given a hero's welcome, but soon his celebrated status dimmed and he found himself left without means of gainful employment. Great struggles came to his family, and soon he was left a widower with several children to raise. Sadly, he was ill equipped to navigate the dreadful days of the Great Depression. He became a casualty of this terrible economic time like many other Americans, whereas twenty years earlier the Germans could not defeat him on the battlefield. Ultimately he returned his Medal of Honor to Washington, D.C., as a protest with the terse observation that the medal couldn't feed his family. The remainder of his life is one of pathos, cut short at the age of forty-four.

Following Thomas Neibaur's nearly unmatched heroism, eight other Mormons have been honored and recognized. For four of them, this recognition came after they had laid their lives on the altar of freedom and, as Abraham Lincoln declared, "gave the last full measure of devotion." Americans of other religious denominations also contributed to this gallant list of heroes. These nine Mormons are now also singled out for their service and valor "above and beyond the call of duty."

While this story is perhaps not unique in the annals of military history, for all of us it is a sobering reminder that we should never tire of paying tribute to the returning warrior who gives so much and asks for so little in return. At Margraten Cemetery in the Netherlands, established for American soldiers after World War II, appears the poignant reminder: "We gave our tomorrows so you could have your todays." And, oh how these men gave.

August 2011
Brigham Young University

INTRODUCTION

August 1967

Some days I recall this memory as though it were yesterday. The scene is vivid and alive with all the sights, sounds, and color of real life—even more now when looking back to that time using the spectacles of maturity, wisdom, and experience. Yet it was more than forty years ago; and I was young—a month short of twelve years old.

I recall very clearly that it was a typical lazy Utah summer morning. I was still drowsy and half asleep as morning broke bright and sunny in this desert land. It was still cool before the penetrating summer rays burned into your brain, baked your skin to a cherry red, and left your mouth parched by the oven-like heat. The Wasatch Range cast its purple shadow down upon a thin strip of flat valley land between the mountains' high grandeur and placid Great Salt Lake a few miles to the west of my home of Layton.

I was always a "morning person" even as a young kid. But this particular morning I was still in bed even though the sun had already risen from its slumber to exact activity from all living creatures.

As I lay there, I heard footfalls, the heavy steps of my father coming up the steep stairs of our split-level house. I heard the creak of the door and saw his roundish, pudgy face poke in. My older brother Roger was fast asleep in his twin bed next to mine.

"Sherman," he said in his normal voice—he did not think to whisper. "Do you want to go out to breakfast?" he asked with a half smile. "At the Sands Café?" Wow I thought! I jumped to the floor, smiled, nodded, and began to jam my feet into my shoes. Who needed socks? I slept in my shirt and cut-off shorts. Why change? It was summer, and I was a child of the sun.

As we climbed in our 1957 Pontiac station wagon, Dad looked at me through his dark sunglasses. Glenn Ottis Fleek—a thirty-year career veteran himself—always wore sunglasses a lot, even inside, because he had lost an eye and sunlight bothered his remaining eye.

"Before we go to breakfast, we need to do one thing," he said.

"Run an errand?" I asked.

"No. Attend a ceremony."

I sat back in the seat and looked out the window, "*Drat!*"

Twenty minutes later I stood among forty or so other people surrounding a large thing, covered with a white sheet or cloth. There were some men in blue uniforms, Air Force uniforms, and others in Sunday dress, suits; the few women and girls wore nice dresses. It seemed like a church thing, but it was not. Dad always dressed nicely, slacks and collared shirts. As for me, who cares? I was only eleven and this was not my thing anyway.

There were flags on staffs and rifles on military shoulders—an honor guard with no shooting. It was not a funeral. There were flowers on stands and a huge red, white, and blue ribbon tied around that strange thing shrouded by the cloth. I had no idea what it all meant. All I cared about was breakfast at Sands Café just down the road on Main Street in Clearfield. Yet there we stood at South Clearfield Elementary School.

The pledge of allegiance, and words and more words, speeches, the ribbon cut, the cloth removed from the waist-high monument, shaking hands, laughs and smiles; and then, finally we were off in our Pontiac.

Though I was not terribly interested in the entire affair, as we drove away, I asked Dad a question: "Why was the main guy—the guy they talked so much about—why was he wearing a medal around his neck? What was that thing?"

Dad looked at me, his eyes peeking over his sunglasses, and said, "Sherman, that is the Medal of Honor."

The Medal of Honor. I repeated the title.

"Who was that guy?" I ventured one more question as my stomach growled.

"Major Bernard Fisher. They just dedicated the park in his honor."

* * *

That was my first memory about the Medal of Honor, the highest decoration and honor the United States can bestow on a person. More than forty years later, retired Colonel "Bernie" Fisher is still with us, living quietly in Idaho, and well into his octogenarian years.

At age eleven I did not know or realize that Hugh B. Brown, a member of the LDS Church First Presidency, was in attendance that day representing the Church. Nor did I know that "Major" Brown had served in the Canadian Army during World War I. His attendance demonstrated a thin line in Utah—the Church and its unique connection in all civil and military affairs in Utah. Mormons as a people and the institution of the Church have always been deeply patriotic, despite historic experiences when they were victimized by state militias and government officials. They maintained that patriotism even as the rest of the nation plunged into bitter opposition to the Vietnam War. The Mormon people have never discarded their ideals of service, commitment, and duty for popular movements. President Brown was a symbol of that collective commitment. That connection is a central part of the story this book tells: LDS servicemen and their valor.

Since that time as a citizen, a professional soldier, and a military historian I have come to learn the incredible significance of the Medal of Honor. As all Americans should, I have the greatest respect, not only for the decoration, but also for the men who received this supreme award of valor.[1] This highest of all American awards and decorations, it is unlike other prominent awards or forms of recognition because it means that the recipient has performed an act of valor at great personal risk and peril. Since its establishment in 1861 during the Civil War, 3,477 Medals of Honor have been presented; nineteen individuals have received two separate awards of the medal. Nearly a fifth, some 600 of the recipients, died during the action for which they were later recognized. Four of the LDS recipients died in action and never knew they had received their nation's highest decoration posthumously.

The Americans who have been awarded this supreme decoration are themselves imperfect, normal humans with all the common talents, frailties, goodness, and weaknesses that are part of life. Most of them led exemplary lives after their acts of valor; a few did not. Those failings do not diminish their act of valor nor tarnish the honor of the medal itself. The gap between a shining moment and what may be years of frustration or adversity is part of human life. After all, the Medal of Honor is not a lifetime achievement award.

For nearly 150 years, the United States has recognized military heroes for extreme acts of gallantry during an armed conflict against the nation's enemies. Compared to the tens of millions of Americans who have served in times of peace and war, Medal of Honor recipients form a select and unique class of citizens. One example readily comes to mind; some four million American citizens served in World War I; only 124 received the Medal of Honor. The Distinguished Service Cross for the Army, the second in precedence after the Medal of Honor, has been presented to 13,000 individuals since that same time; whereas some 150,000 Silver Star Medals have been awarded.[2]

This is a book about nine American fighting men, who among other connections, have two common cords that bind them together. They are each a recipient of the Medal of Honor, and they are also baptized members of the Church of Jesus Christ of Latter-day Saints, commonly called Mormons. There are many connections and common threads that provide association, but these two are unique. Few Americans have received the Medal of Honor, and the Mormon community is a small but growing minority among the vast citizenry of this nation. Therefore, these two associations are narrow and also significant.

One of the purposes of this book is to tell the story of valor, to demonstrate to current and future generations what a real hero is. There are many types of heroes, and being a hero has different meanings to people. Some seem confused. Sports figures, entertainers, politicians, artists, authors, the wealthy, and powerful people are not actual heroes; they may be popular, successful, influential, and serve as role models to some, but they are not heroes in the true sense of the term. Heroes are individuals who willingly risk their lives in an act of bravery to save comrades and fulfill a mission. Police and firemen also share this distinction. Heroes can also be any citizen who, at the risk of his or her life, attempts to save others in danger. Some heroes have paid the ultimate price by sacrificing their own lives on the altar of freedom, selfless service, and devotion to duty. These are true heroes.

* * *

The service and sacrifice of Mormons in war began with the Mexican War (1846–48). Though Latter-day Saints served in state militia units in Missouri, especially particularly during the Mormon War of 1838, and in the Nauvoo Legion in Illinois in the early 1840s—the Mormon Battalion was the first time LDS people were enlisted into federal service during a declared war. Since that time, Mormons have served in all of America's wars, at home and abroad. The Mormon view of war aligns most closely with mainstream American ideals encompassing devotion to duty. Service to one's nation is a sacred duty and an article of basic LDS faith. In fact, there is no basis for pacifism or grounds to claim conscientious objector status, according to LDS doctrine. Individuals who do are making a personal choice. At times the Church has modified its basic programs to conform to military and political needs, such as limiting the number of missionaries during the draft years of the Vietnam War to make more men available for military service.

Mormons have served bravely, proudly, and sincerely in time of war. Mormon doctrine pronounces that Saints should "denounce war and proclaim peace" (D&C 98:16). Yet Mormon scripture, especially in the eclectic Book of Mormon, tells of warrior-prophets and of mighty soldiers serving in vast and bloody wars, and the desolation of entire peoples and lands as the result of warfare. These stories, like Joshua and David, prophet-generals in the Bible, provide examples of religious people taking up arms in defense of nation, liberty, family, and their people. Mormons from the early foundation of the Church to modern times have been nurtured on stories of the valor and heroism of soldiers. This has not changed. The compelling stories of these LDS Medal of Honor awardees need to be told to secure their memory and their sacrifice for the future. Hopefully, generations will to come to know and appreciate these brave warriors, imperfect as they may be, and will continue to inspire others as they inspire us today.

* * *

The history of the Medal of Honor is a proud story. The accounts of valor are compelling and sometimes heart-wrenching. It is best to let the story speak for itself. The final truth is that people, citizens, and especially soldiers, respect awards of valor. Whether jealousy, disappointment, or other human emotions follow for some people, there is great honor attached to elite decorations, especially the Medal of Honor.

The young American republic had no military system of awards and decorations for nearly a hundred years from the beginning of the American Revolution. Many Americans and patriots felt that medals, honors, and military orders were unfitting for a new republic because they smacked of European aristocracy and elitist grandeur. Yet, even General George Washington, the commander-in-chief of the American forces, established a Badge of Military Merit and awarded it to at least three enlisted soldiers in 1783, just before the Continental Army was disbanded. This was the only American military decoration until 1861.[3]

During the American Civil War, the U.S. Congress established "a medal of honor" for U.S. Navy sailors for bravery and meritorious service at sea. Then in 1862, another Congressional act established the Army medal "to such noncommissioned officers and privates as shall most distinguish themselves by their gallantry in action, and other soldier-like qualities, during the present insurrection." A year later, Army officers were included and the first awards were made. However, the Navy did not authorize the Medal of Honor for officers until 1915. Some 2,500 medals were awarded through the course of the Civil War. Many were bestowed for lesser acts of valor by later standards, mainly because the government had not established criteria that would further define the high standard. Many awards presented during the Civil War and the frontier wars would most likely not have merited a Medal of Honor under the modern process. That does not mean these individuals of the past did not deserve their recognition. It merely means that standards and the nomination criteria have evolved, just as the military has. In fact, after the Battle of the Little Bighorn in 1876, many awards were presented, some of questionable merit. The Army later convened a special board that advised: "The conduct which deserves such recognition should not be a simple discharge of duty, but such acts beyond this that if omitted or refused to be done, should not justly subject the person to censure as a shortcoming or failure."[4]

Another aspect that changed the Medal of Honor nomination process occurred in the 1890s when there was a rush of awards presented to Union veterans who individually submitted their own applications for the Medal of Honor to the War Department. There were so many that it became nearly a fad. With minimal review and oversight, hundreds of medals were presented, or in most cases, mailed to the self-nominees. One of these self-applicants was Joshua Lawrence Chamberlain, the hero of the Little Round Top at Gettysburg in 1863, who led the famous 20th Maine Volunteer Regiment. Many of these individuals deserved the award, but the "self-nomination" process was flawed; it diluted the high ideals represented by the medal. Later Congress established by law the requirement that nominations originate through the military chain of command and not the individual. Also, "gallantry and intrepidity" beyond what is normally expected of a soldier became a standard.

In 1916 the War Department convened a board that eventually revoked 911 Civil War and Indians war decorations and again provided more guidance.[5] In 1917, Congress, at the Army and Navy Departments' urging, began to establish other awards for different levels of valor or meritorious service. This year was an interesting one because the United States entered World War I in 1917; and it soon became obvious that, in such a large conflict, the armed forces needed to reorganize its award system. Thus, the "triad of valor and service" was established with the Medal of Honor, along with the Distinguished Service Cross (and the Navy Cross) for extraordinary heroism, and the Distinguished Service Medal (Navy version in 1919) for exemplary meritorious duty and service. The Silver Star Medal has a curious evolution. It was first established by the Army as the "Star Citation" and consisted of a miniature star pinned on the Victory Medal awarded to World War I recipients. Later in 1932, the Silver Star was established by Congress as a separate decoration as it appears today; the Purple Heart came forth in the same year. Other decorations followed such as the Bronze Star Medal and Legion of Merit in 1942 during World War II.[6]

Air Force   Army   Navy

Medals rendered by Hyrum H. Fleek, 2011.

The standards, criteria, and process for nomination for the Medal of Honor have become very stringent in recent years. Starting in 1972 (the last year of major combat in Vietnam), no combat survivors were awarded the Medal of Honor. That changed in 2010 when Army Staff Sergeant Salvatore Giunta received the Medal of Honor. Sergeant Giunta's courage in Afghanistan was such that after nearly forty years the Medal of Honor award was bestowed upon a living recipient.[7] Others have and will follow.

A final comment about the Medal of Honor is its title and official designation. No matter how this title and name has permeated our culture and official records, the real name and only name of this decoration is the "Medal of Honor," not the "Congressional Medal of Honor." Yes, it is bestowed in the name of Congress by the president but it has never been the Congress's medal. Congress has established two dozen military decorations. The people who are awarded the medal are "recipients" or "awardees." No one "wins" or "earns" the medal. It is not an academic degree or a footrace; every profession has its own vocabulary. These may seem like petty points, but when discussing matters of life and death, honor and valor, proper language and titles should be used.[8]

* * *

Nine Mormons have received the Medal of Honor for valor and gallantry above and beyond what is expected of a soldier in combat.[9] Although each one has a harrowing story of service and courage, some are more intense than others. Four lost their lives. One or two survived by what seem miracles, given their amazing actions and circumstances. All four branches of the service are represented: five Army (one was a pilot with the Army Air Forces during World War II), two Navy, and one each of the Marine Corps and Air Force. Four were military professionals who made the service their careers; five were not career-minded or we do not know because three died at an early age. They were mostly from Utah and Idaho, although one hailed from California, and another, a convert, came from Chicago. Only one served a proselytizing mission for the Church. Two were pilots; one commanded a battleship at Pearl Harbor; two fought in the South Pacific during World War II; one fought in France during the Great War; one served in Korea, and two served in Vietnam.

As for individual gallantry, as the reader will see, their stories are unique. One recipient landed his aircraft to rescue a downed fellow airman; another bashed two enemy soldiers' heads togehter and killed two others with his bare hands; another was a medic who treated dozens of wounded over a two-week period, repeatedly risking his life for others, and left the battlefield only after he was severely wounded; three recipients single-handedly stopped an enemy advance or attack; two of them perished in the act; one, though severely wounded, flew back to a base in England; his aircraft was so damaged that it was literally a heap of junk afterward; and, finally after an all-night action when enemy troops attempted a landing, one Mormon soldier disobeyed orders and remained at his fighting position; and then sadly, an LDS soldier experienced such personal tragedy and adversity after the war that he returned his Medal of Honor to Congress in protest.

***

This book describes each LDS Medal of Honor recipient in chronological order in a separate chapter. Each serviceman had a different military experience, but my focus is on the military story leading up to the day or events that resulted in the awarding of the Medal of Honor. This book is not a full biography of each person; therefore, their lives before and after the military story are briefly summarized with the fullest detail being given to the relevant military action. I have also, where appropriate, included religious or faith-promoting characteristics where they form part of the military story.

The most challenging problem I faced in this study was identifying and locating biographic material—especially official military documents to tell the story. In some cases there was ample material. Three of the nine individuals already have biographies written about them. Sadly, a few have little information because they died so young and so long ago that most of the family and friends who knew them are no longer alive, and documentary records are sparse. Here I had to rely on secondary accounts, more background and general information, to capture their valor and service. Regardless, each of these individuals performed incredible acts of courage—selfless service in the face of extremely dangerous combat conditions against great odds. They risked their lives to help their comrades-in-arms and fulfill their military mission.

My other hope is that those who read these accounts will find anew or reinforce a sense of awe and profound respect for the level of valor and devotion that the Medal of Honor requires, not only on paper but in the hearts and souls of Americans. The purpose of the Medal of Honor is to recognize and reward gallantry and intrepidity that are so rare that even the most battle-hardened combat veteran would recognize and be awed by such acts. Every generation needs heroes, and before us are nine Latter-day Saints who were heroes.

Notes

1. Technically, one woman, Dr. Mary Walker, a civilian contract surgeon, received the Medal of Honor after the Civil War. Later in 1916, the award was rightfully rescinded on the grounds that she was a civilian and that it was awarded based on meritorious service, not battlefield courage. Therefore, she was not eligible. She refused to surrender it. In 1977, President Jimmy Carter, bowing to political forces, reinstated the award.

2. US Army Center of Military History, http://www.history.army.mil/html/moh/mohstats.html (accessed September 5, 2009).

3. During the Mexican War and for a few years after, the Army awarded Certificates of Merit to soldiers for acts of valor in combat; also, during this era, the Army rewarded faithful service and valor with "brevet" honorary promotions.

4. Peter Collier, *Medal of Honor: Portraits of Valor beyond the Call of Duty*, 282.

5. Ibid.

6. The "silver star citation" was a small star device awarded for valor and attached to the Victory Medal during World War I. In 1932 Congress established the Silver Star Medal and also the Military Order of the Purple Heart. The Distinguished Flying Cross had been established in November 1918 for aerial service and gallantry.

7. Dana Hegeth, "Medal of Honor Is Bittersweet, Soldier Says," Washington Post, September 16, 2010, A-4.

8. Collier, *Medal of Honor*, 283–84.

9. In this book the term "soldier" may be used at times to represent all service-members of the separate branches of the armed forces.

Acknowledgements

"Feeling gratitude and not expressing it is like wrapping a present and not giving it."—William Arthur Ward

Without the assistance and generosity of many people, especially the families of the Medal of Honor recipients, there would be no *Saints of Valor*. I am deeply indebted to those who provided papers, letters, photos, and personal accounts, and especially official military documents and personnel records, and copies thereof. Without these and the great support of family, friends, and others, than it would have nearly impossible to ferret out the material and conduct the research required.

The list to thank is long, but the need to recognize is just as important. The guiding light and support of Robert ("Bob") Freeman, professor of history and doctrine at Brigham Young University, was crucial and very helpful. It was he who first alerted me to Thomas Neibaur and his story back in 2005, and then followed up with mentions of Edward Michael and Larry Maxam. His connections with so many LDS veterans and families were very important to this project. The surviving daughter of Thomas Neibaur, Marian Neibaur Hunkerford of Ohio, and his nephew Anthony Gardner of St. Anthony, Idaho, helped place me on the journey of LDS Medal of Honor recipients. From that connection, my biography of Private Neibaur emerged.

The two young men who lost their lives in the Pacific Theater during World War II, Nathan ("Junior") Van Noy and Leonard

Brostrom both from Preston, Idaho, was a challenge to locate and obtain any information at all because all the family and friends are long since gone. Jay McKenzie, a lawyer in town, came to the rescue. He was instrumental in obtaining, scanning, and then sending me dozens of documents on Van Noy and a few items about Brostrom. He was also the steward of PFC Brostrom's actual of Medal of Honor for several years.

Louise Michael, the widow of Lt. Col. Edward Michael, USAF (Ret) provided many documents, photos, and great assistance in research on this brave bomber pilot. At one point, she exclaimed that I needed to come to California because she had so many papers that I needed to sort through them myself, then I could decide what I needed. Gayle Alvarez of the Idaho Military Museum in Boise assisted with all four of the Idaho heroes over several years. She was especially helpful with information on Brostrom and also Sergeant David B. Bleak. Without her help, biographical research would have been very challenging. The Fisher families of Idaho and Utah sent me reports, accounts, and studies of Colonel Bernard ("Bernie") Fisher's story, not only during Vietnam but also of the rest of his life.

A special thanks goes to several individuals who helped me learn the story of Corporal Larry Maxam and his gallantry during Vietnam. I first learned of and then made contact with Larry's younger brother, Robin Maxam, residing in Australia. He also sent me copies of letters, documents, and photos of his older brother. He recommended that I contact Lt. Col. John B. Long, USMC (Ret), who provided me with copies of the actual Medal of Honor nomination packet and other critical information. I also talked with or corresponded by email with several Marines who served with Maxam in Vietnam. The crowning moment for me came in April 2010 when I attended the dedication of a Burbank City park in Corporal Maxam's honor. Hundreds were in attendance, including a half dozen older but still gung-ho Marines who had witnessed Maxam's courage. What a surreal experience it was for me to meet gallant men whose names already appeared in my book, to shake their hands, and offer them my heartfelt thanks. For several hours I listened as they recounted the exploits of their friend and buddy.

This book is pioneering in some ways but not in all. Of the nine LDS awardees, three already have biographies written about them. In 2007 Gary Toyn published, *The Quiet Hero*, about the Navy corpsman George Wahlen whose bravery and medical service on Iwo Jima saved dozens of wounded Marines. Sadly George Wahlen passed away in 2009. Gary reviewed and blessed my chapter on Wahlen. To well-known author and student of history Jerry Borrowman, I owe special thanks for his assistance and encouragement. Jerry was the true pioneer and trail blazer for LDS Medal of Honor history when he co-authored *Beyond the Call of Duty* with Bernard Fisher in 2004. Jerry also took time to read and comment on several of the manuscript chapters.

I would like to thank my good friends and discriminating readers of much of what I have written: John Roller of Stafford, Virginia, Randy Madsen of San Diego, California, and especially my mentor as a historian, retired Army Lt. Col. Joseph Whitehorne, Ph.D., of Virginia's beautiful Shenandoah Valley.

I received photos, documents and especially oral history interview transcriptions of several of these individuals from government sources; namely Dr. Jan Herman of the U.S. Navy Medical History Office in Washington, D.C., and Ron Still, historian of the U.S. Army Medical Department History Office at Fort Sam Houston, Texas.

Of course, I need to thank Lavina Fielding Anderson, one of the most distinguished and accomplished editors on earth. She and I wrestled with several points, facts, and that exasperating bibliography; but as she said, "The stories were riveting." The production team at Greg Kofford Books, headed by designer/typographer Loyd Ericson and production manager Angie Breeland met a demanding schedule with creativity and professionalism.

As a father, I take great pride in my young son, Hyrum Hinckley Fleek. His incredible skill, talent, and patience with me, produced wonderful graphic representations of some thirty decorations, both foreign and domestic, including ribbons and badges. By taking samples from on-line and other sources, he crafted these superb graphic designs that are not only striking but accurate and proportionately correct. He also developed and drew most the maps and some of the diagrams that help tell the story. What a wonderful experience it was for both of us to spend hours in front of his computer tweaking and creating these pieces of art in nearly perfect detail. I am so proud of him.

Sherman L. Fleek
September 2011
West Point, New York

PART 1
THE GREAT WAR

AN INTRODUCTION TO
WORLD WAR I

At 11:00 A.M., on the 11th day of the 11th month, November, 1918, the artillery guns, the rifles, the grenades, and the machine guns fell silent across the Western Front—roughly the border between present-day France and Germany. After fifty-two months of slaughter, some ten million men were dead, many millions more were wounded and brutally scarred for life. Families were devastated. The quiet sound of peace rolled across the land. The "Great War" effectively wiped out the military-age generation of men of most of Europe. It had started with the tragic and senseless assassination of the Austro-Hungarian heir-apparent by a group of teenage radicals in Sarajevo, the capital of Bosnia-Herzegovina, and had ended four years later with four major empires vanquished, several monarchies vanished, and the entire world changed in such a way that an atlas published in 1914 was obsolete by 1918. The entire map of Europe was changed.

The assassination of the Archduke Franz Ferdinand and his wife, Sophia, was the spark that fired an inferno that had been ready to incinerate the world for years. Radical politics and near-revolutions; socialism; the arms race of new machines of war; vast professional armies with manpower reserves of millions of citizens standing by; the relentless drive of colonial imperialism--all of these factors had ignited a "cold-war" conflict in which the slightest incident would erupt into international carnage. These factors were only topped by the ego and arrogance of nationalism, racism, and boundless, greedy financial capitalism that created a tinderbox, all too ready for a match.

The imperfect Treaty of Versailles, signed in June 1919 after silence loomed over the Western Front, was a reason for the birth of a German monster that preached an evil ideology that nearly destroyed Europe twenty years later. Thus, the Great War sired a second great war.

When guns opened fire in August 1914, they were the sounds, not just of a European war, but of a true world war. British and French colonial soldiers chased and fought German colonial forces through the lush verdant regions and grasslands of southeast Africa; British and German fleets fought major sea battles off the coast of Chile and Argentina; submarines preyed on merchant shipping across the Atlantic; Turkish troops of the Ottoman Empire defended Palestine, present-day Iraq, and Egypt from Allied armies. Even far-off Japan invaded German colonies in the Bismarck Islands of the south Pacific, wanting to be full allies in the war against the Central Powers.

Not only was it a global war, but it was a new war, a modern war of attrition that the world had never seen before. The war was the first great war of the industrial revolution where countries conscripted mass armies of millions of men, equipped with factory- and assembly-line-produced rifles, machine guns, gas masks, motor-vehicles, submarines, battleships, aircraft, and especially artillery. Projectiles and guns by the millions were produced in a relative quick time.

Today when people think of World War I, they envision four years of stalemate, trench lines, artillery barrages, and mass assaults across "no man's land" repulsed with hundreds and sometimes thousands of casualties. All this is true, but the war was much more than that in many ways. The new hellacious demons of "poison gas," "barbed wire," "aero bombs," "trench-foot," "U-boats,"

Soldiers of the 167th Infantry Regiment in the Western Front trenches. Photo courtesy of U.S. Army Signal Corps Collection.

and "tanks" entered the vocabulary. The Great War, like all wars, seemed endless and fruitless.[1]

Americans were fortunate to avoid the slaughter of the first three years, especially on the Western Front; yet they read about and dreaded the horror in Europe. Battle after battle, campaign after campaign, year after bloody year rolled on until the names, the places, and the body counts seemed meaningless. Yet like a magnet the insatiable pull eventually dragged the United States into this bloody nightmare. In early 1917, the German Emperor, Wilhelm II, agreed to a military stratagem, a risky gamble. His warlords promised that they could starve Great Britain by cutting it off from its food chain. Germany would conduct unrestricted submarine warfare against neutrals, including the United States. The intent of this plan would, they urged, then spell doom for France and finally defeat the Entente (Allies), resulting in victory for the central powers. However, this politico-military gambit failed.

After years of changing German neutrality policies with increasing numbers of American vessels and lives lying in briny tombs, American forbearance was exhausted. The Germans also tried a dastardly attempt through furtive conspiracies and diplomacy to lure revolution-racked Mexico into a war against the "Norteamericanos" to reclaim lost territory and cause a diversion. Such behavior, secret or not, was too much. On April 6, 1917, after President Woodrow Wilson asked Congress for a declaration of war, the American gauntlet fell.

Most Americans were ecstatic; a few were not; millions of young men enlisted; while some families dreaded the realities, the "Yanks" and "doughboys" sailed "over there" into a war. Few knew the full pain and misery that greeted them. Some 4.7 million Americans served, including women for the first time, in uniformed service; 116,000 did not return; nearly double that number were wounded; and 124 men received the Medal of Honor.

A twenty-year-old farmer from Idaho, an LDS-raised soldier, Thomas C. Neibaur, was one of them.

Notes

1. There are hundreds of quality books concerning the battles, campaigns, politics, and results of World War I. Perhaps among the best single-volume editions on the overall war are John Keegan, *The First World War*; and Martin Gilbert, *The First World War*. An excellent study of the American involvement is John S. D. Eisenhower, *Yanks: The Epic Story of the American Army in World War I*.

Private Thomas Neibaur after the Great War.
Courtesy Marian Neibaur Hunkerford Collection.
Unless otherwise noted, all of the photos in this
chapter are from the Hunkerford Collection.

Chapter One

PRIVATE THOMAS C. NEIBAUR
AND THE GREAT WAR

Slowly and with the assistance of a couple of German soldiers, the wounded American soldier climbed down the battle-scarred hill; his right leg was a bleeding mass. His face grimaced with pain, but he also showed a touch of relief as he finally realized that he would live. He had somehow survived the most deadly ordeal of his life. And although he was injured, he was also the victor. Huddled around him were eleven, frightened German prisoners; some were still holding their hands up high in the gesture of surrender. They were still puzzled about how one lone "Amerikaner" had been able to stop and defeat a counterattack of some forty-five of their comrades and then capture the survivors. The grimy Germans looked at him in wonder; they were also glad the war was over, at least for them; they, like the American, had survived.

The wounded, victorious American needed their help down the hill, staggering towards the American lines. In the soldier's hand was his pistol, that deadly small firearm with which just minutes before he had dispatched four Germans to the eternal realms. Now the watchful American held it to the head of one of the de-

9

feated "Huns" as a reminder not to try something stupid because—
though wounded and in pain—the young soldier-boy from Idaho
still had fight in him.

* * *

Thomas C. Neibaur was the first Latter-day Saint to be awarded the Medal of Honor. In France on February 9, 1919, General
John J. Pershing, commanding the American Expeditionary Force
of some 2.2 million soldiers in Europe, presented Neibaur and
seventeen other soldiers their medals. Neibaur stood in the shallow snow as the great general walked down the line of valor; the
citations were read, the medals pinned on tunics, and then hearty
handshakes were administered.[1]

Neibaur was twenty years old. Twenty years later, at age forty,
Thomas Neibaur would mail his prized Medal of Honor and six
other awards to Congress in Washington in a statement of protest
and anger. From the time he received the medal, his life changed,
as such a unique distinction has changed the life of every recipient.
He was a hero, applauded, loved, adored, and championed. His
first twenty years ended with an astonishing experience. The following double-decade would have thrills of popularity for Thomas, besides the joys of family life. Then dread adversity took three
small sons in sad accidents, along with injury, ill health, and personal ruin as the Great Depression threatened the very fabric of life
for all American families.

Of the nine Latter-day Saints awarded the Medal of Honor,
Private Thomas Neibaur's personal story is the most poignant. Of
the thousands of Americans presented with this medal, few, very
few, have rejected or cast off this decoration as a gesture of protest;
Thomas Neibaur was one of those few.

* * *

General John J. Pershing awards the Medal of Honor to Private Thomas Neibaur.

Thomas Neibaur was born of steadfast Mormon stock. Alexander Neibaur, Thomas's great-grandfather, mingled with prophets and leaders of early Mormondom. Alexander was born beside the majestic Rhein River in Germany, near Koblenz, in 1808. Alexander was a Jew, as was his father, Nathan Joseph *Neubauer,* "new farmer" in German. Nathan served in Emperor Napoleon's army as a surgeon in a Prussian corps allied to the French. Alexander became a doctor and dentist; at the time, the two professions were often combined.[2]

Alexander studied in Berlin and gained a university education in medical science. He also had a gift for languages, for he mastered several, including his native German, his household Hebrew, French, Latin, Greek, and Spanish. Migrating to Preston, England in 1830, Dr. Neibaur established a flourishing medical and dental practice, yet fate opened an interesting door for him.

Alexander was one day listening inattentively to work-women when he heard them speak of this new gospel preached by Americans. He jumped up from his leisurely repose on a couch and soon located the Mormon elders led by Heber C. Kimball. In 1837 in Ohio, the struggling Mormon faith under its young founder and first prophet, Joseph Smith, had decided to send missionaries to Great Britain.[3] Within weeks, Alexander was convinced that the Mormons preached the true gospel of Christ and was ready to be baptized and travel to America. Ellen, his English wife of German-Jewish descent, however, was a different matter. It took months of serious study and reflection before she accepted the new American church. Alexander and Ellen were the first people of Jewish descent to espouse the Mormon faith. Eventually, the Neibaurs made the difficult passage to the new world.[4]

The Neibaurs flourished in Nauvoo, Illinois, where Alexander became a close friend and instructor in Hebrew to Joseph Smith. After the assassination of Joseph and Hyrum Smith in 1844, the Saints were on the move again. The Neibaurs went with them, first spending some tough seasons along the Missouri River, then trekking to Utah in 1848.[5]

Alexander and his family began again in a strange land. One daughter, Rebecca, married a young businessman named Charles W. Nibley who was called to serve as a General Authority in the Church. One of their grandchildren would be the renowned Hugh Nibley, a man of letters and educational prominence in ancient studies, philology, and philosophy during the twentieth century.[6]

The Neibaur clan grew and soon spread beyond the boundary of Utah. By the late 1880s, James Neibaur, head of one Neibaur branch, and his family, had moved to the Bear Lake region of Idaho. On May 17, 1898, his wife, Elizabeth Croft Neibaur, gave birth to their ninth child and first son, Thomas, born in Sharon, Idaho, just across the border from Utah.

In 1905 James and Elizabeth moved to Sugar City, Idaho, a new town five miles north of Rexburg and some thirty miles west of the towering Teton Mountains. This rural town was built around a new sugar beet factory established by the Utah-Idaho Sugar Company. This enterprise had been heavily bankrolled by the LDS Church and wealthy and successful businessman like Charles Nibley, Thomas's great-uncle.[7] The Neibaur family would be affiliated with the sugar beet factory for the next thirty years. So was Thomas, after his return from World War I.[8]

Thomas was just an ordinary Idaho kid who loved the outdoors and farming and had a marvelous talent for music and singing. By 1917, on the eve of America's entry into World War I, he found the desire to serve in the military.[9] Fortunately for posterity, he wrote letters home from his initial military training and also while in France at the front lines. He also wrote a clear, detailed, and frank account of his military service soon after he returned home.

"I enlisted on March 30, 1917, as a volunteer in the National Guard of Idaho," wrote Thomas Neibaur. Thomas traveled first to Boise, the state capital, to be mustered into service, "but was not accepted until April 8, 1917" into the Army of the United States.[10]

* * *

Private Thomas Neibaur joined M Company of the 2nd Idaho Infantry Regiment; and because the war had just been declared, he was mobilized or ordered to active-duty service in the U.S. Army. Most of the men in his company were from small towns in eastern Idaho such as Rexburg and Idaho Falls. Soon, he and hundreds of others had started training in Boise. Then he went to Fort George Wright, near Spokane, Washington. The fort was an old military garrison dating from the frontier era. At this time in the Army, there was no standard basic training or "boot camp."[11] The training of new recruits was the responsibility of company and regimental leaders, junior officers, and mostly noncommissioned officers—the sergeants and corporals who were the backbone of any unit. These men were trained in the "school of the soldier," which was dismounted drill, marksmanship, camp hygiene, hand grenades, bayonet drill, and hand-to-hand combat. Thomas loved soldiering

and wrote home, "I would not change my position for that of a civilian." Soldiering was also a manifestation of his patriotism: "Well
dad I am not sorry that I joined when I did for I still believe it is a
duty that I owe my country."[12]

Soon after some months' training and a first duty assignment
of guarding railroad bridges and tunnels in northern Idaho and
eastern Washington, his unit was ordered to Camp Mills, New
York. He was assigned to the 41st Division, a regional organization
of Idaho, Oregon, Washington, and Montana guardsmen.

This newly assembled training camp was a tent city with tens
of thousands of soldiers from all across the nation. Here soldiers
learned the Army's "building block" approach to unit training:
squad, platoon, company, and then combined arms training with
machine gun companies, mortars, and artillery. After a few weeks
at Camp Mills, Neibaur and his fellows were transferred to Camp
Merritt, New Jersey, in early January 1918.

One of the minor decisions made at these camps would have
great significance in Thomas's life later. He had been trained on the
standard infantry weapon, the Model 1903 Springfield, bolt-action
rifle in caliber, 30.06. But now he was reassigned to an automatic
rifle team with a gunner, loader, and spotter or observer. Months
later in France, his small team of three would make history.

Arriving in France, Thomas joined thousands of others from
various divisions. The 41st Division would never see combat. It
became a "depot division" where the officers and men served in
logistical and training functions well behind the lines.[13] Neibaur
was assigned to Company M of the 3rd Battalion of an Alabama
National Guard regiment, the 167th Infantry. They were a rough
bunch of down-home country folk. Neibaur wrote after the war,
"They were a bit rough and a bit rowdy. But there were no boys
who'd stand by closer.... They were full of life and pep they had to
be doing something all the time. If there was nothing doing, then
they'd have to do *something*. They'd raise hell."[14]

Along with the 167th, three other regiments made up the 42nd
"Rainbow" Division. Two regiments, the 165th Infantry from New

Private Thomas Neibaur, 1917.

York and the 166th from Ohio, were part of the 83rd Infantry Brigade; whereas, the 167th, and 168th Infantry Regiment of guardsmen from Iowa were in the 84th Infantry Brigade. Besides the infantry, there was an artillery brigade, machine gun battalions, field hospitals and ambulance units, and a host of support soldiers.[15] An American division in World War I was a colossal monster of some 27,000 men.

* * *

In March 1918 the Germans launched Operation Michael, the first of five major attacks that are now known as the "Ludendorf Offensives." After defeating Russia in late 1917, the Germans moved a million men, tens of thousands of artillery pieces, and

Army Unit Table of Organization 1917

Unit	Commander	Officers/ Enlisted	Organizational Structure	Arms/ Equipment
Company	Captain	250	4 Platoons 58 men	Riflemen, automatic weapons, mortars
Battalion	Major	1,200	4 companies	
Regiment	Colonel	3,720	9 rifle, 1 machine-gun companies, 3 battalions	Machine-gun company
Brigade	Brigadier General (one star)	8,211	2 infantry regiments, machine-gun battalion	
Division	Major General (two star)	27,082	2 infantry brigades, artillery brigade, engineer regiment, signal battalion	72 artillery guns, 260 machine guns

Source: Gregory J. W. Urwin, *The Unites States Infantry: An Illustrated History, 1775-1918* (New York: Sterling, 1991), 161.

42nd Division Units (Neibaur's Chain of Command)

Unit	Commander	Status Experience
M Company	Captain Maurice W. Howe	Alabama National Guard
3rd Battalion	Major George A. Glenn	Alabama National Guard
167th Infantry Regiment	Colonel William Screws	Regular Army (Alabama native)
84th Infantry Brigade	Brig. Gen. Douglas MacArthur	Regular Army
42nd Division	Maj. Gen. Charles Menoher	Regular Army

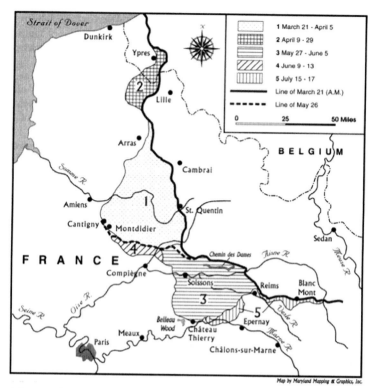

The Ludendorf Offensives were Germany's last gamble to win the war before the Americans intervened effectively. Used by permission of Simon and Schuster.

mountains of provisions and supplies to the Western Front. The grand architect behind the German spring offensives was the brilliant and austere Eric von Ludendorf, the Quartermaster-General of the German Army, a type of chief of staff for the general staff. The Germans hoped to crack the backs of the French and British before the Americans could intervene effectively. They nearly succeeded.[16]

The American effort, the American Expeditionary Force (AEF), was under the command of General John J. Pershing. "Black Jack" Pershing graduated from West Point in 1886, served on the frontier, and fought in Cuba during the Spanish-American War. In 1916, he led the American effort to protect the border during the

American soldiers in combat; the soldier on the left, fires the French-made Chauchat automatic rifle, the same type that Neibaur used. Courtesy U.S. Army Signal Corps.

Mexican revolution. President Woodrow Wilson appointed him commander of the AEF in May 1917.[17]

Pershing had his hands full in late 1917 and early 1918, and it was not only with the Germans. One of his major fights was against the allied field commanders. They wanted bodies—soldiers—and did not care to have American units fight in large formations. The French and British had bled themselves white against German guns and bayonets for four years, and all they wanted were replacements.[18] Yet Pershing steadfastly refused to break up his army.

During the spring and summer of 1918, Private Neibaur and the 42nd "Rainbow" Division fought in several major campaigns. These were mostly defensive in nature against the huge German onslaught. It proved to be a desperate time for the Allies, even though the German army was crumbling from within after four years of fighting along two major fronts, besides assisting the Austrians against the Italians in the Alps. The German people on the home front were weary and losing faith. The Ludendorf Offensives were their last hope.

In July the Germans reached what is called a "culminating point," the time and place during a battle or even a war, where resources, tactics, morale, popular will, and the ability to sustain the effort at the same intensity or "operations tempo" became impossible. It was like a long-distance runner hitting the wall. The Germans had reached their limit; cracks were forming in the seemingly impervious German armor. Yet the Germans retained the important operational principle: the initiative. Soon it would be time for the Allies to wrestle the initiative away from the Germans and end the war.

Thomas had just turned twenty in May 1918. He wrote home on June 10, "I'll tell you folks this is a funny life. I did not think a few months ago that I could ever have stood it."[19] He had been in the "trenches four different times and came through each time without a scratch." According to Neibaur, "We got in there [Chalons-sur-Marne] on the 4th of July. On the 3rd we were planning for a celebration of the Fourth, about ten miles behind the front lines."[20] He also philosophized a bit about his service and the mission of the allies and war effort: "We have a lot to deal with but still I would not miss it for I think we are over here in performance of a great duty to mankind and we should not take any notice of a little thing."[21] But the July 4th celebration was cancelled. The Germans were preparing their last offensive.

The night of July 14-15, 1918, was one of the most significant moments of the war. Neibaur related, "We were there in the front trenches for ten days anticipating an attack. We didn't know who was going to attack, we or the Germans, but on the night of the 14th after a big French celebration, we got word through prisoners we had taken that the Germans were to attack that night and that the barrage would start at 12:15, midnight."[22] The "big French celebration" was the anniversary of Bastille Day, July 14, the national holiday commemorating the French Revolution of 1789. Neibaur wrote after the war that the American officers decided to launch an attack with their artillery at exactly midnight and jump the German gun. "We beat them to it by just fifteen minutes," wrote Neibaur. "For awhile bullets were falling so fast and guns shooting so rapidly that if one had attempted to count the large shells that struck close to us, he would have had a big job on his hands."[23]

The transition from the defensive to the offensive is one of the difficult factors of war. "The next morning at 6 o'clock the Germans came over in one of their famous mass formations," Neibaur wrote, "We didn't think we would ever be able to stop them."[24] July 15 and 16 were a bloody struggle in which German tanks, heavy artillery, and massed infantry attacks threw themselves against the American position. German aircraft swarmed in flights of a dozen or more. Private Broc Hill of the 167th Infantry from Gadsden, Alabama, shot down a German aircraft with his rifle.[25] Corporal Chester Baker of the 28th "Keystone" Division of Pennsylvania wrote concerning July 15: "We saw ambulances overturned, their cargoes of wounded men—some still on their stretchers—now beyond all help. Tanks, twisted and useless, sat silent with their crews hanging dead from the tops of them; field artillery, battered into useless junk, their firing crews bloated corpses in the hot sun, the stench . . . the overwhelming stench that made us fight to keep our gorges down, and, most horrifying of all the clouds of vultures circling in the azure sky over the battlefield."[26]

The Germans led with a heavy artillery barrage against the forward line units. The 167th Infantry occupied the second system of defensive lines along the Aisne River and soon met a German bayonet charge. Historian James Cooke wrote, "All along the line, it was hand-to-hand fighting of the worst type, the first of its kind for the Americans, and the Alabamians held."[27]

Then the Allies counterattacked.

July 18 was possibly the war's turning point. Believing correctly that the Germans had reached their culminating point, French Field Marshall Ferdinand Foch, the Supreme Allied Commander, directed his staff to order the units in the Aisne-Marne sector to counterattack that same day. Two American corps, about 100,000 men, and several French divisions, including colonial troops from Morocco, attacked. Tens of thousands of allied troops "went over the top" sometimes at the same time, from their hastily prepared defensive positions. The Germans—exhausted, mauled, and at the breaking point after five major offensives and months of attacks—fell back, lost ground, and made a few spoiling counterattacks, but then began to retreat.

"It is not often possible to say of wars just when and where the scales wavered, hung, then turned for good," wrote American General Hunter Liggett after the war, "but when, at half-past ten of the morning of July 18 [1918] . . . the Americans and Moroccans [French colonial troops] had carried the plateau that gave artillery command of the main highway from Soissons to Chateau Thierry, the war's great divide was topped."[28]

Thomas recorded his version of the battle: "We were fighting in conjunction with the French, but the Germans kept coming on, wave after wave, until, I think, about 8 or 9 o'clock in the evening, they kept up a steady fire. Finally they quieted down and we made our counter-attack, and drove them back a distance of about fourteen miles on a forty-mile front." On July 18, the Rainbow Division was relieved, left the line, and rested for two days, then boarded army "motor trucks" for movement to a new sector: the Ourcq River.[29]

The division had its first serious tally of casualties: 256 killed, 71 died of wounds, and 1,240 were wounded. Most of these losses occurred on July 15.[30]

* * *

In August 1918, Pershing convinced Field Marshal Foch that the Americans were ready to man a sector of the line with their own field army, headquarters, and subordinate corps. Thus, the AEF prepared for a sixty-mile move south to the St. Mihiel salient. Pershing also organized part of the AEF into the U.S. First Army; he cleverly assigned himself as commander of the field army while retaining command of the AEF.

Since 1914 when the German forces first invaded France, a bulge in the line developed near the small city of St. Mihiel on the

Meuse River south of the principal fortress city of Verdun. This was the sector and mission Pershing sought—to reduce or break this "bulge" in the line.

It was a mammoth undertaking to move some 150,000 "Yanks," several divisions, and mountains of supplies hauled by hundreds of trucks and horse-drawn wagons, and then to launch an offensive on September 12, 1918, but the AEF succeeded. The Germans, unknown to the Allies, had already decided to withdraw from the St. Mihiel area in order to shorten their lines and reduce forces. So when the Americans attacked, the Germans conducted only a superficial defense and then withdrew. Tens of thousands of German prisoners surrendered to the Americans. "We had very easy fighting at this time," Thomas Neibaur wrote, "It was merely nothing. Some of the German officers would look around and try to find some officer of the American Army when they would surrender their men to us." The Americans reached their objectives quickly and pressed on. "We gave them heavy barrage and our barrage scared them." By "them" he meant the vast number of prisoners the Americans took.[31]

"I'll tell you folks this war sure is hard on a man," wrote Thomas in early October 1918, just a week before the heroic action that would change his life, "and nobody but a real man could stand it. One night a man is sleeping in a good warm place and the next night he's sleeping in a shell hole with nothing to [for] cover."[32] Such was Army life, and such was war.

Neibaur's regiment remained one of the two in the 84th Infantry Brigade; and by this time, it had received a new commander—Brigadier General Douglas MacArthur. Not to be outdone for future military fame, during the St. Mihiel attack, the 42nd Division was supported by a new developing arm of modern warfare: the tank corps. The feisty commander of the 1st Tank Brigade was Lieutenant Colonel George S. Patton. His tank brigade was support for the 84th Brigade's attack at St. Mihiel. Another famous military figure involved with the St. Mihiel offensive supporting the 42nd Division was Brigade General William ("Billy") Mitchell.

He commanded the U.S. Army Air Service units in this sector that provided limited ground close air support, besides keeping German aircraft from observing and reporting American operational movements and deployments. By late September 1918, the St. Mihiel campaign was over, and the AEF was on the move again.[33]

"I sure am delighted at the success we are having," Thomas Neibaur wrote home. "It seems as if the Germans cannot stand the awful fire of our artillery and the charges of our cavalry and infantry." Though written in early October 1918, just days before his last action, Thomas could sense the reality of the German collapse and the war winding down. As many others knew, the conflict was racing to a conclusion. "It does not seem as if this awful war can last much longer as the numbers of prisoners we are taking is so great that the German army must be getting somewhat weaker while ours is getting stronger all the time." He concluded in a realistic tone, "But still it is going to take lots of men and money."[34]

The Allies were planning a major operation, the final great offensive of the war. The American sector, the Meuse-Argonne, was one of the key sectors during that major campaign.

The best way to describe the terrain that the American forces faced would be comparing it to a lane in a bowling alley. The Meuse River Valley was only ten or fifteen miles wide at various points and ran north for some fifty miles to Sedan and the German border. On the right, was the unfordable Meuse. Rivers are always difficult propositions in war: a dangerous natural obstacle. On the left was the dense Argonne Forest, another natural barrier where the Germans had deployed many units and had very complex defensive positions.

The Germans fortified the Meuse-Argonne region with three separate but mutually supporting defense lines—a well-planned defense in depth. The German operational planners were clever in their name selection for the defensive lines, designating them in succession after the three witches in an opera by the German composer Richard Wagner: the Giselher, Kriemhilde, and Freya Stellungs. *Stellung* means "position or line" in German.[35] The first

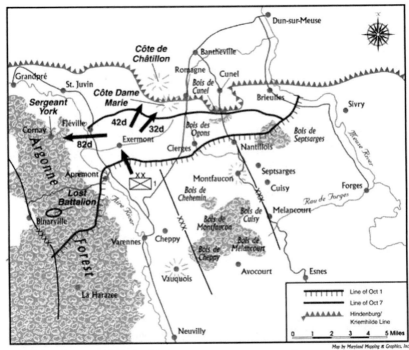

The AEF attack into the Meuse-Argonne sector, September- October
1918. Used by permission of Simon and Schuster.

defensive line, Giselher Stellung, had concrete emplacements
manned with machine guns among multiple trench lines, with wire
obstacles covered by artillery and mortar fire. Next came the main
defensive line, six kilometers back, the Kriemhilde Stellung, that
ran along the Romagne Heights, a rocky line of hills. Kriemhilde
was the strongest line of defense, because of the Romagne hills,
including Hill 288, Côte Dame Marie and the Côte de Châtillon,
where Neibaur's action would occur. The Kriemhilde Stellung
had formidable defensive measures and was not really a "line" of
entrenchments but rather "an elongated honeycomb of entrenchments," according to historian John S. D. Eisenhower.[36] Finally,
Freya Stellung was eight kilometers behind the Kriemhilde with
fewer emplacements, trenches, and gun positions. Of course, there
were tens of thousands of hardened, battle-worn Germans defending the "witches."

General Pershing wrote in his official report after the war's end: "The enemy's position had been strengthened during a period of four years by every known artifice in field fortifications, and was covered by a dense network of wire entanglements, with many concrete machine gun emplacements and dugouts."[37] Colonel Hugh Drum, the Chief of Staff of the U.S. First Army, called the Meuse River Valley "the most ideal defensive terrain I have ever seen or read about."[38]

The "dough-boys" crossed the line of departure, called the "jumping off line," on September 16, as scheduled. The first major objective was the town of Montfaucon, a key position at the southern portion of the valley. Montfaucon was nested on a high hill that dominated the surrounding terrain. The schedule called for it to be taken by noon on the first day. Instead, it took two days of serious fighting. The war was now evolving. Not since August and September of 1914 had the Western Front seen this switch from static trench-lines to maneuvers.

The Americans soon realized that the Meuse-Argonne was not to be like St. Mihiel; the Germans meant business this time. The American offensive basically ground to halt on October 4, after a week of horrendous fighting and losses. No one knew it yet, but the Meuse-Argonne battle of some seven weeks would be the bloodiest single battle in American history; some 26,000 Americans would be killed in action with triple that number wounded.

As the tactical situation developed, the significance of Côte-de-Châtillon became apparent. The senior American officers took more interest in the low, forest-covered hill, soon developing plans and allocating units to seize and hold it. MacArthur himself made a personal reconnaissance and offered the following account:

> This salient was dominated by the Côte de Châtillon stronghold which raked the Allied flank and thus stopped the advancing line of the American attack. Every effort to go forward had been stopped cold by this flanking fire. I carefully reconnoitered the desolate and forbidding terrain that confronted my brigade. There were rolling

hills, heavily wooded valleys of death between the endless folds of ridges. . . . I saw at once that the previous advance had failed because it had not been recognized that the Côte de Châtillon was the keystone of the whole German position; that until it was captured we would be unable to advance.[39]

The 84th Brigade planned its attack for October 14 to capture the crest and eastern slopes of Côte-de-Châtillon. The 83rd, its counterpart brigade, was to attack oriented to the north and advance toward Landres-et-St.-Georges across a wide, open plain of farmland and pastures.[40]

At 0830 on October 14, two American divisions, the 42nd and 32nd, attacked, but soon a gap developed between them. Gaps are frightful tactical problems. In military terms, it is ideal and critical to find the enemy's "seam" between two units especially in a defending force, to penetrate this seam, and thus "roll up the flanks." A seam or gap between units on the offensive is not as critical, but it is still a major tactical concern because the enemy can exploit it in a number of ways, especially by a counterattack. The "tie-in" or cooperation of two large units such as divisions was a critical tactical, coordination, and leadership imperative.

The first objective of the day for the Alabama 167th was La Musarde Ferme (farm) at the southwest base of Côte-de-Châtillon; whereas the Iowa 168th Infantry's assignment was to take La Tuilerie Ferme at the southeast base of Côte-de-Châtillon. The two French farms were like the base of a triangle with the summit or crest of the hill to the north as the point or the apex.

The German fire was deafening. Dozens of machine-gun positions in strongly developed networks swept the entire area from Côte-de-Châtillon. The Germans also employed well-directed artillery fire from Côte-de-Châtillon and other hills that blasted and enfiladed the 167th Infantry's flank as it crossed the low ground towards La Musarde farm.[41]

Neibaur wrote, "We lay there until the 14th [October] and then went over the top. We lost an awful lot of men in this fight, and didn't gain an inch of ground. The 15th the same." He continued, "We did not seem able to drive the Germans back an inch—they had too many machine guns."[42]

After the day's bloody butchery ended, a dramatic episode of comedic theater occurred at General MacArthur's headquarters. Major General Charles Summerall, the V Corps commander, visited without notice.[43] MacArthur recalled fifty years later that Summerall was "tired and worn, and I made him drink a cup of steaming black-coffee, strong enough to blister the throat." "'Give me Châtillon, MacArthur,' he suddenly said, his voice strained and harsh. 'Give me Châtillon, or a list of five thousand casualties.' His abruptness startled me." A list of five thousand names would be half of MacArthur's brigade. MacArthur's account ended with, "'All right, General,' I assured him, 'we'll take it, or my name will head the list.'"[44] This rejoinder was sheer bravado, soldier's whimsical talk, half ego, half foolish, asserted with total emotion at the frustration and horror of war. Thus, plans were made for the attack the next day.

* * *

October 16, 1918, Day of Days

Morning broke gray and misty after the rain stopped. Since the Americans were advancing across the open ground of the Meuse Valley, there were no trenches, no fixed positions and dugouts as in previous battle areas. The soldiers fought, advanced, and, when halted, took cover in shell holes or any other place they could. "Where available we got corrugated iron to put over the top and keep the rain out as best we could," Thomas related. "The ground was soaked with water, and whenever we lay down, our clothes would absorb the moisture from the ground."[45]

Some time in the early afternoon, word went from foxhole to foxhole and along the regimental line that an important mission was under consideration. An automatic weapon team was to silence a group of German machine-gun positions that were raking

the front of Neibaur's M Company and the 3rd Battalion with ferocious and accurate fire from about midway up Côte-de-Châtillon. Captain Maurice W. Howe, commanding M Company, asked
for volunteers to eliminate the German threat.

Thomas Neibaur and his team volunteered.

When asked ten years later why he volunteered, Thomas replied, "I don't know. A sudden rush of patriotism to the head I
guess." Neibaur, manning the heavy and second-rate French Chauchat automatic rifle; Boscarino, a big New York City Italian; and
a small blond soldier, whose name unfortunately is lost to history,
stepped forward. Captain Howe directed Neibaur's team to maneuver toward the sloping face of the northern spur on the hill to
flank German machine gun positions that were facing the battalion's lines.[46]

Côte-de-Châtillon was a low, round knoll that was forested on
most sides of the top at that time. The elevation of the hill rose to
270 meters above sea level or approximately 800 feet. The slope of
the entire hill mass was gradual. Coming down the hill were several
V-shaped spurs, two of which were on the western slope facing the
3rd Battalion. The southernmost of these spurs was important to
the Neibaur story. This "V" opened nearly due west with the point
aiming due east. Its two arms were northwest and southwest, almost at a 45° angle.[47]

The exact strength of the German forces in this sector was not
known. The Germans would have had a half dozen observation
posts with machine guns and riflemen forward of the main defensive positions. From Neibaur's own account, the Germans had several machine guns at the apex of the "V" that covered a frontage of
a kilometer or more off the hill. "On the right of this knoll [spur],"
wrote Thomas, "there was a nest of machine guns shooting down
on us, on an angle, and we were in a position where we could not
advance and strengthen our lines until that nest of machine guns
was cleared out." The objective was to destroy the machine-gun
positions so the 3rd Battalion could advance to mop up the last
resistance in the area.

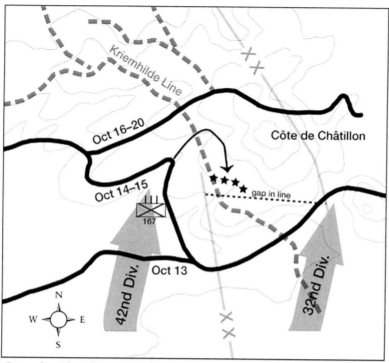

Côte-de-Châtillon October 16, 1918. Used by permission of
Utah State University Press.

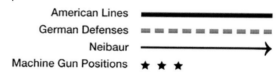

"I, with my scout [observer] and loader, crawled to the top of
the hill [north spur] where we encountered barbed wire entanglements," Thomas recalled.[48] The distance was approximately 150
meters (yards). Barbed wire and other obstacles are not meant necessarily to stop an attack but to delay and channel enemy forces so
that weapon systems can engage them, as in this case. It was hard
going, crouching, crawling from shell crater to shell hole, carrying
their weapons and ammunition. Neibaur lugged the twenty-pound
Chauchat automatic rifle. The three men tried to keep low to avoid

detection by the Germans; but crossing the north wing of the V, they were in full view of their own comrades.[49]

Then the Germans saw them and opened fire.

Neibaur, Boscarino, and the blond soldier, were all hit. "In getting over this wire entanglement I was shot in the thigh of my right leg three times, three bullets passing through the leg without breaking any bones, however," he wrote. "My loader and scout were both killed at this wire fence." The blond soldier died instantly. Neibaur crawled over to Boscarino, who was wounded several times; he soon expired.[50]

Realizing that his wounds were not serious, Neibaur crawled along the ragged landscape of shell craters to a small pile of dirt, tailings from a trench, and found cover behind it. He was armed with two full clips of twenty rounds each and a half-loaded clip— fifty rounds total. He also carried his personal weapon, a M1911, .45 caliber semi-automatic pistol of seven rounds, plus one in the chamber. The Germans then "counterattacked" Private Neibaur, who was a hundred or more meters from friendly lines and observed by his company and most of his battalion.

"I looked up. . . . I saw about forty to forty-five Germans coming up directly toward me," he recorded. "I quickly turned my automatic rifle on them and fired about fifty shots."[51] After the war, when author James Hopper asked if he were "hitting" any of the Germans, Thomas answered, "Yes, I was. Oh, I know I was! I could see them drop. But the others were still coming." With fixed bayonets, the Germans charged as Neibaur continued to fire, killing or wounding many of them. As he fired the remaining rounds of the third clip, his Chauchat jammed.[52] "I saw there was no chance whatever for me to get them all . . . so I turned and made the attempt to get back over the shell holes to my company" at the bottom of the ridge spur.[53]

Ten years later in the interview with Hopper, he explained, "Then I gave up. . . . I dropped the damned old gun right there, and started down the hill toward my own guys below me." His comrades provided covering fire as Neibaur crawled and half stumbled down the spur toward friendly lines. The German fire was intense. Pieces of dirt and earth sprayed up all around him as he negotiated this private "no-man's land."

Suddenly a fourth round pierced his right hip, crossed through his lower abdomen and lodged in his left hip near his spine, where it would remain the rest of Thomas's life.[54] Private Thomas Neibaur fainted and collapsed.

"This shot seemed to stun me just for a minute," Thomas recalled, "I fell on my face in the mud, and then the Germans, fifteen in number, came up and took my pistol away from me." Thomas recounted later that he was "in the hands of the Germans for about half an hour."[55]

"I was without anything to defend myself, and I certainly expected either to be killed or to go back to a German prison," he wrote. Meanwhile, his fellow soldiers continued their covering fire, forcing the fifteen German captors to take cover. In doing so, the Germans left Thomas unguarded and either failed to pick up his Colt .45 automatic pistol or merely dropped it.[56]

"About this time the Germans kept getting up . . . and the boys of my company saw them and fired a volley at them. None of the Germans were killed, but it scared them badly and they got down out of sight in the shell holes." Thomas saw his pistol and quickly realized that the opportunity to escape, or at least defend himself, was before him.

The fifteen Germans were so close by that Neibaur yelled at them in English to surrender, with no effect. Presumably the Germans had not scattered so much as to be unable to rush in a group, and there stood a wounded and defiant Private Neibaur with eight rounds in a pistol against fifteen German bayonets. "Why did they not fire?" the curious James Hopper asked rhetorically in 1928. Whatever the reason, "They didn't, and to this day Neibaur wonders why." Were they out of ammunition? Perhaps they did not realize he had retrieved his pistol.[57] In his own words Thomas wrote, "I then shot four of the Germans who were in the front attack and all this time I was calling on them to hold up their hands!" Regardless of language and historical era, belligerents understand the common signs or calls to surrender. "When they saw that four out of the fifteen were killed, the other eleven threw down their rifles, knocked off their helmets and raised up their hands," Thomas explained.[58]

He then marched his eleven prisoners off the hill. Some of the Germans had to assist him as he limped along.

* * *

Entering the friendly lines of his 167th Infantry, Thomas was undoubtedly shaken, excited, also in pain, and physically and emotionally drained. His officers asked him if he could escort his prisoners back to the prisoner collection point in the rear. He said he could. In the next few hours, Thomas faced extraordinary situations with officers of his own regiment and division. Thomas in his own words narrated this surreal episode:

> I took them back to the battalion headquarters, a mile or a mile and a half in the rear of the front line, and I expected to find my old Captain in charge of the battalion. He had been promoted to a Major, and was in charge of the battalion, as I thought, and I spoke to him rather familiarly, more so, perhaps than I should have done.
>
> I said, "Cap, I have about a dozen boys out here. Would like to have you look them over."
>
> The Major was a stranger to me, and as he popped his head out of a hole in the ground, he said, "This doesn't happen to be Cap, it is Major of the First Battalion."
>
> I told him I had some prisoners. He came up to the prisoners and looked at them, and at the insignia on their collars. He said, "Which one speaks English?"
>
> I said, "I don't think any one of them does, as I have been trying to talk to them."
>
> He said, "You don't know anything about it."
>
> That made me rather sore, but he examined them and tried to ask them some more questions. Finally he turned to me and said, "Did you take these prisoners?"

I answered, "Yes, sir."

"How did you do it?"

I said, "They attacked me, and I made a counter-attack."

He said, "How did you do it?"

I told him the story and then his attitude changed altogether. He said, "Son, give me your name and serial number, and when you get to the hospital write me a letter. Anything you want on this side you can have it. I will get it for you no matter what it costs."[59]

Thomas Neibaur then walked nearly three more miles to an aid station, finally boarded an ambulance, and was admitted to a field hospital. He was soon cleaned and washed, underwent an operation, and found himself in a bed with white sheets and a mattress—the first in nearly a year.[60]

* * *

"I received your letter today," wrote Thomas to his parents from Base Hospital #13 located in Limoges, France, on January 3, 1919. He continued after the normal salutations with this statement, "I suppose you were very much surprised to hear that I have received a medal [of Honor] for bravery." Then Thomas made an observation that many soldiers who received such high honors have repeated, "I am very proud of myself and I am going to try and live up to the reputation that I have made for myself altho it was nothing that any of my comrades would not have done under the same circumstances."[61] From his hospital bed, he wrote several poignant and touching letters.

Neibaur's wounds were not serious or life threatening, but they were incapacitating, and he never served at the front again. In late November 1918, a ghastly infection set in; and he had a second surgery. The army doctors decided to not remove the "magic bullet" that entered his right hip and passed through his lower abdomen to lodge near his spine on the left side.

During this time, the officers of his company, battalion, and regiment soon recommended Thomas Neibaur for the Medal of

Honor. The action had occurred on October 16; and by the end of November, the nomination was before President Woodrow Wilson for approval. This was an exceptionally quick nomination considering that the fastest method of communication in 1918 was the transatlantic telegraph. In early December 1918, the Neibaur family in Idaho received a letter from the War Department and first learned of Thomas's nomination and approval for the Medal of Honor.[62] For the next several months, family and friends in Idaho anxiously awaited Thomas Neibaur's return.

After recovering sufficiently to walk, Private Neibaur and seventeen other officers and soldiers were awarded the Medal of Honor by General Pershing at the AEF headquarters in Chaumont, France. Neibaur also had lunch with the general before returning to Base Hospital #13 in Limoges, in west-central France.[63]

Finally, in late April 1919, Thomas sailed home to the United States. He spent some time in hospitals at Norfolk, Virginia, and Detroit, Michigan. In May 1919, the Army discharged him from active service at Fort D. A. Russell, Wyoming, now Francis E. Warren Air Force Base.

* * *

On May 27, 1919, "upwards of 10,000 people gathered at Sugar City to do honor to the returning hero," published the *Rexburg Journal* on May 30. Among the distinguished visitors were Idaho Governor D. W. Davis, Lt. Governor C. C. Moore, the LDS Church's Presiding Bishop Charles W. Nibley (Thomas's great-uncle), mayors of local towns, military officers, and other dignitaries. Three high school bands played patriotic songs and marches. A procession and parade led the throng from the railroad station to the city park, where music filled the air and little girls suspended in a basket at the entrance of the park dropped carnations on the people as they entered. Governor Davis gave a speech and declared the celebration as "Neibaur Day" following his earlier official proclamation establishing May 27, 1919, as a state holiday. Then, at the apex of the ceremony and festivity, Private Thomas Neibaur stood up and, in his humble but direct way, explained what happened that day in France in October 1918. In awe the crowd of thousands listened.

"My friends, you can't imagine just what a pleasure it is to me to be back with you again," the *Rexburg Journal* quoted, "and realize all this has been done for me. . . . It is beyond words to express to see so many faces that I know and to see so many people that are out here for the purpose of welcoming me home."[64]

Renowned Idaho author and award-winning novelist Vardis Fisher recorded his memories of that special day, "when Tom Neibaur came back from the war. Of all the names in Idaho, his was on most tongues that day. His was the hand everybody wanted to shake; he was the man to whom everybody wanted to give a job."[65] Tragically, except for some speaking engagements, a few public events, and some veterans' conventions, this day, May 27, 1919, would be Thomas Neibaur's apex of fame and public acclaim. What followed was a slow slide into a downward spiral of adversity.

Thomas Neibaur was a gifted musician who also had a marvelous singing voice. At age twenty-one, a war hero, young, active, handsome, he and his two brothers, Leslie and Earl, and two cousins formed a band and hit the road playing at music halls, inns, and theaters across the Mountain West. In November 1919, he married, and his carefree days in a band came to an end.

One very important task Thomas performed during that summer of fun and frivolity was to write his personal account of his military service and especially his actions at Côte-de-Châtillon on October 16, 1918. His great-uncle, Charles Nibley wrote the introduction and arranged for the *Improvement Era* to print it. Thus, Thomas became the author of a personal article titled "How Private Neibaur Won the Congressional Medal of Honor," that appeared in July 1919.

Sarah ("Lois") Sheppard, four years Thomas's senior, married him on November 4, 1919. She was a strong and faithful member of the LDS Church all of her life, while Thomas had slipped away from active attendance even before joining the National Guard during his late teens. Soon children began arriving: Faye, then Marian, and then seven boys in a row. Thomas wanted to be a farmer but did not have the means to purchase sufficient acreage. He and Lois lived in Logan, Utah, during 1921-22 and 1923-24, where Thomas took some classes in agricultural science at Utah Agricultural College, later Utah State University; he did not graduate.[66]

Thomas was back in Sugar City and working in the sugar beet factory as an oiler on the heavy cutting machines, when the Neibaurs suffered the first of several tragedies. On October 18, 1925, eighteen-month Thomas Phil Neibaur, their oldest son, wandered out of the family yard, fell into an abandoned cesspool, and drowned. The family was devastated.

By this time, though only in his mid-twenties, Thomas was having difficulty with his wounds from the war. Further compromising his health were two separate episodes of gassing on the Western Front, his long-time habit of cigarette smoking, and bouts of frequent drinking.

Adversity struck the family again in 1928 when Neibaur was seriously injured in a work accident at the sugar beet factory. His right arm got caught in a cutting and slicing machine and was mangled terribly. Workers had to disassemble the heavy machine to free his arm, which became increasingly crippled over the remainder of his life. After two weeks in the hospital in October 1928, Thomas was home recovering when he had a special visitor, James Hopper from New York City, an author who published *Medals of Honor* the next year. Hopper interviewed Thomas and his parents and made some poignant observations about their family and home life.[67]

Hopper described Thomas and Lois's home: "The house was gay with cleanliness; the sun poured in through the wide windows; white starched curtains completed the effect of lightness and clearness." He described Lois Neibaur as "young, pink-cheeked, an overworked mother and housewife who refused to look overworked." Hopper wrote that Thomas sat at the table, arm bandaged, for the interview: "My first surprise was at his youth. . . . What struck me next were his eyes, clear gray-blue eyes in deep orbits—the eyes of a sharpshooter." Hopper added, "Now that I know Thomas Neibaur I think it would be good if the entire United States turned Mormon—his kind of Mormon."[68]

By the end of 1929 when America entered the "Great Depression," the Neibaur family was already in great need. The extended family assisted as best they could, but Thomas could hardly work. In November 1929, twin boys were born, bringing the children to six living offspring, all under age ten. The last two boys, Doyle and Gene, arrived in the early 1930s, rounding off the total of nine children, including their dead Thomas Phil.

In 1933, six-year-old Gordon Keith suffered from a rare disease that destroyed his sense of touch. Unable to feel pain, cold, or heat, he crawled up on the wood-burning stove one morning, suffered terrible burns, and died days later from infection.[69]

By 1935 the family moved to Boise due to dire economic challenges. Thomas was making $150 a month from his Medal of Honor pension and his clerical job in the Workers Progress Administration (WPA). Lois helped by doing laundry and sewing, but they were slowly sliding into poverty. In 1937, Thomas was on a job site away from home, and Lois went to visit him. Two-year-old Doyle toddled out of the yard of their rented home, was struck by an automobile, and died at the scene.

The Neibaurs moved several times in the Boise area, each time to a smaller, cheaper, and less adequate dwelling. They were not making it. Distraught and near the end of his options, Neibaur called on journalist Vardis Fisher, later one of Idaho's most famous literary luminaries. Fisher had an office in Boise at the time and was working for the Federal Writers Project. Thomas asked Fisher for a job. Fisher recalled, "He came into my office in Boise, a dirty and starved and ragged man, and asked for a job. Because he had had little formal education I could not give him a job on that project." Fisher still wanted to help, so "I hiked over to lay his case" before associates and colleagues at the state capital offices. "The Gov-

The day Thomas Neibaur sent his decorations to
Congress, 1939.

ernor said he would give Neibaur a job. . . . God knows Neibaur
needed it; he had a family and he was starving."[70] But Thomas had
no marketable skills, no formal education beyond high school, no
management or administrative experience. His only advantage was
his fame as a recipient of the Medal of Honor.

By 1939, many people felt sorry for his condition. Therefore
a combination of friends and others convinced the Idaho delega-
tion in Congress to submit a bill in Neibaur's behalf to have him
promoted to the rank of major in the Regular Army and add him
immediately to the retired list. The pension was about $2,250 per
annum. This measure was defeated in committee, mostly by the
influence of the War Department. When this negative message arrived in Boise, Neibaur was ready to act; he had already formulated

a plan. He called a small press conference of sorts and announced that he was returning his Medal of Honor and other decorations to Congress because he could not "eat them." In a cover letter he wrote to Idaho Senator William Borah, on April 10, 1939:

> I am sending you, under separate cover, my medal of honor and propose that you see to it that it is given to Secretary of War Harry Woodring, who no doubt has performed a much more patriotic duty to our country by saving the people the few dollars necessary to pay this claim than I did when I stopped an enemy counter attack and saved the lives of a number of American soldiers October 16, 1918, in the Argonne forest of France. I am trying to support a wife and seven children on the pay of a W. P. A. laborer, and the small disability allowance that I now receive, and I find that that [illegible] is not sufficient to support a medal of honor.[71]

Thomas wrote to a magazine journalist in Iowa in April: "I for one would be glad to exchange my medal [of honor] and all it has ever brought for a good job where I can make a living for myself and my family." Neibaur's frustration no doubt stemmed from his sense of responsibility as a father and breadwinner. His desire to support his family was commendable, though his methods, especially engaging the public in such a way may have been misplaced. "I have been trying for the past month to land a job with the state," Neibaur lamented, "but it seems they have no use for a broken down soldier."[72] His error was in listening to the assurances of friends and others that a Congressional act would authorize him a Regular Army pension. Secretary Woodring was correct—Thomas Neibaur did not deserve a full military pension—he did, however, receive the highest award for what he deserved—valor on the battlefield.[73]

Two days later, Neibaur received a call from state officials who offered him a position as a night watchman at the state capitol at double the income he was receiving, an offer he accepted. But he never saw his Medal of Honor again.

For the first time in years, the Neibaur family seemed to attain a degree of stability and the means to support itself, but another

The Neibaur boys in a Michigan orphanage in
1942. Left: Gene, twins Leo and Cleo, and Lamar.

tragedy was just around the corner. In May 1940, Lois Neibaur, his
good and enduring wife, died at age forty-eight, broken in health
by adversity and relentless work. Thomas had lost his anchor. The
family began to unravel. The two older daughters were already
married and gone, leaving Thomas and the four younger boys alone
in the house.

Thomas's health continued to decline until he could no longer
work. Thomas married Lillian Golden in 1941, a woman he met
in Boise. Later that year he entered the veterans' hospital in Walla
Walla, Washington. His four beloved sons were sent to a veterans' orphanage in Eaton Rapids, Michigan, because Lillian could
not care for them. They never saw their father again. Thomas C.
Neibaur died on December 23, 1942, at age forty-four as the result
of his war wounds, particularly the German mustard gas, and his
own habits that had further eroded his health.

Months after Thomas's death, his awards were returned to his
wife, Lillian Neibaur, who donated them to the Idaho State Historical Society in Boise.

THOMAS NEIBAUR

Rank and organization: Private, U.S. Army, Company M, 167th Infantry, 42d Division. Place and date: Near Landres-et-St. Georges, France, 16 October 1918. Entered service at: Sugar City, Idaho. Born: 17 May 1898, Sharon, Idaho. G.O. [Government order] No.: 1 18, W .D. [War Department], 1918.

Citation

On the afternoon of 16 October 1918, when the Côte-de-Châtillon had just been gained after bitter fighting and the summit of that strong bulwark in the Kriemhilde Stellung was being organized, Pvt. Neibaur was sent out on patrol with his automatic rifle squad to enfilade enemy machine gun nests. As he gained the ridge he set up his automatic rifle and was directly thereafter wounded in both legs [sic] by fire from a hostile machine gun on his flank. The advance wave of the enemy troops, counterattacking, had about gained the ridge, and although practically cut off and surrounded, the remainder of his detachment being killed or wounded, this gallant soldier kept his automatic rifle in operation to such effect that by his own efforts and by fire from the skirmish line of his company, at least 100 yards in his rear, the attack was checked. The enemy wave being halted and lying prone, 4 of the enemy attacked Pvt. Neibaur at close quarters. These he killed. He then moved alone among the enemy lying on the ground about him, in the midst of the fire from his own lines, and by coolness and gallantry captured 11 prisoners at the point of his pistol and, although painfully wounded, brought them back to our lines. The counterattack in full force was arrested to a large extent by the single efforts of this soldier, whose heroic exploits took place against the skyline in full view of his entire battalion.

Notes

1. In 1919 after General John J. Pershing arrived home to the United States, a grateful Congress passed legislation establishing the rank of "General of the Armies"—what would be the equivalent of a "six-star" rank. The only other American officer to hold this rank was George Washington, posthumously promoted in 1976 by another act of Congress, without back-pay and with an earlier date of rank than Pershing. It was not until the late 1930s that the Medal of Honor medallion would be suspended under the star-bedecked, sky-blue ribbon as a neck device so common today.

2. Susa Young Gates, "Alexander Neibaur," 52–62.

3. Ibid.

4. Fred E. Woods, "The Life of Alexander Neibaur," 23–36.

5. Alexander Neibaur, Journal, February 5, 1841–March 20, 1848.

6. Woods, "The Life of Alexander Neibaur," 23–36.

7. Matthew C. Godfrey, "Charles W. Nibley, 1907–1925," 101.

8. Leonard J. Arrington, "Launching Idaho's Sugar Beet Industry," 17–28.

9. Neibaur Family genealogical records, family organization and LDS Family History Library, Salt Lake City; copy in my collection.

10. Ironically, April 6, the day the United States declared war is a special anniversary for Mormons; the LDS Church was organized on that date in New York State in 1830.

11. Sherman L. Fleek, *Place the Headstones Where They Belong: Thomas Neibaur, WWI Soldier*, 42–44.

12. Thomas Neibaur, Letter to Mr. J. C. Neibaur, May 14, 1917, in Thomas C. Neibaur Letters and Papers.

13. *The United States Army in the World War 1917–1919: Military Operations of the American Expeditionary Forces*, 2:265.

14. James Hopper, *Medals of Honor*, 211.

15. The famous "fighting 69th" New York Volunteer Regiment during the Civil War was now the 165th Infantry during World War I; later in the 1950s the Army Department redesignated the 165th back to its famous New York militia roots of the 69th Infantry as it is known today. Jim Dan Hill, *The Minute Man at War and Peace: A History of the National Guard*, 265–68.

16. Anthony Livesey, *The Historical Atlas of World War I*, 150.

17. Frank E. Vandiver, *Black Jack: The Life and Times of John J. Pershing*.

18. S. L. A. Marshall, *World War I*, 307; John S. D. Eisenhower, *Yanks: The Epic Story of the American Army in World War I*, 119.

19. Thomas Neibaur, Letter to Neibaur Family, June 10, 1918, in Thomas C. Neibaur Letters and Papers.

20. Thomas C. Neibaur, "How Private Neibaur Won the Congressional [sic] Medal of Honor," 784.

21. Thomas Neibaur, Letter to Neibaur Family, June 10, 1918, in Thomas C. Neibaur Letters and Papers.

22. Neibaur, "How Private Neibaur Won the Congressional Medal of Honor," 784–85.

23. Ibid., 785.

24. Ibid.

25. Henry J. Reilly, *Americans All: The Rainbow at War, The Official History of the 42nd Division in the World War*, 270–71.

26. Chester Baker, quoted in Eisenhower, Yanks, 170.

27. James J. Cooke, *The Rainbow Division in the Great War*, 107.

28. Ibid., 162.

29. Neibaur, "How Private Neibaur Won the Congressional Medal of Honor," 785.

30. Reilly, *Americans All*, 302.

31. Neibaur, "How Private Neibaur Won the Congressional Medal of Honor," 786.

32. Thomas Neibaur, Letter to Neibaur Family, October 7, 1918, in Thomas C. Neibaur Letters and Papers.

33. General Billy Mitchell would be court-martialed in 1925 for defying official army policy in regards to aviation training, doctrine, and safety. General MacArthur served on the court-martial board.

34. Thomas Neibaur, Letter to Neibaur Family, October 7, 1918, in Thomas C. Neibaur Letters and Papers.

35. Vandiver, *Black Jack*, 2:956.

36. Eisenhower, *Yanks*, 251.

37. *Report of the First Army, American Expeditionary Force: Organization and Operations*, 38–39.

38. Eisenhower, *Yanks*, 200. Fort Drum in New York would be eventually named after Hugh Drum.

39. Douglas MacArthur, *Reminiscences: General of the Army Douglas MacArthur*, 66.

40. Cooke, *The Rainbow Division in the Great War*, 170.

41. Ibid., 171.

42. Neibaur, "How Private Neibaur Won the Congressional Medal of Honor," 786.

43. A corps is a tactical unit above the division and, from the British and French military practice, is designated by Roman numerals.

44. MacArthur, *Reminiscences*, 66.

45. Neibaur, "How Private Neibaur Won the Congressional Medal of Honor," 786.

46. Hopper, *Medals of Honor*, 229.

47. I made a personal visit to Côte-de-Châtillon in France on October 16, 2006, eighty-eight years to the day when Private Neibaur fought on Côte-de-Châtillon. The terrain description is mine.

48. Neibaur, "How Private Neibaur Won the Congressional Medal of Honor," 783.

49. Hopper, *Medals of Honor*, 221.

50. Neibaur, "How Private Neibaur Won the Congressional Medal of Honor," 787.

51. Ibid.

52. Hopper, *Medals of Honor*, 224.

53. Neibaur, "How Private Neibaur Won the Congressional Medal of Honor," 787.

54. Hopper, *Medals of Honor*, 225.

55. Thomas Neibaur, Letter to Neibaur Family, October 28, 1918, in Thomas C. Neibaur Letters and Papers.

56. Neibaur, "How Private Neibaur Won the Congressional Medal of Honor," 788.

57. Ibid.

58. Ibid., 789.

59. Ibid.

60. Ibid., 790.

61. Thomas Neibaur, Letter to Neibaur Family, January 3, 1919, in Thomas C. Neibaur Letters and Papers.

62. Colonel E. G. Davis, Office of the Chief of Staff, Department of War, Letter to J. C. Neibaur, November 20, 1918, Idaho State Historical Society.

63. Thomas Neibaur, Letter to James Neibaur, February 22, 1919, France, in Thomas C. Neibaur Letters and Papers.

64. "Neibaur Day Was a Big Success," *Rexburg Journal*, May 30, 1919.

65. Vardis Fisher, "Roses, Roses all the Way," [*Boise*] *Idaho Statesman*, January 4, 1943.

66. Fleek, *Place the Headstones Where They Belong*, 164.

67. Hopper, *Medals of Honor*, 207, 229.

68. Ibid., 210.

69. Fleek, *Place the Headstones Where They Belong*, 173.

70. Fisher, "Roses, Roses all the Way."

71. Quoted in Walter R. Bottcher, United Press, "Idaho's World War Hero, Eking Out Existence on WPA, Returns Congressional Medal of Honor to Congress," April 10, 1939. Photocopy of clipping from unidentified newspaper in my possession.

72. Quoted in ibid.

73. Fleek, *Place the Headstones Where They Belong*, 179–80.

PART 2
THE GLOBAL WAR

An Introduction to
World War II

What can one write about World War II that has not been written already a hundred times? Following an earlier world war, "The Great War," this second conflict was greater, longer, bloodier, and much wider spread. It was truly global. All oceans and most continents saw combat in some form. If World War I changed the map of Europe and the Middle East, World War II changed the world's.

The war was all encompassing and universal with some 16 million Americans in uniform. Latter-day Saints served in all the theaters of war, all the areas of operation, all combat zones, all branches of services, and for many of the nations at war—including the German forces. At the beginning of the war, the LDS Church membership was some 880,000 and by the end of the war in 1945, more than 100,000 Mormon men and women had served in American uniform.[1] Several thousand did not return home.[2]

From this war, five Mormons received the Medal of Honor, three of them posthumously. Mervyn Bennion was a professional officer, a graduate of the U.S. Naval Academy, who died while in command of a battleship at Pearl Harbor. He refused to leave the bridge despite being seriously wounded and continued to command his ship and inspire his crew until the end. Edward Michael was not a member at the time of his valiant service as bomber pilot in England. He was able to pilot his heavily damaged B-17 hundreds of miles back to England despite his own wounds, saving his crew members. Eighteen-year-old Nathan ("Junior") Van Noy died while repelling a Japanese night assault on "Scarlet Beach" with only the support of his machine-gun loader. Leonard Brostrom went from the LDS mission field to the battlefield, the only one of the nine LDS Medal of Honor recipients to serve a mission. He was killed assaulting a Japanese machine-gun position on the island of Leyte. George Wahlen, the last LDS recipient of World War II, was not a warrior, but a naval corpsman (medic) who for nearly two weeks treated dozens of marines on Iwo Jima. Despite being wounded three times, he refused to be evacuated. Only after a third and very serious wound would he allow others to remove him from the combat area. Junior Van Noy and Leonard Brostrom, by coincidence, were from the same small town. Today a monument marks their graves and valor in Preston, Idaho.

The following chapters and stories tell of heroism at Pearl Harbor, in the air over Germany, in the Philippines, Iwo Jima, and New Guinea. Two served in the Navy and two were Army, though one was a pilot in the U.S. Army Air Forces which later became the Air Force. The biographical and official information and material available about these five individuals varies. George Wahlen has already been a subject of a biography while only the sketchiest information exists about Leonard Brostrom.

These Latter-day Saints proved their mettle and willingness to serve and sacrifice.

* * *

For the United States and the Allied powers, the world conflict was divided into several theaters of war. The European Theater of Operations (ETO), which also included Africa and the Middle East, became the main and first priority. The objective was to defeat Hitler's Nazi Reich, which the Allied political and military leaders considered the most dangerous and important of the enemy Axis powers: Germany, Italy, and Japan. This consolidated war aim or international strategy became known as "Europe First."[3] Only a few dozen select government leaders, scientists, and military officials among both the Allied and Axis leaders knew about the potential development and use of nuclear weapons. The Allies believed correctly that Nazi Germany had the capability of developing this weapon. Therefore, a highly secret arms race occurred with two objectives: to defeat Hitler's Germany and to develop an atomic weapon themselves.[4]

Yet the war was fought with conventional weapons—rifles, tanks, aircraft, bombs, and ships across most of the world.

* * *

It was Adolf Hitler and his diabolical regime and ideology that caused the war. After Germany's crushing defeat in the First World War and the harshly punitive reparations and restrictions imposed on it, it defined itself as a victim and faced a political, economic, and moral vacuum. The Treaty of Versailles allowed the evil of National Socialism to spawn and grow. Hitler tested the will of the Allied powers to resist German rearmament and aggression by conducting several successful bloodless invasions. The fighting war began when Poland in September 1939 resisted Nazi incursions. By America's entry into the European war in late 1941, Germany was at the height of its power and success. Fortunately, Hitler insisted on an ill-fated and foolish strategy to invade Soviet Russia in June 1941 that landed the German army at the gates of Moscow. Only Great Britain had survived the Nazi juggernaut, but the Russian winter halted the German advance. Hitler's gamble to quickly annihilate the Communist menace of the Soviet Union failed. It took months of preparation, but the United States declared war in December 1941 as a result of the Japanese attack on Pearl Harbor and was promptly engaged in both theaters of war. Because isolationist sentiment had slowed American armament, it scrambled to put the home front on full

war-time production. American soldiers hit the beach in North
Africa in November 1942, then advanced to Sicily, then crawled
up the boot of Italy. Fascist Italy fell in September 1943, but Germany regrouped and fought a superb defensive campaign in Italy
for nearly two more years.[5]

The vast steppes of eastern Europe were the epicenter for the
rest of the war. Ukraine and Russia saw the ultimate and immense
battles of modern warfare. Millions of soldiers served in the German Wehrmacht and Russian "fronts," opposing each other during four grueling summers and winters that saw millions perish.
The names of Stalingrad, Leningrad, Kiev, Kursk, and Warsaw
are seared into German, Russian, and eastern European collective
memory. The United States and its citizens never saw, imagined,
or suffered the conditions of the eastern front.[6]

* * *

Japan was a brutal and difficult enemy to face and the main
characteristic of this theater of war was the huge Pacific Ocean, a
watery battlefield of millions of square miles, thousands of miles
across, surrounded by mainland continents and dotted by tens of
thousands of islands, small and large. Thus, the Pacific was divided
into two major areas: the Southwest Pacific Area under General
Douglas MacArthur, and the Pacific Ocean Areas under Admiral Chester Nimitz.[7] Both were Americans who also commanded
hundreds of thousands of Allied men, hundreds of ships, and tens
of thousands of Allied aircraft. The Pacific war was a daunting logistical challenge. What is called now the "operational art" level of
war evolved into an island-hopping strategy, moving from island
chain to individual islands in an inexorable and bitterly fought
advance toward mainland Japan. Some of these islands or groups
were huge—like the Philippines or New Guinea. Others were essential staging areas for forward bases and future operations. Iwo
Jima was one; Okinawa was perhaps the bloodiest fight. The Pacific was a naval war unparalleled in history. Vast fleets battled each

other by carrier and land-based aircraft, or surface engagements. Sleek, silent submarines, the jackals of the deep, carried out deadly attacks on commercial vessels and warships.

While the war in the Pacific was fought across a nautical arena, most of the troops in the Allied and Japanese efforts were ground forces. The United States trained and equipped six Marine Corps divisions to fight in the Pacific,[8] partnering with the U.S. Army's twenty-one combat divisions.[9]

The enemy was not only Japanese soldiers but beriberi, malaria, dysentery, and malnutrition. Americans served in beautiful, exotic tropic scenes and also nasty, sweltering jungles. Guam, Guadalcanal, Tarawa, and Saipan—names the soldiers and Marines had never heard two years earlier—became as familiar as Cleveland, Chicago, and Boston. Though Europe was a higher priority overall, the Navy and other branches received vast stores of provisions, ammunition, most of the naval craft, and several million troops. The way to Tokyo was long, slow, and difficult.

* * *

While the Pacific war's main characteristic was a huge ocean, the ETO's climate covered extremes: the harsh deserts of North Africa, the fertile farmlands of Italy, France, Germany, and the Low Countries, the rugged Carpathian Mountains and towering Alps, and lastly, the great steppes of the central continent, itself an ocean of ice and snow.

This global war was also a war of technology, gadgets, and devices: radar, napalm, radios, armored vehicles, and immense numbers of everything from toilet paper to hand grenades, from mountains of supplies to landing craft that could carry an infantry regiment along with their tanks. Bombers and German V–1 and V–2 rockets, jet aircraft, and airborne operations involving thousands of parachute troops landing behind enemy lines to wreak havoc were some of the facets of industrialized warfare. The Germans were innovative, but it was the American scientists who beat them to the ultimate prize: the atomic bomb. Beyond the atomic bombs, conventional bombs leveled scores of cities in Japan and Europe; tens of thousands of civilians died from fire-bombs, rockets, and calamitous after-effects of disrupted food and water supplies, inadequate clothing and shelter, and epidemics without enough doctors or drugs.[10]

By far the worst calamity that humankind has ever faced in world history was the Nazi holocaust. Millions perished in this methodical, organized, state-planned, state-directed, and popularly supported mass murder. Massacres have always characterized human warfare, but this campaign against Jews and other state-labeled "undesirables" was the lowest point in humanity's grim history. It is impossible to imagine that such a crime occurred, but it actually did.[11]

Finally, after six years the guns fell silent, the gates to the concentration camps opened, the bombs ceased falling, and the assembly lines of war and destruction stopped. Those who survived returned—but not to what they had left. Everything had changed.

* * *

In all these theaters of war, lands, campaigns, battles, and types of warfare, Mormons served. We, of later generations, the sons, daughters, and grandchildren of these veterans, sat around the firesides and kitchen table to hear the endless and marvelous tales of "the war." With pride, sorrow, and even a little bitterness, our parents and grandparents passed on their memories. Many did not tell their stories; their demons perished with them. Yet as a people, Latter-day Saints shouldered arms and marched off. Even in the hell of war, there were heavenly moments. Converts were baptized, chapels built, food shared, covenants kept, scriptures read, services held, and knees bent in sincere prayer.

What follows is the story of five Mormons who received the Medal of Honor for courage and valor above and beyond what is normally expected.

Notes

1. Robert C. Freeman and Dennis A. Wright, eds., *Saints at War: Experiences of Latter-day Saints in World War II*, 6.

2. An estimated 4,000 Latter-day Saints in the U.S. armed forces died in World War II. Statistical Report, *LDS General Conference Report*, April 1946, 168.

3. Richard W. Stewart, ed., *The United States Army in a Global Era, 1917–2003*, Vol. 2 of AMERICAN MILITARY HISTORY, 84.

4. John Keegan, *The Second World War*, 582–84.

5. Ibid., 460–68.

6. Ibid., 473–76, 512–15.

7. Keegan, *The Second World War*, 290. Nimitz also commanded two relatively quiet areas that experienced little combat, the North and South Pacific Areas.

8. Thomas Parrish, ed., *The Simon and Schuster Encyclopedia of World War II*, 649.

9. Stewart, *The United States Army in a Global Era, 1917–2003*, 123.

10. Keegan, *The Second World War*, 581–82.

11. Ibid., 288–89.

Captain Mervyn Sharp Bennion. Unless otherwise noted, the photographs in this chapter are from the U.S. Navy History Institute.

Chapter Two

CAPTAIN MERVYN SHARP BENNION AT PEARL HARBOR: THE APEX OF A DISTINGUISHED CAREER

W hen it comes to history, Hollywood films are seldom right. Add military history to the formula and Hollywood is rarely correct, no matter how exciting, how large in scale, how impressive the cast and talent, and how much money producers bankroll for the three-headed god they worship: to make a profitable, entertaining, and artistic film. History is hardly a priority when juxtaposed against these three. Such is the case with the 2001 film, *Pearl Harbor*.

The film had all the makings of a great historical epic: a compelling story—the Japanese attack on Pearl Harbor; huge star power (actors Ben Affleck, Cuba Gooding, Jon Voight, Kate Beckinsale, and newcomer Josh Hartnett); money to burn (a $150 million budget); established director Michael Bay; technical assistance and props from the U.S. Navy; and a timeless plot—a romantic triangle. The formula was unbeatable; and the teasers, or trailers, were incredibly appealing. Yet after viewing the film, we military historians found little to praise. Historian Max Boot pronounced

Pearl Harbor as "simply execrable."[1] Though *Pearl Harbor* raked in hundreds of millions of dollars, it was a historical flop, not reaching the mark of an epic film telling an epic story. One only wonders after the successes of *Saving Private Ryan*, HBO's *Band of Brothers*, and *We Were Soldiers*, why Hollywood screwed up this film so much. The film's problems with history were legion, and it would take chapters to explain why. Yet there was one redeeming quality that *Pearl Harbor* inadvertently included in the Japanese attack. Dramatic scenes portrayed a battleship commander, wounded and dying, but still in command.

In the film, as Japanese aircraft, "Kates," "Vals," and "Zeroes," are bombing, strafing, and dropping torpedoes, Cuba Gooding, playing the part of real hero Mess Attendant 3rd Class Doris ("Dorie") Miller, climbs to the bridge of the USS *West Virginia*. Miller in history was a mess steward and served food not only for the crew but also to the commanding officer of the 34,000-ton battleship. The film depicted a wonderful quality of loyalty and respect between the captain of the ship and his immediate staff, a true relationship. Miller, played superbly by Gooding, is shocked when he reaches the bridge, just minutes after the first bombs fell, to find his commander sprawled on the deck, mortally wounded, in a spreading pool of blood. Horror and regret visibly well up inside him. (In the film, it was a torpedo that slammed into the battleship at the water line, causing the destruction to the bridge thirty feet above—which is not true and factual).

With firm courage and composure, the captain, a thirty-one-year veteran of the Navy, instilled strength and confidence not only in Miller but also in all the crew members and officers who saw him that tragic morning. However, the scriptwriters improvised on the truth and had the mortally wounded captain tell Miller to get word to the executive officer to immediately assume command of the ship. Then, Miller manned an antiaircraft gun, though untrained in gunnery, and began to engage Japanese aircraft. In the film, actor Cuba Gooding seemed to be enjoying the fun and wild

Mess Attendant 3rd Class Doris Miller who treated Captain Bennion and later received the Navy Cross for bravery.

excitement of firing a twin Browning .50 caliber machine gun. Later the real Doris Miller received the Navy Cross for his gallantry.

This commanding officer was played by veteran British actor Peter Firth, who, for some reason, spoke with a southern accent. His lines and portrayal were contrary to a dozen eyewitness accounts. The real captain maintained command of the damaged ship, directed the crew, refused to be removed, and issued warnings and orders until he succumbed. That is why he was later awarded the Medal of Honor. Of course in films, time is often hurried to develop plot and storyline, but this expedient was unfortunate.

The naval officer who remained at his station, commanded the USS *West Virginia,* inspired his crew, and then died, was a Latter-day Saint and the second Mormon to receive the Medal of Honor. His name: Mervyn Sharp Bennion.

* * *

Of the nine LDS Medal of Honor awardees, Captain Mervyn Bennion was perhaps the most professionally trained and best-prepared service member of them all at the time of his action. He was a U.S. Naval Academy graduate, an officer who had served on four vessels—all battleships—that were sunk or damaged on that infamous December morning: the *Tennessee, Arizona, California,* and *West Virginia.* He had held posts of great distinction and re-sponsibility as he climbed the ranks of the Navy—gunnery officer, executive officer, positions at Navy headquarters, destroyer com-mander, gunnery expert at the Bureau of Ordnance for three duty tours, and later commanding officer of two destroyer divisions. Then at the apex of an already stellar career, he assumed command of the mighty USS *West Virginia* just months before he was killed at Pearl Harbor.

Born to a struggling family in arid, rural Utah of second-gener-ation Mormon pioneers, Mervyn posthumously received the high-est award for valor that America could present, a decoration he never saw and never wore.

Yet he was among the elite as a naval officer and also as a Mor-mon. He married a daughter of a presiding authority of the LDS Church. He served in several Church positions of responsibility and rubbed shoulders with prominent Saints. Thus, Mervyn Bennion, compared to the other eight LDS recipients, was at the zenith of his career when death claimed him and honor was accorded him.

* * *

Israel Bennion had gone to bed for the night in Salt Lake City when he felt a "premonition" that he could not ignore. He felt strongly that his little boy, Mervyn, was in danger. He had just arrived in the city that day from his home in the small, rural town of Vernon, Tooele County, some seventy miles to the southwest, to buy goods for his own small store. It may not have been a long distance; but at night in the 1890s, returning home entailed a short railroad trip, then hiring a team or buggy, and driving the twelve miles to Vernon. Israel Bennion tried to dismiss the sensation.

But he couldn't.

Israel rose, dressed quickly, and ran down to the Denver and Rio Grande train station on Sixth West Street near downtown Salt Lake City. No passenger or scheduled trains were running this late. He miraculously arrived just as a freight train was leaving the station, sprinted after it, and jumped aboard the caboose. He rode on the train through the night to the closest station to Vernon. No horses or teams were available at that hour, so he walked and ran as fast as he could. He arrived in mid-morning, rushed into his store, and asked for Mervyn. A moment later, Israel ran in the back "where there was a ladder and a trap door leading to the loft, just in time to see the child's foot disappear from the opening overhead. He [Israel] mounted the ladder with a bound and grabbed the child just as he was reaching for a piece of cheese doused with strychnine to destroy mice. A moment's delay and he would have been too late."[2]

The Bennion family regards this incident as a miracle.

The Bennions were of good Mormon pioneer stock. John Bennion, Mervyn's grandfather, was born in 1820 at Moors Lane township, Hawarden Parish, Flintshire, Wales, six miles from Chester, England. In 1840, he heard Mormon elders John Taylor and Joseph Fielding preach the new gospel in Liverpool. He joined the LDS Church the next year. A year later, John and his wife, Esther Wainwright Bennion, also Welsh, sailed for America, then made their way to Nauvoo, Illinois. In 1847, they trekked to Utah in the John Taylor and Parley Pratt company and arrived in the Salt Lake

Valley on October 5, 1847.[3] They were among the first few hundred Mormons to winter in the Valley of the Great Salt Lake.

John married his second of three wives in 1857; she, too, was an Esther from Wales, Esther Ann Birch, and had crossed the plains the year before with a handcart company. Eventually, some of the Bennions settled in Rush Valley, in the small central Utah town of Vernon, a dry and lonesome land of cattle herds and sagebrush.[4]

Israel Bennion, the son of John and Esther Birch Bennion, was born in 1860 in Taylorsville, Utah. He married Jeanette Sharp, and they started their own family. Mervyn was their second child and eldest son, born May 5, 1887. Mervyn was a brilliant child, quick-witted, intelligent, resourceful, and diligent. He excelled beyond his companions in the one-room log schoolhouse that he and his siblings attended in Vernon. It was a setting straight out of nineteenth-century morality novels. At age fourteen, just entering the new twentieth century, Mervyn began attending the Latter-day Saints High School in Salt Lake City. Though he had to miss one entire year of school because of lack of funds while living away from his family, he graduated with high marks, excelling in all his subjects, and won a scholarship from a local banker named Heber J. Grant, who later became the president of the LDS Church. One of his grammar school teachers wrote, "Mervyn was a stalwart young fellow at ten years. Larger than his associates at the same age. Erect in posture and particular about his appearance. Straight dark hair. Expressive eyes. Long nose. Even square white teeth. Suntan complexion. A most sensitive boy. Reserved. Deliberate in his thinking as well as in his speech."[5]

During the summers, Mervyn worked hard as a cattleman in the high pasture ranges of Utah and also occasionally herded sheep. He learned the value of hard work, sacrifice, and "roughing it."[6] His younger brother, Howard Sharp Bennion, wrote of him years after his death, "From his earliest days, Mervyn was generous, manly and stalwart, truly a leader in our little tribe."[7]

Soon Mervyn was considering his future education. Years earlier he had heard of the marvelous and "free" education provided by "West Point" which was very appealing to him. So he took the examinations for the class beginning in 1906 at both the U.S. Military Academy at West Point, New York, and also the U.S. Naval Academy at Annapolis, Maryland. Later, he received a nomination to attend the Naval Academy before he heard from West Point, so he took it.[8]

Mervyn Bennion's life was about to change forever.

* * *

Except for Salt Lake City, Mervyn had never visited a large city such as Washington, D.C., and Baltimore, Maryland. In June 1906, he reported at the Naval Academy at Annapolis, just a few miles east of Baltimore on the Chesapeake Bay. The academy was built on the grounds of an old Army post, Fort Severn, on the Severn River. Established in 1845 as a naval version of West Point, the U.S. Naval Academy soon carved out its own destiny and educated a corps of naval officers not easily equaled in the world. He entered the hallowed halls and walked the manicured lawns and historic grounds of one of the most prestigious colleges in America. Mervyn's timing could not have been better. He arrived just as a major construction and expansion program was underway, replacing old buildings and structures with new, modern edifices to accommodate the growing academy.

The first few days were maddening, filled with the issuing of uniforms, being marshaled into companies and battalions of midshipmen, and learning the austere discipline, language, and tradition of the proud U.S. Navy. Shortly afterward, he and some 185 other future naval officers were mustered and boarded training vessels to learn nautical terms, seamanship, leadership, celestial navigation, and the rigid culture of the naval service. Midshipman Bennion was assigned to the USS *Severn*, an old-fashioned tall-masted schooner. For several weeks that summer, he gained the skills and experience that would serve him for the next thirty years.[9]

Back at the academy, the new students began their classes in an extremely rigid and austere environment of discipline, training, and accountability. One of the lasting and special qualities of the academy was the associations, friendships, and bonds that Mervyn and other midshipmen developed. One classmate later recorded these impressions:

> He was very even tempered. . . . He was able to concentrate mentally to a degree I have never seen equaled. He could read over a thing once and he had it. He had a perfectly marvelous brain and mental processes. Naturally it was not very long until the news spread around that Mervyn was the fountain source of knowledge; and, as I remember it, for three years promptly at nine thirty (release from study hour) in would come half the company or more to get straightened out on the knotty parts of the lessons for the following day. Mervyn would patiently listen to everything anyone had to say and then finally turn them out with the correct information.[10]

Bennion attended the Naval Academy during its golden age when classes were small, intimate, and highly competitive. Everyone knew every midshipman in all four classes. Competition thrived, not only in the classroom, but in athletics, leadership, and military training. Mervyn gained a letter "N" in the two-mile cross-country team and excelled in leadership. During one of the summer training cruises as a midshipman, Mervyn had an incident that both clarified his leadership and also his humility—sometimes a rare combination in a military officer and warrior. A midshipman came aboard in the dark of night, tired and careless, making a lot of noise in search of his hammock. Mervyn rose to assist him but soon offered his own hammock to the weary newcomer. The next morning his mates found Mervyn asleep on a table in the galley.[11]

He was always near the top of his class during his four years. One day during a monthly oral examination in French and Spanish, the instructor asked Bennion a question which at first he was unsure how to answer. The instructor began reciting the French lesson. Mervyn then took over and began reciting the story in French, line after line. He had memorized the entire story. Without skipping a beat, he switched to Spanish. His instructor stopped Bennion after it appeared that he would go on for pages. He asked Mervyn, "What does 'Ojala' mean?" Mervyn looked at him and said, "would to God." The naval officer than said, "Ojala that I had your memory."[12] Entering the final examinations of his senior year, he was fifth in his class. When the final grades were posted, he graduated third in the class of 1910 of some 130 midshipmen. He was awarded a sword from the Daughters of the American Revolution for outstanding leadership and excellence in seamanship and international law.[13]

The age of sail was over, gone into the pantheon of naval history and lore. Yet the tradition and legacy of John Paul Jones, Stephen Decatur, William Preble, Matthew Perry, and David Farragut lived on in the halls and classrooms at Annapolis. The first ironclads were built during the Civil War, and the powerful dreadnaught class of warships ruled the waves. The ships of iron with coal-burning boilers and metal plates for gun decks had replaced the graceful wood hulls and flying sails. Huge caliber guns rained gigantic projectiles a dozen miles away at equally immense iron vessels in deadly surface battles between dreadnaughts.

Mervyn Bennion determined to become an expert in naval gunnery and ordnance. He loved the precision and science of ballistics that gunnery officers and battleship men experienced. The thrill of handling huge shells and hurling them at targets miles away with an accurate, predicted mathematical outcome was powerful and exciting.

Mervyn soon made his first of many cruises to foreign ports, visiting strange and exotic places. In late 1911, he made his first voyage into the Pacific Ocean and arrived at Honolulu, Hawaii. He was still a midshipman, a rank in the Navy, and not yet a commissioned officer. Nevertheless, he had duties, responsibilities, and leadership challenges.

From Pearl Harbor, on December 7, 1911, ironically also a Sunday morning, which the Japanese would attack exactly thirty years later, he wrote a letter home, describing his recent activities: "Last week we took a cruise around the island of Oahu," he wrote, explaining that U.S. Army officers were on board who "spent the time studying the coast line with a view to finding out the best way of fortifying it." He was aware of the natural wonder of the island, saying, "It was beautiful." Then as a dutiful Latter-day Saint, he added, "Am sending a check for tithing. It's time to close my accounts for the year."[14]

Coincidentally, he was writing abroad the USS *California*, (officially designated as BB–44). It was one of the great battleships damaged or sunk at Pearl Harbor thirty years later. Along with the *California*, Bennion would eventually serve aboard the battleships *Tennessee* and *Arizona* and command the *West Virginia*, all of them damaged by the Japanese at Pearl Harbor. After two years of apprenticeship training as directed by law, Mervyn Bennion was finally commissioned an ensign in the United States Navy on March 7, 1912, aboard the *California*.[15]

Another special achievement and surprise came for the Bennion family of Utah that year. Mervyn's younger brother, Howard Sharp Bennion, who had received an appointment to West Point, graduated as number one—the top cadet in his class of 140 cadets, in June 1912. He was the first LDS cadet to do so.[16] It was extraordinary that a ranching family in a small rural town in central Utah had two sons who achieved high marks and standing at two of the most prestigious and challenging educational institutions in America.

From 1914 to 1915, Mervyn Bennion served aboard the protected cruiser USS *St. Louis* as it patrolled along the Pacific coastline of California and Mexico.[17] The *St. Louis* had been commissioned in April 1906 and was reminiscent of the "dreadnaught era" of technology and classes of warships. It measured 426 feet in length and was 60 feet at the beam, with a displacement of 9,700 tons. The *St. Louis* was a four-stacker that carried fourteen six-inch guns, eighteen three-inch guns, and a complement of 673 officers and sailors.[18]

At this time, Mexico was in the midst of a dreadful and bloody revolution that had started in 1910 and would last roughly ten years after a revolutionary movement ousted President Porfirio Diaz from office in 1911.[19] Eventually the United States, which shared a lengthy border with Mexico, was sucked into this unfortunate conflict. American involvement in Mexico ended with the declaration of war against Germany in April 1917.

Ensign Bennion patrolled the coast for many boring and unpleasant months in 1912–14 and had his own opinion about the United States' entanglement in Mexican and Latin American politics. He wrote to his family in Utah from Guaymas, Mexico, on May 27, 1913:

> I wish these Americans would go back where they belong. Then these bloody-minded people could fight to their hearts' content, I am more and more a believer in nonintervention. It is a busybody that fusses with other people's affairs. Nine times out of ten he gets beaten up for his pains. I'd like to let the Mexicans work out their own salvation. I'd say to them by way of advice, ["]Thus did your Uncle Samuel. If you would become a great nation, profit by his example." If they were too blind or stubborn to see the point, I'd wash my hands of the whole business.[20]

Bennion wrote the next letter just days after the "Great War" erupted in Europe in August 1914. Naturally, he and most of the world were caught up in the opening days of hostilities as France invaded Germany, Germany invaded Belgium, then Russia marched west against Germany with Great Britain entering the fray.

From Acapulco, Mexico, on August 16, 1914, Ensign Bennion recorded even firmer noninventionist opinions: "Least of all do I like to see Japan stepping in (to world war I) [sic]. The Japanese have no business whatever in European politics. Of course their sole purpose is to put England under obligation to help them in the next war. The parting advice of our first president, 'Beware of entangling alliances,' still holds true. A well-defined policy of minding one's own business, coupled with a firm attitude toward meddlers from without, should carry our nation through to safety."[21]

What bothered Bennion was Japan's saber rattling about capturing German possessions in the Pacific. Ever since the

Spanish-American War of 1898 and America's entry into territorial expansion by taking control of the Philippines, Guam, Hawaii, and some portions of Samoa, the United States faced direct political and economic competition with Japan. The Empire of Japan, just a decade earlier, had won a decisive victory in 1905 against Russia, one of the great European nations. Modern Japan instilled pride, ambition, and aggressiveness in its people, rekindling the "Samurai" military culture of earlier centuries. Little did Mervyn Bennion know that, in less than three decades, he would become one of the first fatalities in the war with Japan.[22]

The next several years were hectic and eventful for Mervyn Bennion. In March 1915 he was promoted to lieutenant (junior grade) in a temporary billet and was assigned to the Naval Academy for postgraduate advanced courses in ordnance. This training would establish the course of his career and all future assignments as a gunnery expert, commander, and fire control officer. In July 1917, he was promoted to the rank of lieutenant (temporary) while serving at the Washington Naval Yard for technical training in gunnery and ordnance.[23]

Lieutenant Bennion was a young, up-and-coming officer in demand. He was on temporary duty with the ordnance bureau when, in January 1918, the captain of USS *North Dakota*, his assigned ship at the time, wrote, "His services can ill be spared." The Chief of Bureau of Ordnance similarly reported: "Lt. Bennion [is] making great headway. Work must stop if he is taken away." The Ordnance Bureau won the fight. Realizing Bennion's brilliance, it solicited his services in the research, development, and testing of new systems and methods. He spent much of the last months of World War I in Washington, D.C., working with ordnance procurement projects.[24] This professional tug of war proved to be a great blessing to his personal life.

* * *

Mervyn's years at the ordnance bureau in Washington allowed him to establish a regular pattern and routine in his social and religious life, something that had been haphazard and infrequent while serving at sea. The nation's capital had a small but growing Latter-day Saint population of transplanted professionals and their families from the Rocky Mountain region. There were many Mormons who were civil servants in the government, the military, and private business. Among them were LDS Apostle and U.S. Senator Reed Smoot, future hotel and hospitality tycoon J. Willard Marriott, and J. Reuben Clark Jr., former Solicitor of the Department of State. Utah-born and raised, Clark had attended Columbia University law school in New York City and carved out an illustrious reputation as a brilliant attorney. During World War I, he had served as a major in the Army's Judge Advocate General Corps, dealing with selective service laws and procedures.[25]

In 1920, Clark was in private practice, and on occasion he and his family lived in Salt Lake City. In the Clark family was a bright-eyed, wonderful daughter, Louise. After months of friendship and fun, Mervyn offered marriage, and they were married in a civil ceremony at Louise's home on February 5, 1920. Later their union would be sealed in the Salt Lake Temple.[26] For the next few years, Mervyn and Louise began their family life amid the excitement of several moves and new assignments. Mervyn served in Norfolk, Virginia, and then at the Navy's primary gunnery and research center at the Naval Proving Grounds in Dahlgren, Virginia.

Promoted to lieutenant commander in March 1922, Mervyn gained greater responsibility and authority. He was detached from the USS *Florida* (BB–30), a battleship, for this duty. Louise and Mervyn had one child, Mervyn Jr., born in April 1925. Finally after several years, he returned to sea in 1926 aboard the USS *Tennessee* (BB–43) as gunnery officer. He was responsible for the training, management, and proper employment of all of the battleship's guns during battle. Ironically, many years later at Pearl Harbor, the *Tennessee* was berthed alongside the USS *West Virginia* as the

Japanese attacked, and it was shrapnel from the *Tennessee* that killed him.

* * *

In 1955, a fine film opened in theaters, *The Court-Martial of Billy Mitchell*, with the great Gary Cooper playing Colonel William ("Billy") Mitchell. Other stars in the cast were Rod Steiger, Ralph Bellamy, Jack Lord of *Hawaii Five-0* fame, and a young Elizabeth Montgomery, later the funny lead in the TV sitcom *Bewitched*. Though loose with history and the record, the movie adequately portrayed the atmosphere, politics, and impact that the famous 1925 court-martial had among Americans, and even decades later when the film opened.

After serving with distinction in World War I as a pioneering military aviator, Billy Mitchell became distraught at the lack of funding and professional development of the Army's Air Service. Climaxing in 1925, Mitchell's main fight was to prove that air power—aerial bombing—could sink "unsinkable" battleships and that the United States needed a separate air force. He also argued strenuously that Army and Navy aviation was under-funded and unsafe.

In the film, which follows the real story rather accurately, the climax occurred when the ornery prosecuting attorney, played by Rod Steiger, hammered Gary Cooper for his actions and disobedience, then entered into a dialogue with Cooper about the future. Trying to demonstrate that Mitchell was crazy or unbalanced, Hollywood scriptwriters recorded Billy Mitchell's actual prophecy. Cooper, playing the scene for emotional intensity, predicted that the Empire of Japan would someday bomb and destroy the United States fleet at Pearl Harbor unless adequate funding, training, and modernization improved Army and Navy aviation. For the audiences of 1955 and generations since, who knew about the actual attack on Pearl Harbor in 1941, this was an astounding moment. But in 1925, such a prediction was the accepted wisdom, not prophetic or outlandish. The strategic concept that envisioned war between the United States and Japan in the vast Pacific Ocean had actually originated in 1903. The American armed forces had developed plans and carried out war games based on that possibility. The plans were revised to fight Japan, with or without an attack at Pearl Harbor. And in fact, the idea of an attack at Pearl Harbor was indeed remote in 1925, because the Pacific Fleet was home-based at San Diego and would remain so until 1940.[27]

It had been the United States of America that had opened the Empire of Japan to the West in 1850s. For another half century, America's main interest in the Pacific was whaling and limited commerce. In 1898, the United States gained possession or governance of Hawaii, Guam, and the Philippines, which then ensured that it would pay more attention to the Pacific Ocean region.[28]

Even before World War I, planners in both the Navy and the War Department had assigned designations and color-coded files for the major powers involved in Pacific strategic games: "Red" represented Great Britain, "Black" for Germany, "Green" for Mexico, and "Orange" for Japan. These nations were not necessarily foreseen as enemies, but their importance was based on their geographic prominence (Mexico) or on their sea power (Britain, Germany, and Japan). Slowly but surely, plans evolved and soon focused on Japan, especially with the demise of the German High Seas Fleet after World War I. Thus, "Plan Orange" grew and expanded, but the main focal point was always Pearl Harbor, the Pacific Fleet in California, and how to defend American interests.

Eventually, Congress provided millions of dollars to establish a forward naval base in Hawaii, deluxe with modern berths, dry docks, training areas, airfields, hangars, and permanent facilities.[29] The Army also was closely involved in all these decisions and plans because of the Washington Treaty, signed in 1922, which limited signatory nations to certain tonnage of ships, sizes, and types— a body-blow to Japan, since it limited the size and number of its capital ships (battleships, aircraft carriers as they developed in the 1920s, and cruisers). Critically, this treaty simultaneously allowed the United States to improve defensive measures in Hawaii. Japan signed the treaty but soon ignored the limitations of 315,000 total tonnage and of aircraft carriers to 35,000 tons maximum.[30]

Military planners recognized with the advent of aircraft carriers in the 1920s that, theoretically, as aviation capabilities advanced, the seemingly huge Pacific Ocean became smaller and smaller. By the 1930s, Japan, Great Britain, and United States had modern aircraft carriers from which dozens of bomber or torpedo bombers could be launched. These aircraft could strike targets hundreds of miles away with devastating effect and live to fight again. This was the reality of the future Pacific war by 1939 when war erupted in Europe.

* * *

For the next dozen years through the late 1930s, Mervyn Bennion continued his career. Rank, positions, and responsibility increased as the years rolled by, as did assignments far and near. In 1929 the Navy promoted Bennion to the rank of commander, the equivalent of a lieutenant colonel in the Army or Marine Corps. He was serving as navigator aboard the USS *Maryland* (BB–46) when the Secretary of the Navy presented the Navy's annual award for gunnery efficiency to the crew for outstanding scores and gunnery evaluations. The *Maryland* was another battleship later attacked at Pearl Harbor.

Bennion also visited Great Britain and even had the opportunity to meet King George V in person. Bennion then also visited Scotland, Denmark, and many other European ports. By 1930 he was assigned for the second time to the Bureau of Ordnance in Washington where the Bennions and Clarks were again united. His services in the technical world of gunnery, ordnance, and mechanical engineering were recognized. A classmate of 1910, William W. Brown, wrote, "Mervyn had the busiest and orneriest desk in the Bureau. In charge of turrets, all designs, etc., and all machinery. . . . The engineers who worked in his section were unanimous in their praise of him. He would seldom give them a direct order. . . . [A]fter listening to their opinions, he would lay the whole problem so bare that they would see that there was but one logical solution and adopt it as their own." Brown concluded: "In fact, I have never met anyone, junior or senior, who served with Bennion that wasn't loud in his praises of him."[31]

In Washington, Bennion had the opportunity to serve more consistently in LDS Church callings and positions in the small Washington D.C. Branch. For years aboard ships and in foreign ports, if he could not always meet with the Saints for services, he would gather with other Christians and share in their worship services. Often he and the ship's chaplain were the only officers attending. As Church membership grew around Washington, D.C., he became the supervisor of some thirty families in the new "ward teaching" concept recently developed at Church headquarters in Salt Lake City. Mervyn served in his priesthood capacity as he did with his naval service—with zeal and vision. If his ward teachers could not visit their families, he and his companion would sometimes visit all the families themselves. His efforts blessed many families as the small branch grew. In 1938, while on his last tour at the Bureau of Ordnance, the Washington Branch was divided, and the Chevy Chase Branch was created.[32]

Not only did Mervyn receive callings or positions of responsibility in government and the LDS Church, but so did his father-in-law, J. Reuben Clark. In 1928, Clark became Undersecretary in the Department of State, appointed by President Herbert Hoover, and the next year became U.S. ambassador to Mexico. His crowning service came in 1933 when he was called and sustained as second counselor in Heber J. Grant's First Presidency. Interestingly, Clark served for more than a year in the First Presidency before his ordination as an apostle in October 1934, an unusual circumstance in a very formal and authority-based Church.[33]

The Saints in the Washington, D.C., area were blessed in 1933 with a marvelous chapel on the five-street intersection of 16th Street and Columbia Road. The majestic building, known as the 16th Street Chapel, was constructed from 16,000 blocks of Utah granite with a single lofty spire topped by a golden Angel Moroni. The distinctive design replicated the spire and statue of the Salt Lake Temple. In 1940, the Washington Stake was organized with Ezra Taft Benson, who worked in the Department of Agriculture, as its first stake president.[34] Mervyn was ordained a seventy in the stake seventies quorum, and later served in the quorum's presidency. He then was called to serve as second counselor in the branch presidency. When the branch became a ward in 1940, Mervyn was called to serve as first counselor in its bishopric. This was his last Church calling prior to his assignment to Pearl Harbor in July 1941. Bishop Riley A. Gwynn wrote years later, "His willingness to serve knew no bounds. I have never known a more dependable man. He was willing to be the servant of all. I say without reservation that he was a great man and a noble character."[35]

* * *

Commander Mervyn Bennion had positions of leadership and responsibility for much of his career; but until a professional military officer becomes a commanding officer, he really has not had the full opportunity of leadership, command, and responsibility. Thus, it was a major step when, in 1932 Bennion assumed command of the USS *Bernadou*, a destroyer, and then the USS *Biddle*. In 1934, he attended the Naval War College at Newport, Rhode Island, and then taught on faculty for a year. This appointment was an assignment for the elite and most successful officers in the Navy.

He then assumed the position of "XO," or executive officer, of the USS *Arizona* (BB–39), an important and responsible duty as second in command of a huge and complex battleship. For a long but significant year, beginning March 30, 1936, Bennion basically ran the administrative and logistical requirements of this monstrous "battlewagon" of some 1,400 officers and men. His commanding officer later praised Bennion's "disregard for hours of work in looking after the interests of the ship . . . and a long history of kind attention to the needs and best interests of his men."[36]

In 1937 he received another major duty assignment, the command of Destroyer Division One of some four destroyers, and later Destroyer Division Nine. These assignments took him from the Atlantic Coast to Europe, and from the Caribbean to the Pacific. His expertise and experience grew immensely, preparing him for his final command. He returned to Washington, D.C., in 1938 at the rank of captain, the equivalent as a colonel in the Army and Marine Corps. In 1941, at the zenith of a distinguished career, he received command of the illustrious warship, the USS *West Virginia*, with the Pacific Fleet at Pearl Harbor.[37]

* * *

In 1970 the epic film, *Tora! Tora! Tora!* opened in theaters; and after four decades, it remains an accurate reconstruction of the attack on Pearl Harbor. Among the large and amazing sets, battle sequences, cinematography, vintage props, and riveting action, the producers made a valiant attempt to employ proper aircraft, weapons, equipment, and history. The film also provided a reasonably in-depth account of the planning, causes, and background of the war, the attack, and the players involved. The film was especially impressive with Japanese actors speaking Japanese, directed by Japanese movie-makers, and being filmed at Japanese locations.

There was a balance to the film. It did not strike a moralistic pose about whether World War II in the Pacific was justified or an act of aggression. Rather, the film attempted to lay out the facts of the politics, diplomacy, military build-up, preparation, and the attack itself objectively. There is no doubt that the film accurately depicts the near flawless execution of the Japanese attack on Pearl Harbor and other targets. It also correctly shows how confused, muddled, chaotic, and inept American preparations and defense were. Given excellent Japanese planning and deplorable American failures, thousands of Americans died that day; families were crushed; and many brave acts of selfless service and valor occurred. Then Americans rose up in moral indignation and focused will that carried them to victory nearly four years later. It is impossible to depict in any film the complex facts, time span, and hundreds of real historical characters, both of great and lesser military and political rank, who were involved with the planning of the attack or the defense of Hawaii.

* * *

The mastermind and architect behind the attack on the U. S. Pacific Fleet was Admiral Isoroku Yamamoto who commanded the Imperial Japan's Combined Fleet in 1941. Having lived, studied, and served in America, he knew the strengths and weaknesses of America. Yamamoto did not want war with the United States—in fact, dreaded the thought of it. He knew, however, that the only way to win was to cripple the Americans with a surprise attack at its heart: the Pacific Fleet. The main objective was the fleet itself; however, the prizes were the aircraft carriers, then the battleships, and also aircraft, both carrier and land-based. He hoped that, with the fleet destroyed and no means to strike back for several years, America would sue for peace after a few months.[38]

The politics and diplomacy leading up to the attack are long and complicated; but simply put, Japan, as an ally to Germany and Italy, sought power and resources in its own region for its growing form of nationalism, economy, and military development. Japanese nationalism and militarism overrode common sense, morality, and diplomacy in foreign relations and governance. In 1931, Japan invaded and occupied Manchuria, then moved into Indo-China after France fell to Germany in 1940. These aggressive moves appalled Americans. When the U.S. Navy countered by moving the Pacific Fleet to Hawaii in 1940, the militant warlords in Japan considered it a blatant provocation. When the United States also decreased resources and then curtailed the fuel it would sell to Japan—especially petroleum, coal, and iron ore—it was the last straw for Japan. The move to war was led by the Minister of War, General Hideki Tojo, in the summer of 1941. By that time, Admiral Yamamoto's plan was nearly finished. He had anticipated that, if there was to be a war, Japan had to strike first. He and many of his colleagues knew, despite military bluster and proud nationalism, that Japan could not fight a long, defensive war.[39]

* * *

A driving force behind the scenes was the brilliant Japanese staff officer and planner, Commander Minoru Genda, who perfected Admiral Yamamoto's concept, even though he was not on Admiral Yamamoto's direct staff. When he saw the admiral's initial plan he remarked: "The plan is difficult but not impossible." His genius and incredible memory for facts and details went a long way to allay fears about and correct false assumptions that many senior Japanese officers had about the overall plan.

Several different operational theories balanced the two main factors that the Japanese planners were most concerned with: (1) how to destroy the Pacific fleet in a surprise attack, and (2) how to do so without losing their own aircraft carriers. The main planning factor became the range of the strike force. The aircraft had a fuel range of about 300–400 one-way miles from the carriers. How far could the carriers go to launch their aircraft and wait while they made the attack? How far could the planes fly, loiter if necessary for other targets of opportunity, and then safely return to the carriers before running out of fuel? Most of the time, key military decisions boil down to a similarly simple factor.[40]

Another factor that was of major concern to the Japanese fleet, Yamamoto, and Genda was the depth of Pearl Harbor—a comparatively shallow forty feet. Most torpedoes of the time required at least seventy feet when dropped even on a shallow run; therefore, torpedoes were ineffective at Pearl Harbor. Yet in November 1940, obsolete British Swordfish bi-plane torpedo bombers damaged, destroyed, or sank several Italian battleships and cruisers at Taranto, Italy, demonstrating the vulnerability of a stationary fleet to aerial attacks. Eventually the Japanese solved the depth problem by affixing wood fins to the rear of their Type 92, Model II torpedoes.[41] These fins provided buoyancy and more stability to the metal torpedo.

The next major decision was how to deploy the strike force. One of the extreme tactical options was called the "all out" or "one way" plan. Some admirals considering this plan proposed that the carriers should launch the strike force about 500 to 600 miles from Oahu, almost the limit of the planes' fuel range. After delivering the attack, the pilots would ditch in the ocean on their return leg wherever they ran out of fuel. Submarines or small surface craft would then rescue the airmen. This was one of several "suicide-type" scenarios.

Genda dismissed this plan, however, cleverly calling it the "Great All-Out Battle" and comparing it to the great nineteenth-century set-battles like a naval Waterloo or Austerlitz. The two military forces would mass, attack, and struggle to the death. The winner of the battle and also the war would be the force with the most pieces still standing. Genda questioned why the admirals were willing to sacrifice hundreds of fine aircraft and endanger a thousand trained airmen on this one-battle theory.[42]

Instead, Genda countered with several major planning imperatives. It would be a surprise attack, during daylight, preferably early in the morning. The preferred date would be an American holiday or a weekend—especially a Sunday.[43] The main target would be U.S. carriers and the fleet. The secondary target would be land-based aircraft. Every available Japanese aircraft carrier should be involved. The attack would combine torpedo bombers, dive bombers, and fighters. The plan would require total secrecy.

The final major imperative Genda demanded was that the air attack must be followed by a ground invasion of Hawaii. Why destroy the fleet if the enemy could rebuild and restore the harbor, ports, and island resources? "We should follow up this attack on Hawaii with a landing," Genda said. "If Hawaii is occupied, America will lose her largest and best advance base and, furthermore, our command of future operations will be very good."[44] Genda prevailed on all of the other conditions, but not this one. The logistics of moving thousands of troops and supplies for a land invasion were simply too great to follow immediately on the air strike.

Eventually, four heavy aircraft carriers of Japan's total of ten—the largest number owned by any nation in 1941—and two light escort carriers, would be the nucleus of the main strike force. The Japanese Navy had to create a new organization, the First Air Fleet, to concentrate its carriers under one command, thus taking organic carriers from each fleet. Some admirals were vehemently opposed to this move.[45]

The Carrier Strike Force of the First Air Fleet was commanded by Vice Admiral Cuichi Nagumo, a seasoned officer with little operational aviation experience. The strike force also had two fast battleships, two heavy cruisers, a destroyer squadron, submarines, tenders, tankers, and some 465 aircraft, but no army ground invasion forces. Japanese ground troops were spread rather thin because the empire was also launching simultaneous operations against the Dutch East Indies, British Malaya, Burma, Borneo, American Guam, Wake Island, and the Philippines. Hundreds of thousands of soldiers, dozens of warships, and hundreds of troop transports were involved in these invasions. Most of the attack and covering aircraft were land-based from Japan or from newly occupied French Indo-China.[46]

The aviation plan at the tactical level was developed by another brilliant Japanese officer, Commander Mitsuo Fuchida, staff air officer for the strike force. A thirty-nine-year-old career aviation officer, Fuchida was prominently portrayed in *Tora! Tora! Tora!* The attack would consist of two main waves, launched some 230 miles northeast of the Oahu. Some 183 aircraft would participate in the first wave: forty-three A6M Zeke Type 0 ("Zero") fighters; fifty-one D3A Type 99 ("Val") dive bombers; and forty-eight B5N Type 97 ("Kate") high-level bombers, followed by an additional forty Kate torpedo bombers.[47] The first wave would approach

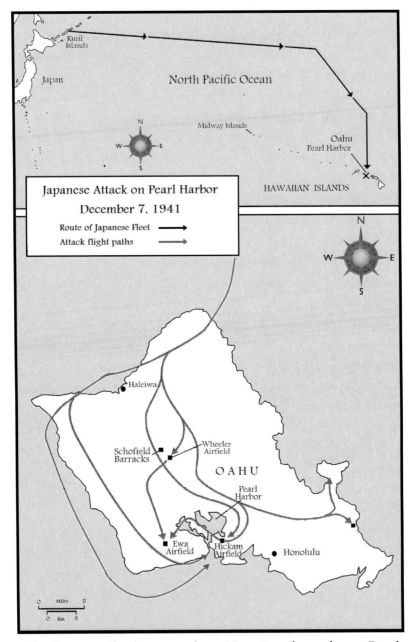

The Japanese fleet's approach to Hawaii and attacks on Pearl Harbor. Cartography by Hyrum H. Fleek.

Oahu from the north, fly along the island to the westward, and then strike Pearl Harbor from the west along the coastline. One squadron would separate just west of Oahu and fly overland to hit Wheeler Army Air Field, Schofield Barracks, and Bellows Field far to the east. The second wave of 162 planes would arrive approximately an hour later and have nearly the same target profile but approach from the east and fly over the center of Oahu and past Diamond Head, a highly visible landmark. What the first wave did not destroy, the second attack would finish.[48] Planning was so detailed that each aircraft, each flight section, and each squadron had a specific or group of targets, whether an aircraft carrier (mercifully not docked at Pearl Harbor on the fatal weekend), battleships, airfields, fuel tanks, harbor facilities, or hangars.[49]

As for anticipated Japanese casualties and the loss of ships, aircraft, and airmen, the Japanese planners could only speculate. Genda, Fuchida, and Yamamoto based everything on one assumption or planning imperative: *surprise*. Flight leader Fuchida was so taken by this critical factor that he developed a code word or signal for that very moment if they achieved surprise: Tora! Tora! Tora!, or Tiger! Tiger! Tiger![50]

* * *

As in any large organization, people are evaluated during their careers. Below are some comments from Captain Bennion's officer evaluations:

> December 1939: He has handled this financial work thoroughly and efficiently. His knowledge of ordnance requirements of the fleet [was] particularly helpful in obtaining funds from Congress. Good Judgment.
>
> December 1940: He has handled this financial work thoroughly and efficiently. He is accurate and has excellent judgment.
>
> March 1941: Captain Bennion . . . handled arduous work in highly efficient manner. Thorough and untiring in devotion to duty.

Cooperative and considerate of others. Personal and military character excellent. Recommended for promotion.

    July 1941: Captain Bennion . . . performed duties in a manner
leaving nothing to be desired.[51]

From the time of his promotion to captain, Mervyn Bennion
had been at the Navy Department for his third tour of duty. His
officer evaluations cited above describe an efficient, intelligent,
and meticulous officer and also an outstanding leader. In the days
before formal selection boards for command and assignments,
the way an officer received command of a battleship was through
performance, experience, and education but also by the support,
sponsorship, and politicking of influential leaders, admirals, and,
in some cases, politicians.

    Whatever the process at work in this case, Captain Mervyn
Sharp Bennion, graduate of United States Naval Academy class of
1910, born in Utah, faithful Latter-day Saint, and the son-in-law
of a LDS apostle and member of the Church's First Presidency, was
selected from among many potential candidates to command the
USS *West Virginia* (BB–48), one of the great prizes of the Navy.

    The *West Virginia's* keel was laid on April 12, 1920, and it was
commissioned on December 1, 1923. This Colorado-class battleship was a mighty machine of war, even by 1941 standards after
nearly twenty years of service. Captain Bennion was now responsible for an elite warship, a "battlewagon" with a crew of 1,407 officers and men. The "Wee Vee," as many called it, was 624 feet long
and 97 feet at the beam. It displaced some 33,950 tons and could
reach a speed of 21 knots, or about 27 miles an hour. This class
of warship was the transition between the old "dreadnoughts" of
the late nineteenth century and new modern battleships like the
Bismarck, *Yamato*, and the *Missouri*-class ships. The *West Virginia*,
called a "super-dreadnought," had massive sheets of armor and carried an amazing array of armament: eight sixteen-inch guns in four
turrets; twelve five-inchers; and eight three-inchers in turrets or
gun positions. There were also dozens of anti-aircraft guns of various calibers, two torpedo launchers, and depth-charge racks for

The USS *West Virginia* leads the U.S. Pacific fleet under the Golden Gate Bridge during the 1930s.

enemy submarines. The ship was a monster of steel, guns, technical wonders, and sophisticated power.

On August 12, 1941, Captain Bennion reported aboard and assumed command of the *West Virginia*. The great battleship was also the flagship for the commander, Vice Admiral William S. Pye, of the Battle Force or Task Force 1, comprised of the battleships of the Pacific Fleet). Admiral Pye would later assume command of the Pacific Fleet after Admiral Husband E. Kimmel was relieved following the attack.[52]

To recount, explain, and try to understand all the failures, close calls, and ineptitude of American defensive measures that allowed a large Japanese fleet to arrive only 230 miles away from Hawaii, launch several hundred aircraft, and strike a dozen military targets with total surprise will probably never be explained completely. The only honest response is that the chain of failures ran from the White House to the duty officers on shift that morning in Hawaii. The attack was not a complete surprise; for weeks the U.S. Armed Forces and the State Department knew that the Japanese were planning, preparing, and deploying for such an attack. They did not know exactly when, although they were fairly certain that Pearl would be the target. A particularly lamentable failure was that the War and Navy Departments had cracked the Japanese signal communiques using a decrypting machine called "Magic" but failed to fully understand and share this intelligence. In fairness, despite the brilliance and importance of this break-through, most of the decrypted messages were diplomatic communiques with no tactical and operational information that the commanders in Hawaii needed.[53]

The Army was responsible for local security of the island chain, for air patrols guarding the approaches, Pearl Harbor, and, hence, the fleet, whereas the Navy deployed its few aircraft carriers on quick sorties to patrol at long range. In late November, intelligence sources learned of several large Japanese convoys of troop transports with heavy escorts heading south toward either the Philippines, Malaya, the Dutch East Indies, or Singapore. They were, in fact, en route to all of these locations.[54]

As diplomatic message chatter increased and intensified, the American commands—the Army and Navy in Hawaii—were on constant alert. In late November 1941, the intelligence experts and analysts were convinced that the Japanese would attack Oahu on November 30. They were wrong. With radars scanning and searching the horizon farther than humans and aircraft could view, with air patrols and submarines ranging far and wide, the Americans missed the fleet until the Japanese formations were winging their way on their bomb and torpedo runs a week later.

As in the Japanese Navy, the United States Navy also had a galaxy of mid-level, trained, and experienced staff officers who conceptualized new tactics, weapons, and breakthroughs. The admirals and generals often gain the fame and credit for the innovations and the great staff work of their subordinates. The American Navy at Pearl Harbor had an intelligence and communications genius, Edwin T. Layton. Like Genda, he was an eccentric and informal officer, a lieutenant commander on Admiral Husband Kimmel's staff in the intelligence shop. Born and raised in Nauvoo, Illinois, and a 1924 graduate of

The USS *West Virginia* in camouflage paint.

the Naval Academy, Layton had lived in Japan for several years as a naval attaché and was fluent in Japanese. It was Layton's difficult task to make sense of the communiques from Washington that came to his section. His knowledge of Japanese culture, the Japanese Navy, and its people helped, but the maze of messages was still overwhelming.[55] In Washington, Army Colonel Rufus Bratton and Navy Lt. Commander Alvin Kramer were also immensely involved in the signal traffic, providing critical analysis as best they could.[56]

For Captain Bennion, the last few weeks had been hectic with short sorties and intensive training of his crew. He was anxious about the intelligence information he received and also realized that he did not know the entire picture. Mervyn kept his crew aboard the night of December 6–7, except for those few officers and men who had families in quarters ashore. He himself accepted a dinner invitation from Ralph Woolley, president of the LDS Oahu Stake, on Saturday evening. The Woolleys invited Mervyn to remain overnight and attend church services with them. He declined, being anxious to return to his ship.[57]

* * *

December 7, 1941, Day of Days

The combat action and events at Pearl Harbor are complicated, confusing, and almost impossible to understand completely. The following narrative will reconstruct the events involving Captain Bennion, his crew, and his ship on that day of days.

At about 0755, Captain Bennion was in his quarters shaving, dressing, and preparing to go ashore to attend services; it was Fast Sunday for Latter-day Saints. An alarm sounded aboard the USS *West Virginia*: "Away Fire and Rescue Party!" Bennion ran from his quarters to the conning tower near the flag bridge, his battle station, to better appraise the situation. As soon as he learned that Japanese aircraft were attacking, he checked the readiness of his gun crews. Within a minute or two, Japanese aircraft were spotted converging on the fleet at low levels, making torpedo runs. Over the intercom, Captain Bennion ordered, "Battle stations!" and "General quarters!"—both signals of an all-out emergency—followed by the fatal message that explained everything: "Japanese air attack!"[58]

Lt. Commander Shigemaru Murata leading the torpedo force of the first wave, zeroed in on this huge ship—his assigned target, and led several of his Type 97 "Kates" in a disciplined and precise torpedo run. They dropped their torpedoes (called "fish" in Navy slang) in the water. The *West Virginia* was berthed outside and alongside the *Tennessee* with a dock mooring between them. In quick succession, three torpedoes slammed into the port (left) side of the *West Virginia*. The huge battleship shuddered with the concussions and impact. The first struck in the stern, smashing the steering gear and separating the rudder from its mountings. Within moments, three more torpedoes struck the ship. One or two penetrated the hull below the armor belts, causing gaping holes. In fact, it is believed that a later torpedo entered a hole from a previous hit and struck directly amidships, causing huge fires that burst out in the galleys.[59]

Following the wave of Kates, Japanese dive bombers came screaming out of the sky, aiming toward their specified targets, releasing their ordnance of various sizes. They waited so long to pull up that they nearly struck the steel masts. Smoke and flame engulfed many ships. Sirens, bomb blasts, thick black smoke, racket from anti-aircraft guns, and men screaming in pain filled the air. The *West Virginia* took on water quickly and began to list to port. This tilt became worse as the minutes ticked off. Lt. Commander T. Beattie, the ship's navigator, just a few minutes after the torpedo hits, made his way to the bridge, briefed Captain Bennion, and recommended counter-flooding. Bennion agreed and ordered, "Go do that!"[60] More and more bombs blasted nearby. Shrapnel struck the vessel. Neither officer knew that two junior officers had already commenced counter-flooding without orders, on their own initiative.

Bennion ran outside to the lateral walk-way to observe the action and check the condition of the damage. Within moments, a bomb struck a turret of the nearby *Tennessee*, spraying the area with shrapnel. A large splinter struck Bennion in the upper abdomen, slicing his stomach in half and lodging near his spine, immediately paralyzing his legs.

Bennion collapsed to the deck but gripped the splinter and pulled it from his body. Then with "nerves of steel [he] put back in place the entrails that had spilled out." Blood began to flow from his wound; the pain must have been excruciating. He lay there for some time in agony.[61] The battle had been raging for no more than twenty minutes, and he was mortally wounded.

A pharmacist's mate came to Bennion and bandaged his wound with a temporary dressing. Bennion then ordered him away to treat the other wounded. As the confusion of battle intensified, he lay on the deck, receiving a stream of reports from several of his officers and sailors to whom he issued orders. He inspired confidence in all who saw him. The highly trained and efficient crew soon overcame the initial shock of battle and went to work.[62]

As aircraft zoomed overhead, antiaircraft guns blasted away and acrid gun smoke choked the air. The *West Virginia* began to list to port more steeply, taking on more water. Smoke billowed

The USS *West Virginia* ablaze amidships, December 7, 1941.

from the hits. Just then, a bomb hit the quarter-deck aft of the main super-structure, plowed through the deck's armor plates, and lodged below but did not detonate. As the first attack began to diminish after about a half hour, the battleship was now listing 20° to 25° to port. It would soon capsize.[63]

When Captain Bennion ordered Lt. Commander Beattie to begin counter-flooding, neither of them knew that counter-flooding was already underway, thanks to quick-thinking Lt. J. S. Harper, the Damage Control Officer. Aft Gunnery Officer Lt. Claude Ricketts and Boatswain's Mate 1st Class Billingsley also, without waiting for orders, began flooding compartments. Between the two attacks, the *West Virginia* was saved from capsizing by the quick actions of these men.

Reports, orders, and recommendations were relayed to Bennion as he lay on the lateral walkway alongside the bridge. Several times his crew tried to carry him to the shore where he could be hospitalized, but he refused.[64] Lt. Ricketts later wrote, "The Captain deserves the highest praise for his noble conduct to the last. Although in great pain he kept inquiring about the condition of the ship," especially the fires, the pumps, and fire crews. Bit by bit, Bennion's life ebbed away.[65]

During the lull between the two waves of Japanese attacks, Lt. Beattie and several other officers and enlisted men put Captain Bennion on a cot and tried to make him comfortable. Bennion was still conscious but in great pain. One of the enlisted men who helped move him and then tended to him was Mess Attendant 3rd Class Doris ("Dorie") Miller who often served Captain Bennion his meals. They had a casual and warm relationship. Miller, during the second wave of attacks, jumped to one of the twin-mounted .50 caliber machine-gun positions and opened fire on Japanese aircraft. He later received the Navy Cross, the second highest award for valor in the Navy. He was the first African American to be awarded such distinction. The citation referred to Miller's selfless service in assisting Captain Bennion and his bravery in engaging enemy aircraft without training.[66] Miller died at sea in 1943 when a Japanese submarine sank the escort carrier, USS *Liscome Bay*, on which he was serving.

Fires that had started in the galleys spread amidships and raged in the superstructure. Bravely, the men tried to move Captain Bennion to a clear area, even though they had to lift him up to the navigation bridge as the second attack was underway. It was well after 0930 as they moved him to this location. For another half hour, two junior officers and a pharmacist's mate stayed with him. Mervyn rose up on his elbows at approximately 1000 hours, and uttered his final words, "I'm gone."[67] He expired.

Those on the navigation bridge with him were now in danger themselves from the fire engulfing much of the ship. Those around him had to leave his body as the flames and smoke surrounded them. His body was recovered the next day, untouched by fire. Ensign Graham rigged a rope line from the large starboard boat crane and threw it to his mates who tied it to a railing on the flag bridge. Then they each escaped one by one, hand over hand, above the inferno below them. This was an amazing act of desperate valor.[68] About 1400 hours the *West Virginia* slowly settled on the floor of the harbor, still upright, burning, and abandoned except for the sixty-six dead found aboard when the ship was raised in 1942 and repaired to take part in later World War II engagements. Perhaps one of most tragic tales of Pearl Harbor occurred aboard the *West Virginia*. Salvage crews found the bodies of three sailors trapped in a commissary storeroom below decks. They had survived for sixteen days on stored rations, keeping a calendar until they perished on December 23, 1941.[69]

* * *

Many mistakes were made before the attack—and perhaps some immediately afterwards, especially when Admiral Kimmel and Lt. General Walter C. Short were relieved so quickly without the benefit of a thorough investigation. On December 17, ten days after the attack, President Franklin D. Roosevelt ordered the establishment of America's first unified or "joint" command under Admiral Chester Nimitz. That same day, several senior commanders at Pearl Harbor, including Kimmel and Short, were relieved. Forever afterward, the only thing that these professional officers with stellar careers would be remembered for would be the Japanese surprise attack on Pearl Harbor and their alleged incompetence and negligence.[70]

Louise Clark Bennion and her son, Mervyn, were in Salt Lake City on December 7, awaiting the opportunity to move to Hawaii. Mervyn Jr. was attending East High School. The family learned of Mervyn's death on December 9, two days later. It must have been the worst day of Louise's life. She lived another fifty-six years, dying in 1997 at age ninety-eight. Mervyn's body was eventually interred in Salt Lake City. On Sunday, February 15, 1942, a well-attended memorial service in his honor was held at the 16th Street Chapel in Washington, D.C. Many naval officials besides hundreds of

MEMORIAL SERVICE

Mervyn S. Bennion

Washington Chapel
Church of Jesus Christ, of Latter Day Saints
16th and Columbia Road, N. W.
Washington, D. C.

SUNDAY, FEBRUARY 15, 1942, 7 P. M.

Funeral program for Captain Bennion, Washington, D.C., February 15, 1942. Courtesy of Saints at War Center, Brigham Young University, and the Bennion family.

friends, Latter-day Saints, and others offered their respect to a naval hero.

The U.S. Navy honored the memory and gallantry of Captain Mervyn Bennion by commissioning the USS *Bennion* (DD–662) a Fletcher-class destroyer in his name, on December 14, 1943. Fittingly, both the *Bennion* and the restored and repaired USS *West Virginia* fought in the greatest naval battle in history—the Battle of Leyte Gulf and especially the action at Surigao Strait—on October 24, 1944.

MERVYN SHARP BENNION

Rank and organization: Captain, U.S. Navy. Born: May 5, 1887, Vernon, Utah. Appointed from: Utah.

Citation

For conspicuous devotion to duty, extraordinary courage, and complete disregard of his own life, above and beyond the call of duty, during the attack on the Fleet in Pearl Harbor, by Japanese forces on 7 December 1941. As Commanding Officer of the USS *West Virginia*, after being mortally wounded, Captain Bennion evidenced apparent concern only in fighting and saving his ship, and strongly protested against being carried from the bridge.

Notes

1. Max Boot, *War Made New: Weapons, Warriors, and the Making of the Modern World*, 246.
2. Howard S. Bennion, "Mervyn Sharp Bennion: One of the Lord's Noblemen," 3, Box 4, fd. 20, Bennion Family Papers, 1842–1960, Utah State Historical Society..
3. Ibid., 1–2.
4. Ibid., 2.

5. Ibid, 4.

6. Ibid., 6.

7. Ibid., 4.

8. Ibid., 6.

9. Ibid.

10. Ibid., 7.

11. A. H. Gray, Letter to Louise Bennion, April 11, 1942, Bennion Family Collection.

12. Ibid.

13. James W. Cheever, email to Sherman Fleek, July 15, 2009; Bennion, "Mervyn Sharp Bennion," 8.

14. Bennion, "Mervyn Sharp Bennion," 8.

15. Mervyn S. Bennion, Biographical Summary, Bennion Official Files, in Bennion Family Files, Box 4; hereafter Bennion Official Files.

16. *Register of Graduates and Former Cadets, United States Military Academy*, 2008. In 2009, Brady Deardon became the second LDS cadet to graduate at the top of his class.

17. Prior to World War I, the Navy designated ships by their date of commissioning; later designations involved type as well as number.

18. Naval Historical Center, USS *St. Louis*, 1906, www.history.navy. mil/danfs/s17/st_louis-iv.htm (accessed December 10, 2009).

19. John S. D. Eisenhower, *Intervention: The United States and the Mexican Revolution, 1913–1917*, 329–32.

20. Bennion, "Mervyn Sharp Bennion," 9.

21. Ibid., 9.

22. Louis Morton, *The War in the Pacific, Strategy and Command: The First Two Years. The United States Army in World War II*, 16–17.

23. At this time the Army and Navy issued temporary promotions because of the expanding forces during World War I. Often as personnel and needs stabilized, promotions were made permanent.

24. Bennion, "Mervyn Sharp Bennion," 10.

25. "J. Reuben Clark Jr. and Limited Government," Sutherland Institute, December 13, 2007, http://www.sutherlandinstitute.org/uploads/ reubenclark.pdf (accessed December 4, 2009).

26. Bennion, "Mervyn Sharp Bennion," 10.

27. Morton, *The War in the Pacific*, 22–24.

28. Ibid., 13–17.

29. Ibid., 23–25.

30. Richard W. Stewart, ed., *The United States in a Global Era, 1917–2003*, Vol. 2 of American Military History, 65; Alan R. Millet and Peter Maslowski, *For the Common Defense: The Military History of the United States of America*, 383.

31. Bennion, "Mervyn Sharp Bennion," 11.

32. Ibid., 13–14.

33. *2006 Church Almanac*, 58.

34. Julian C. Lowe and Florian H. Thayn, "History of the Mormons of the Greater Washington Area," 89 .

35. Bennion, "Mervyn Sharp Bennion," 14–15.

36. Ibid., 12.

37. Service of Captain Mervyn Sharp Bennion, Box 4, Bennion Official Files.

38. Gordon W. Prange, *At Dawn We Slept: The Untold Story of Pearl Harbor*, 3–5.

39. Ibid., 9–17; John Keegan, *The Second World War*, 240–45.

40. Prange, *At Dawn we Slept*, 20–21.

41. Ibid., 19–20, 104–5, 159, 321.

42. Ibid., 21–24.

43. Ibid., 25–26.

44. Ibid., 104–6

45. Ibid., 107–9. "Organic" elements are part of the original unit. For example, "organic" elements for divisions include not only the soldiers but supply, medics, transportation, and even laundry.

46. Morton, *The War in the Pacific*, 110, 131–32.

47. Boot, *War Made New*, 241; Morton, *The War in the Pacific*, 131–34; Prange, *At Dawn We Slept*, 381–84.

48. Morton, *The War in the Pacific*, 132.

49. Prange, *At Dawn We Slept*, 375, 381–88.

50. Ibid., 379.

51. Bennion, "Mervyn Sharp Bennion," 12–13.

52. Prange, *At Dawn We Slept*, 66–67; Bennion, "Mervyn Sharp Bennion," 13.

53. Ibid., 80–82.

54. Keegan, *The Second World War*, 256.

55. Prange, *At Dawn We Slept*, 68, 87.

56. Ibid., 80–84.

57. Bennion, "Mervyn Sharp Bennion," 16.

58. Ibid.

59. Prange, *At Dawn We Slept*, 511.

60. Bennion, "Mervyn Sharp Bennion," 16.

61. Ibid., 16–17.

62. Ibid.

63. Commander Ross H. Hillenkoetter, "After Action Report," December 11, 1941, Box 4, fd. 9, Bennion Official Files.

64. Lt. C. V. Ricketts, Statement, December 11, 1941, in Bennion Official Files.

65. Ibid.

66. Prange, *At Dawn We Slept*, 514–15.

67. Bennion, "Mervyn Sharp Bennion," 18.

68. Ricketts, Statement, December 11, 1941.

69. Homer N. Wallin, VADM USN, *Pearl Harbor: Why, How, Fleet Salvage and Final Appraisal*, 238.

70. Morton, *The War in the Pacific*, 144. At this time, the Panama Canal Zone was established as a "joint" command under Army leadership.

Private Nathan ("Junior") Van Noy, ca. 1943.

Chapter Three
PRIVATE NATHAN ("JUNIOR") VAN NOY: WAR—A YOUNG MAN'S FIGHT

"The kid was tow-headed, red-cheeked and 19 years old," wrote Private John McLeod, a U.S. Army journalist. "He joined his outfit as a replacement. . . . The fellows in his outfit didn't pay much attention to him. They hardly knew his name, called him Whitey or Junior." McLeod's piece appeared in *Yank Magazine: The Army Weekly*, on December 31, 1943. This issue of *Yank* appeared barely two months after a very bloody action at Finschhafen, New Guinea, on October 17, 1943. McLeod narrated, as best he could, a night battle in which basically one soldier singlehandedly stopped a small Japanese landing force—an incredible feat. What is also interesting that McLeod quickly zeroed in on a quality of "soldier" that has been true of combat since the dawn of warfare. War is a young man's fight.[1]

"They called him Junior because he looked even younger than he was, because he didn't have much to say," the piece continued, "When he did say something he did so without using the Army's stock phrases of profanity."[2] The private's comrades quickly clued in on a trait of his that was just as unique as his youth—his innocence.

"We kind of figured him as a mama's boy," commented his sergeant, a tough cuss from Brooklyn, New York, who then admitted, "goes to show you how wrong you can be."

Three barges carrying a total of some one hundred Japanese soldiers made an amphibious assault in the early morning hours of October 17, 1943. With only a few minutes' warning, a platoon of Army engineers, along with a group of Australian soldiers, manned their fighting positions at "Scarlet Beach" near Finschhafen, an old Dutch settlement that the Allies had captured a few weeks earlier. The farm boy from Idaho ran to his defensive position, which was well forward of the rest of his mates in a relatively exposed but key position. There he manned a Browning .50 caliber machine gun with Corporal Stephen Popa of Detroit, who was Van Noy's loader.

"Gazing out to sea, the two saw three smudges on the skyline," continued McLeod in his article, "The smudges gradually took more distinct shape as they moved slowly and noiselessly toward shore. They had the decidedly peaked prows of Japanese landing barges."

Within moments, all hell broke loose. Large caliber antiaircraft guns mounted off the beach blasted away at one of the barges which soon began to sink. Dozens of Japanese soldiers jumped overboard. The Americans and Aussies fired at the Japanese in the surf. Up forward on the beach two barges approached the lone gun position where the youthful private and his loader were ready and waiting. Just as the ramps dropped, .50 caliber tracers lit up the black sky. Within minutes several Japanese grenades exploded. The defenders were ordered to withdraw inland to their main defensive line in the jungle tree line. All the defenders eventually scrambled back, including Junior's wounded loader. But Junior had refused to retreat.

For some time the racket of machine gun fire, hand grenades, and fire of the heavy guns continued on the beach. Then it stopped. An eerie silence reigned across Scarlet Beach.

As dawn arrived, the engineer soldiers slowly moved to the beach and found the slaughter of this terrible night action. Every enemy soldier in the assault group was dead; Japanese soldiers lay on the beach or bobbed in the rolling surf near the lone gun position.

Only one American soldier was dead: nineteen-year-old Private Nathan ("Junior") Van Noy. He had been savagely wounded by grenades and small arms fire, but he had apparently fought on despite his wounds.

"All the American buddies and the twenty Australians who fought with Junior Van Noy agreed" with his gruff sergeant who said, "That kid had more guts than all the rest of the Army put together."

* * *

Private Van Noy, a Mormon born in Grace, Idaho, and raised mostly in Preston never married, never had children, did not attend college, did not have a trade or a real profession, and had never had the opportunity to serve a mission for the LDS Church. Junior missed the wonderful opportunities and challenges that life could afford. His own life ended at age nineteen.

Within weeks, about the time the article in *Yank* appeared, Junior Van Noy's nomination for the Medal of Honor was well under way.

* * *

His full name was Nathan Kilby Van Noy Jr. He was one of three sons of Nathan Kilby Van Noy Sr. and Pauline Petersen Van Noy, from Grace, Idaho. Even though nearly every military and many official documents have reported or recorded his name as either Junior Van Noy or Junior Nathan Van Noy, they are incorrect. Much of this confusion came from Private Van Noy himself, because he apparently used "Junior" as his first name when he entered military service and used it on almost all his official papers. But that does not change the fact that the name given him at birth, which appears on the earliest documents of his life, was Nathan Kilby Van Noy Jr.[3] It is not surprising that he was always called "Junior" by family and friends, not only to distinguish him from his father but because, even in youth, he always looked younger than his age. An alternative nickname was "Whitey" because of his light complexion and very blonde hair.

The distressing factor about Nathan Van Noy, like one or two others recipients of the Medal of Honor, is the limited information on him. Private Van Noy died in 1943; and over the next seven decades, nearly every person who knew him also died. There are no living close relatives. An album held by friends in Preston, Idaho, contains dozens of newspaper clippings, a few letters by him, many letters written by others to his mother, Pauline Van Noy, and a few official documents. That is the sum total of a life snuffed out at age nineteen.

Junior's mother, Pauline Justine Petersen Van Noy, was born and raised in Denmark. She converted to the LDS Church in 1893 in Aalborg, a large city on the Jutland peninsula of Denmark, at age nine. It is not clear whether other members of her family converted at the same time and whether she emigrated alone to the United States. She married Nathan Kilby Van Noy, born in 1873 in Richmond, a small farm town in northern Utah's Cache Valley. Nathan died in 1940 while Junior was still attending Preston High School. The Van Noys had five children: Spencer E., William T., Betty Jean, Nathan Jr., and Delaine.

Junior was born August 9, 1925, in Grace, about twenty miles north of Preston. When he was nine, the family moved to Preston, a larger community that its Mormon settlers had named in the 1880s after Preston, England, the town where early LDS missionaries met with great success. The only record available about Junior's LDS membership is his certificate of ordination to the office of deacon in the Aaronic Priesthood in the Preston Second

Ward, Franklin Stake, in October 1936. His father, Nathan, did not ordain him.[4]

Nathan Van Noy graduated from Preston High School in 1942. Coincidentally, four years earlier in 1938, Leonard Carl Brostrom had graduated from the same school and also received the Medal of Honor for actions in October 1944 in the Philippines.[5] (See Chapter 5.) Van Noy soon took a job in the transportation section of the Army Service Forces Depot in Ogden, Utah. In February 1943, Nathan Van Noy received his draft notice to serve in the United States armed forces.[6]

* * *

December 8, 1942, Brisbane, Australia

A year earlier to the day, December 8, 1941, was the worst day in General Douglas MacArthur's career of fifty-two years. The Japanese not only attacked Pearl Harbor but also commenced a well-planned and well-executed invasion of the Philippines. (Despite the difference in the date, thanks to the International Date Line, the two actions happened simultaneously.) MacArthur, then stationed in Manila, was the commander of all U.S. forces—Army, Army Air Forces, and Navy, and the Philippine Commonwealth's armed forces. On that black day, MacArthur had received reports for several hours before the attack that the Japanese were assaulting Hawaii; but indecisively, he did little. The result was that he soon lost half his air force, with dozens of aircraft destroyed on the ground. Although he deployed some of his ground forces to key defensive position, the Japanese wisely landed elsewhere. That had been the terrible situation in December 1941. Now, after a year, late 1942 the situation was . . . still terrible.

In a power-play of politics among the Allies, between the Army and Navy, and among men of huge egos but proven military ability, the Allies divided the world as Charlemagne or Augustus had, among powers, nations, leaders, commanders, and geography. Admiral Chester Nimitz was the over-all commander in the Pacific. He commanded the most important naval force in the Pacific Ocean, especially the aircraft carriers; and he had responsibility for the main axis of advance to Japan—directly across several thousand miles and dozens of key islands and archipelagoes en route. His area was formally designated as the Pacific Ocean Areas headquartered at Pearl Harbor, where he camped out in Admiral Husband Kimmel's former office. Kimmel, former commander of the Pacific Fleet, had been abruptly relieved of duty ten days after the Japanese surprise attack on Pearl Harbor. Nimitz had most of the naval and Marine resources, some army divisions and a growing fleet under his control. Whatever Nimitz wanted, he seemed to be able to obtain. In 1942, his Navy won the Battle of Coral Sea and the crucial Battle of Midway. He had also landed Marines on Guadalcanal, later reinforcing them by an army division. These first actions were essential victories, exactly what the American people needed.

For Douglas MacArthur, it was an entirely different matter.

Perhaps out of political necessity or respect, President Franklin Roosevelt and his advisors carved out a chunk of the Pacific for MacArthur's command, officially designating it as the Southwest Pacific Area (SWPA). It was crowded with huge land masses: Australia, New Guinea, and, of course, the Philippine Islands. MacArthur's daunting task was to invade and secure areas now occupied by the Japanese.

A particular challenge was the hundreds of islands sprinkled over hundreds of thousands of square miles of ocean. These islands and island groups were miserable places to fight a conventional war of divisions and linear combat operations. They included malaria-infested jungles. Some islands were crowned by steep mountains and ringed by barren beaches. Many consisted of little more than atolls with no fresh water and little life. Most of these lands had no roads, few usable harbors, and only primitive airfields.

The Philippines were not only a former American possession and a huge island archipelago; but for MacArthur personally and his family, they were almost home. His father, Arthur MacArthur, was a general in the original U.S. invasion and occupation in 1898–99. Both his father and Douglas governed the Philippines during their careers. When General MacArthur was ordered by President Franklin Roosevelt to leave the Philippines in March 1942, it was a crushing humiliation for the general to leave his soldiers in a desperate fight. When he reached Australia, he declared, "I shall return." For MacArthur, this promise to return to the Philippines was more than a call to action; it was the engagement of his personal honor to free the Filipinos from Japanese aggression and end their brutal occupation.[7]

There were few armed forces available to MacArthur when he arrived in Australia in April 1942. He had no navy, no army forces to speak of, no artillery, only obsolete tanks, and only a few dozen aircraft at his disposal. Most Australian forces were fighting in the Middle East against the Germans or were in Malaysia with the British forces. The Roosevelt administration had assured him that sufficient forces, equipment, and supplies were awaiting him in Australia when it ordered him out of the Philippines. Once MacArthur arrived in Australia and learned the true situation, he was furious with everyone: President Roosevelt, Army Chief of Staff General George Marshal, and others. Privately, he also fumed because he did not command the entire Pacific Theater of War.[8]

Because of its geographical location between Australia and several island groups and its proximity to the East Indies and the Philippines, New Guinea, the largest island in the world after Greenland, was a critical region for the Allies—and, for the same reasons, to the Japanese. Australian soldiers already occupied key regions in southern New Guinea. For more than a century, it had been a colony, first of the Dutch, then of the British. Germany controlled a portion until World War I, then it came under Australian control. In 1942 it was still divided politically into three major portions. Australia administered the southeast territory, Papua, and, exactly to the north, North East New Guinea. The entire western portion of the island was Dutch New Guinea and politically part of the Dutch East Indies—a strip some 1,600 miles long from the eastern tip to the western end. The Owen Stanley Mountains divided N.E. New Guinea from Papua in the east, while the higher Central Range continued westward. These were daunting ranges, reaching more than 10,000 feet in elevation. The first campaign for complete control of New Guinea would be over this high spine of mountains.

After a year of combat operations, General MacArthur had had only one minor victory and the Australians had achieved it. In the spring of 1942 the Japanese launched an overland campaign from the north shore of New Guinea over the high Owen Stanley Mountains along the Kokoda trail to the Australian-held harbor town of Port Moresby. After a desperate fight, the Australians re-pulsed a Japanese assault, killing hundreds; thousands more died from starvation, malaria, and exhaustion. If it had not been for the Australians, there would have been no Allied troops to command. MacArthur knew that the New Guinea campaign for the Austra-lians was like fighting in their own back yard.

The Allied global effort was so critical in the spring of 1942 that it took Australian Prime Minister John Curtin months to convince Winston Churchill to release the Australian divisions from North Africa to come home and defend their own country.[9] Now, by December 1942, with few naval forces to assist and a small and inadequate air force, MacArthur's newly arrived and untested Americans and his seasoned Australians grappled with the Japanese in mortal combat for two key port towns that would become legend in military history—Buna and Gona.

This battle was the first serious American involvement in New Guinea. Buna and Gona were bloody, costly actions which Mac-Arthur swore he would never repeat. He needed more men, divi-sions, fighter aircraft, bombers, landing craft, and a navy.

* * *

Nathan Van Noy received War Department Order Number 10,743, dated February 9, 1943, while he was working in Utah. The message began "Greetings" and continued: "Having submitted yourself to a local board composed of your neighbors for the purpose of determining your availability and service in the land or naval forces of the United States, you are hereby notified that you have now been selected for training and service therein."[10]

This notice was from Local Board #1 for Franklin County, Idaho, based in Preston. Later a new notice ordered him to report at Fort Douglas, Utah, on February 24, 1943. Overlooking Salt Lake City, Fort Douglas had been established in 1862 during the Civil War. The fort was not tied to any military school or training area. Its function was basically administrative; and in this case, it operated as a reception station for inductees.

Van Noy reported as directed, was issued uniforms, and received a haircut that cost him 75 cents.[11] In one of his first letters home, he wrote, "I sure like the army, all but the grub it is to[o] greasy, but maybe I will get used to it." Imagine that! a soldier complaining about army chow. The army, of course, had its downsides, even for Private Van Noy. "Well I just got another jolt, a shot in the arm today," he wrote to his mother Pauline, "sure was the shits but I am getting along alright."[12] Then as only a son would do, he asked his mom for a favor: "If you can get me a little sewing kit please," he wrote, "I sure need it."[13]

After a short time at Fort Douglas, he was transferred to Fort Francis E. Warren in Cheyenne, Wyoming, for basic training, followed by additional skill training. Originally named Fort D. A. Russell, after Civil War General David Russell, killed in the battle of Third Winchester in September 1864, the post was renamed in the 1920s by John Pershing, General of the Armies, for Francis Warren, U.S. Senator from Wyoming, who was also Pershing's father-in-law.[14] Cheyenne was a small town on the wide, high desert plains of windswept Wyoming. Junior was assigned to Company H, 1st Quartermaster Training Regiment. For about six weeks, he underwent the typical basic training regimen of drill and ceremo-

nies, inspections, marching, field and marksmanship training, and
such pleasant diversions as guard duty and "KP" (kitchen police).

"We went into the gas chamber today," Van Noy wrote, "when
we got in they had us remove our masks it was tear gas." He then
explained what it was like to see thirty or forty men "bawling . . .
tears streaming from their eyes, our faces burning and we were all
coughing. They did this to show us the importance of our gas masks,
believe me I sure value mine now!"[15]

Nathan wrote home on March 23, 1943: "Don't get me wrong
I really like the Army, if I had known it was like this I believe I
would have inlisted before. I know when I come back I will realy
be a man and I mean a man." One can feel the youthful exuber-
ance rise from the page of this letter. After his basic training, Van
Noy remained for advance training as a supply specialist in the
quartermaster corps. He learned the duties and tasks of maintaining provisions, supply procedures, requisitioning and forecasting
his unit's requirements, and maintaining an inventory. In other
words, he was not trained as an infantryman, paratrooper, or a
tanker, but as a company supply clerk.[16]

In May 1943, Nathan received notice that he was heading for
the Pacific Theater of War and, like tens of thousands of other
Americans, had no idea where he was going until he arrived. Junior
was eventually assigned to the 532nd Engineer Boat and Shore
Regiment as a supply clerk in Headquarters Company, Shore Battalion, 2nd Engineering Special Brigade.

The young, lean soldier wrote home from an undisclosed location in California on June 11, 1943: "I have been putting on weight
and I feel great, although I still miss your cooking." Wartime censorship and security had created a culture that everyone knew and
understood. Whether he shipped from San Diego, San Francisco,
or Long Beach is not important. Nathan could not, of course, disclose his orders but he hinted: "Well Mom if you don't hear from
me for quite awhile, do not worry because I know I will be alright."
In nearly every letter home, Junior assured his mother that she
need not worry about him. They must have had a close relation-

ship. Junior's older brother, Bill, was a soldier in the Army Corps of Engineers based in England. Soon Pauline Van Noy would receive letters from Junior in the southwest Pacific as General MacArthur, and also Admiral Nimitz, combined forces to capture the most threatening Japanese base in the southern reaches of the Solomon Islands and the Bismarck Archipelago: Rabaul.

* * *

Rabaul was a strongly fortified Japanese base with airfields, harbors, and 100,000 troops on the eastern end of New Britain. The conquest of the Solomon Islands and New Guinea was impossible unless Rabaul could be captured or neutralized. Allied planners named the operation, Cartwheel, a very fitting name for its design and operational concept. At the time, the mission was, "The Reduction of Rabaul."

The entire island-hopping strategy of the Pacific Theater was mostly decided on the basis of where airfields could be captured or established. It was necessary that ground troops, invading forces, and sea lanes be covered by air power. The range of land-based bombers, fighters, and transports became the planning imperative for nearly all operations. Carrier-based air operations were mobile and more flexible but restricted by the number and size of aircraft.

Geography was a monster. The entire continental United States could fit in a mere half of MacArthur's Southwest Pacific Area. Nature created two avenues of approach to New Britain and Rabaul: one like stepping stones and the other a sidewalk. The stepping stones were hundreds of islands in the Solomon Islands group starting with Guadalcanal, where a vicious battle was already underway beginning in August 1942, then proceeding to the Bismarck Archipelago (with Rabaul on New Britain), and finally closing the approach from the west with the Admiralty Islands. The sidewalk was New Guinea, a long narrow island resembling a road-runner, with its head stretched out and tail protruding east and west. These two natural features created avenues or corridors that developed pincer arms, allowing a double envelopment of Rabaul.

In April 1943, the Joint Chiefs authorized the concept for Cartwheel: leap-frogging along the Solomon chain, then invading and occupying the north coast of New Guinea. The operational goal initially was to either destroy or neutralize Rabaul. But as the operation unfolded, the concept changed. It became obvious that capturing Rabaul would be too costly. The alternative plan was to isolate, surround, and thus neutralize Rabaul. At this stage of the war, Allied commanders, especially MacArthur, determined that the best way to limit casualties was to bypass the strong points and place a force in Japan's rear, cutting across its lines of communications and logistics and forcing the Japanese to withdraw from their major bases strongholds or see them cut off.[17]

The key to Cartwheel's success would be the naval and landing craft support required for such a complex operation, led by a brilliant and aggressive commander of the 7th Fleet, Vice Admiral William ("Bull") Halsey. Halsey would command the island-hopping pincer up the Solomon chain toward and then past New Britain.[18] The U.S. Army and Australians would carry most of the burden of MacArthur's southern pincer force.

Until 1943, the Imperial Australian Forces in the southwest Pacific under the command of General Sir Thomas Blamey had done most of the fighting and gained the initiative in the first battles on New Guinea. Blamey was a seasoned officer whom MacArthur respected, but he would not allow non-Americans to command Americans troops.

Once Gona and Buna were captured and Operation Cartwheel was underway, MacArthur decided it was time to reorganize his forces. He first established the U.S. Army Forces—Far East under his personal command, then created the Sixth U.S. Army, nicknamed the "Alamo" Force. He wangled the appointment of an old friend to command it, Lt. General Walter Kreuger from the Third Army in San Antonio, Texas. Kreuger was a veteran of the Spanish-American War and had been in the Army longer

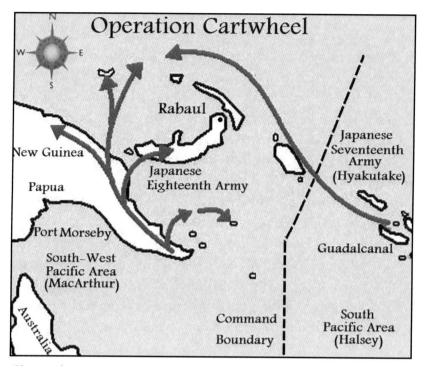

Closing the trap to neutralize Rabaul. Cartography by Hyrum H. Fleek.

than MacArthur. Under Kreuger, MacArthur formed the I Corps under Major General Richard Eichelberger consisting of nearly all the American units, especially the 32nd and 41st Divisions, both of which were National Guard units from Wisconsin and Oregon respectively. Also in the Sixth Army was the 503rd Parachute Infantry Regiment (PIR) providing airborne capability and separate infantry, field artillery, and antiaircraft regiments. Much later in 1943, the famous 1st Cavalry Division and the 24th Infantry Divisions, both from the Regular Army, would join the Sixth Army. MacArthur grouped all four of the Australian divisions under General Blamey into the Allied Land Forces. Whether right or wrong, MacArthur wanted to keep the American troops under his direct control, not under Allied leadership.[19]

To execute MacArthur's leap-frogging along the north coast of New Guinea, the Navy gave him one of its top amphibious experts,

Rear Admiral Daniel Barbey, to command the VII Amphibious Force. Unfortunately, until the spring of 1943, all MacArthur had in the way of an amphibious fleet were a few boats and landing craft provided by the Army's Engineering Special Brigade (ESB). He had no LSTs (Landing Ship Tank) or LCIs (Landing Craft Infantry) or tenders and transports for logistics until Admiral Barbey arrived.[20]

The 2nd ESB, one of three such brigades in the Army, was a brilliant idea. The U.S. Army Corps of Engineers and the War Department had conceived the concept as the war in Europe commenced and the possibility of a war with Japan in the Pacific loomed large. (The 1st ESB served in Europe, the 2nd and 3rd in the Pacific.) The Army needed an amphibious capability. These brigades had shore and boat regiments that constructed harbor facilities, repaired landing craft, and provided engineering support to the units tasked with amphibious operations.

* * *

As the Allies developed their plans for operations against New Guinea, the Japanese area commanders also developed counter-measures to stop Allied advances. The terrible jungle war along the spine of the island was brutal and costly. In late 1942, the Japanese made a determined effort to push inland west of Huon Gulf to the high mountain town of Wau where the Australians tenuously held a pre-war airfield built by a mining company. If the Japanese took control of Wau, then they could wreak havoc on the Allies with air power. The battles were small but torturous. If grenades and machine guns did not kill enough soldiers, then malaria, dysentery, and dengue fever took their toll. The midlands and mountains of New Guinea were crisscrossed with mountain trails hardly wide enough for foot soldiers, let alone vehicles and heavy equipment. The Japanese failed in their effort to capture Wau, losing hundreds in the attempt. Though victorious, the Australian 7th and

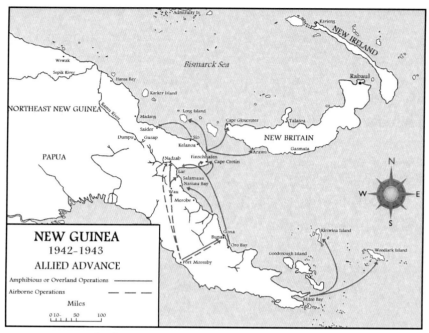

Eastern end of New Guinea. Cartography by Hyrum H. Fleek.

the American 32nd Divisions were sorely weakened after months of fighting in the jungle mountains.[21]

The next obvious Allied targets after the capture of Gona and Buna were the key towns and harbors in the Huon Gulf. The Japanese 8th Army under the command of Lt. Gen. Hatazo Adachi had some 55,000 troops deployed in key points and defensive positions in New Guinea. The main Japanese force in the Huon Gulf was the 51st Division, though not all of its components had reached New Guinea by February 1943. Therefore, the Japanese 8th Area Army headquarters in Rabaul ordered some 7,000 troops, most from its 115th Regiment, to reinforce the 51st Division in the Lae and Salamaua area of Huon Gulf. These men and their equipment and provisions were moved aboard sixteen transports escorted by eight destroyers. The convoy departed from Rabaul on February 28, 1943, with strong air support from several Japanese airfields nearby.[22]

The Battle of the Bismarck Sea occurred due to luck and the sharp eyes of an American B–24 crew. It was also an unusual battle where the Allied forces were mostly aircraft attacking Japanese transports and destroyers. Once again the importance of airpower proved how vulnerable ships can be to air attacks if they are not protected by their own aircraft.

Poor weather provided some cover to the Japanese convoy; but on March 2, the day after it was spotted, twenty-eight B–17 bombers of the U.S. Army Air Force were airborne from bases near Port Moresby, New Guinea, en route to the kill. These magnificent "Flying Fortresses" were from Lt. Gen. George Kenney's 15th Air Force, the air arm of MacArthur's SWPA. They bombed and strafed the barges like ducks on a pond, sinking one transport by thousand-pound bombs. Hundreds of Japanese soldiers were adrift in the open sea. Most drowned, but Japanese destroyers rescued some and evacuated them to Lae on New Guinea.[23]

The next day, March 3, 1943, the Japanese convoy of fifteen troop transports and destroyer escorts was only ninety miles from a friendly coast, but Australian medium bombers and American B–17, B–24, and B–25 bombers attacked again, dropping bombs from low altitudes or making strafing runs. P–38 and P–40 American fighters joined in, fighting off Japanese air support. Several transports were sunk along with four Japanese destroyers. The next day, American PT (torpedo patrol) boats finished off several damaged ships. Hundreds of Japanese soldiers struggled in the water; most of them drowned.

The Battle of the Bismarck Sea was a disaster for Japan. Allied air power sank eight troop transports, and four destroyers. Allied fighter planes also downed dozens of Japanese planes in aerial fights. The Japanese claimed a loss of 3,664 troops, but this figure fails to account for the fact that a few of the transports arrived in New Guinea. The Allies lost four aircraft and had thirteen airmen confirmed killed in action. [24]

* * *

The 2nd ESB was commanded by Brigadier General William F. Heavey, a graduate from West Point in April 1917. His class had graduated two months early, a schedule accelerated to coincide with the United States' declaration of Germany in April 1917. His unique unit was in direct support of the operations against the key Japanese-held towns Lae and Salamaua on the coast of Huon Gulf, just south of the Huon Peninsula. Australian General Blamey planned and orchestrated the campaign to cut Lae and Salamaua off from reinforcements and capture them. One of the key tactical moves was to capture a Japanese airfield at Nadzab, a mountain location assigned to the 503rd PIR, along with ground support from the Australian 7th Division. On September 5, 1,700 paratroopers boarded sixty-four C-47 aircraft at Port Moresby and jumped out at 1,000 feet near Nadzab. They captured the airfield, and the Japanese defenders fled. Allied casualties were three dead and thirty-three injured. All of the injuries resulted from bad landings, not enemy action.[25]

At 0445 on September 4, the day before the Nadzab airborne operation, battalions of the Australian 9th Division under Major General George Wooten boarded twenty-seven LSTs and twenty LCIs at Milne Bay on the far east end of New Guinea. They made a landing near Salamaua, which fell to Allied forces on September 12; Lae was the next target.[26]

General Heavey's EBS was involved with both of these actions providing crucial engineer support, supplies, ammunition, and replacements, besides repairing damaged landing craft and establishing dock and harbor facilities. On September 16, 1943, Lae was cleared of the enemy, thus ending the Lae and Salamaua battles—Junior Van Noy's first action. The Japanese lost some 2,850 men killed, joining another 8,100 casualties totaled by the captures of Wau, Nadzad, Lae, and Salamaua. Allied forces lost 430 Australian and 81 American dead, and 1,120 and 396 wounded, respectively.[27]

A beachhead designated by American and Australia forces as "Scarlet Beach" lay a few miles north of Finschhafen, an old Dutch

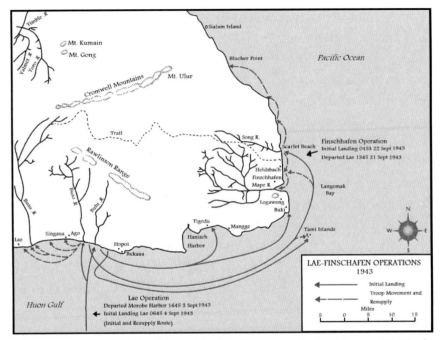

The Huon Peninsula and Finschhafen. Cartography by Hyrum H. Fleek.

colonial town, on the point of Huon Peninsula. Finschhafen was a Japanese strongpoint. The U.S. Army engineers were providing direct support for the 162nd Infantry Regiment and Australians for the invasion that took place on September 22. That same day, Private Van Noy, the 532nd Engineer Boat and Shore Battalion, the Australian 20th Brigade, and the 2nd ESB landed on Scarlet Beach. They met only sporadic fire from the jungle tree line against the first two landings; but the third landing received much heavier fire because the Japanese had time to react. Eventually, the threat on the beachhead was eliminated. Most of the Japanese forces were deployed to the south near Finschhafen or higher in the hills near the Sattleberg peak to the west.[28]

The Allies consolidated their beachhead and began unloading tons of supplies and equipment. Later that day several Japanese aircraft attacked and strafed Scarlet Beach. Junior Van Noy, a supply clerk in Headquarters Company, came under fire. As Japanese Zeke Type 0 fighters ("Zeroes") attacked, Junior jumped to a

Browning .50 caliber machine gun mounted on one of the landing craft and opened fire, singlehandedly accounting for the kill of a Japanese fighter that winged over and crashed not far from the Allied beachhead. This was no small feat, mathematically speaking, considering the ratio of a few three-second bursts of half-inch bullets flying at the Browning's comparatively slow rate of 450 rounds per minute.[29] A belt of .50 caliber ammo was nine yards long—hence the expression, "the whole nine yards." At that time, antiaircraft machine guns were dual, or had four guns ("quads") mounted together that could lay down a serious amount of firepower. Van Noy had had great skill, great luck, or both.

But he did not escape unscathed. Several bomb blasts and enemy rounds sprayed shrapnel, and some flying fragments wounded Junior in the left arm, neck, and shoulder. He was treated at an aid station, and the army physician ordered him off the beach to a hospital in a more secure area. Van Noy refused to go. He convinced the medical staff to release him for duty. His section leader, Sergeant John Fucina from Brooklyn, New York, wrote to Pauline Noy, that Junior had said, "If the Aussies can take [it] so can I." Later Van Noy contracted an unnamed jungle infection, and Sergeant Fucina took him back to the aid station a couple times a day for treatment. Fucina wrote, "I tried to have him relieved of his duty but he out-talked the doctors."[30]

"Just a line to let you know I am well and safe," Nathan wrote his mother after he shot down the Japanese fighter. He did not mention his coup but used the cramped space on the V-mail form to add his usual reassurance: "I can't tell you where I am but don't worry because I will get along alright. I hope you received the rings I sent to you." The rings were a unique story in themselves. Some of Junior's comrades took some of the metal from the Japanese Zero he shot down and fashioned two rings out it. These he sent home to his mother and brother Spencer. For his wounds at Scarlet Beach, Private Van Noy's chain of command recommended him for the Purple Heart. The award was approved the day before his last action, but he never knew about the decoration.[31]

For the next three weeks, the Allies pushed deeper inland against the Japanese 20th Division up in the Cromwell Mountains and against the primary objective of Finschhafen some twenty miles to the south. Two separate Australian brigades supported by American engineers, namely Van Noy's 2nd ESB, and other units, commenced a double envelopment of elements of the Japanese naval garrison and a company of the 2nd Battalion, 238th Infantry Regiment, at Finschhafen. After determined Allied attacks, Finschhafen fell on October 2, 1943. However, driving the Japanese out of the rugged Cromwell Mountains was a more difficult task.

* * *

In war, plans and intelligence are sometimes accurate; but on most occasions, estimates are little more than educated guesses by highly trained experts. The notion of a Japanese counterattack, especially local attacks by seaborne means, seemed unlikely at this time. Reckoning up the appalling defeats and losses of Japanese men and landing craft caused by Allied air attacks, Allied intelligence analysts concluded that such a risky operation was out of the question. But that was exactly what the local Japanese commanders were planning. For two weeks some 2,400 troops in small units marched or were airlifted near the Huon Peninsula to reinforce the Japanese 20th Division and retake the harbors at Finschhafen and at Heldsbach, a few miles to the north.[32]

At this point in the campaign, the Japanese did not have air superiority nor did they have complete freedom of the sea lanes, but they could still bite hard in both. By early October, the Japanese were ready to launch a three-pronged advance. Two elements would come overland, down from the Sattleberg area and converging near Finschhafen. The third element was the most audacious. Some 100 Japanese troops aboard three transport barges would land at Scarlet Beach and at the Song River with the goal of destroying Allied ammunition caches, harbor and landing craft facilities, and heavy engineer equipment. The Japanese 79th Division dispatched an especially trained outfit, the Suginao Boat Unit, to make the amphibious counterattack. On October 16, the landing force boarded the barges and made its way into the seas south toward the Song River and Scarlet Beach. Simultaneously, the overland elements advanced but were challenged by both the terrain and obstinate Australian forces.[33]

* * *

October 17, 1943, Day of Days

On the evening of October 16, 1943, as the Japanese approached Scarlet Beach in their barges, the men of the shore and boat battalion finished their duties and retired for the night. Except for those at observation posts manning fighting positions, most went to sleep. Australian infantrymen along with Americans were deployed along Scarlet Beach and manned defensive positions in the jungle tree-lines and at supporting antiaircraft sites. The combat tempo had deteriorated into small actions well inland and in the highlands well above the coast. There had been no fighting for several days in the vicinity of Finschhafen or along the point of Huon Peninsula.[34]

Thus, the men along Scarlet Beach, after another hard and laborious day in the hot, humid climate, grabbed some chow and stretched their hammocks. Some wrote letters home. The religious among them prayed. In the case of an attack, however, each of these seasoned soldiers, American and Aussies, had an assigned position for small sections, squads, and gun crews at their defensive stations.

The Bismarck Sea was dark and still as Sergeant Fucina and Technical Sergeant Raymond J. Koch of Wabasha, Minnesota, made a call of nature before turning in when they noticed "three smudges on the skyline." Three barges with their high-peaked, double prows, packed with almost a hundred combat-ready Japanese troops and their equipment, slowly cut across the bay toward Scarlet Beach.

The two quickly sounded an alarm and raced to their positions. Junior Van Noy jumped from his hammock and sprinted to his assigned position at a .50 caliber machine gun. In moments, Corporal Stephen Popa, Junior's loader, joined him. Sergeant Fucina and dozens of Australians opened up on the lead barge with a heavy 37mm antiaircraft gun and also a 40mm, Swedish-made Bofors antiaircraft cannon. Small arms fire also crackled out. They made a series of direct hits. A barge caught fire and began to sink. Japanese soldiers jumped overboard and began to swim ashore. Many drowned. The defenders killed many in the surf.

Private Van Noy did not fire. He waited.

As the two other barges approached Scarlet Beach near Van Noy and Popa, the noise of the firefight reached horrific proportions. Hundreds of tracers darted through the black night; grenade blasts, flares, and burning debris illuminated the darkness.

The two remaining barges, with perhaps 50 to 60 troops total, were coming in toward a less contested section of the beach than where the first barge was sinking. Waiting in silence were Junior Van Noy and Corporal Popa. The two barges were only ten or fifteen yards away. All that stood between these two American soldiers and some sixty Japanese soldiers was their Browning machine gun, meagerly sheltered behind a sandbag barricade. The menacing attackers not only had heavy machine guns mounted on the barges and small arms, but two of the Japanese had flamethrowers already ignited.[35]

The two barges ran up on the beach almost simultaneously. The steel ramps slowly lowered into the churning surf.

Van Noy held his fire.

Japanese bugles and whistles sounded loudly among the racket of chaos, and the troops charged down the ramp, into the waves and on to the sand.

And Junior Van Noy opened fire.

Dozens and dozens of .50 caliber rounds in three-to-five second bursts ripped into the attacking enemy. The two soldiers holding flamethrowers were among the first killed. The Japanese soldiers threw hand grenades whose small but extremely lethal denotations blasted in the sand, throwing red-hot shrapnel through the air. The large guns manned by Australians banged away. The Japanese struggling up the exposed beach returned fire with all their might. It was hellish madness.

Then the Allied order was sounded to withdraw to the second defensive position, back into the tree lines. Americans and Aussies fought their way back to where the large caliber guns were positioned, but Van Noy and Popa remained in their isolated position, still pouring belts of bullets through their Browning. They either did not hear the order or ignored it.

The heavy fire continued, tracers and grenades flashing blindingly but briefly against the blackness.

Sergeant Fucina and others yelled at Van Noy and Popa to retreat. Then a Japanese grenade landed in the gun position. Corporal Popa's leg was shattered. Van Noy yelled at Popa to escape while he provided covering fire. Popa crawled up the beach, dragging his bleeding and broken leg behind him. He yelled at Van Noy to follow him to the stronger defensive line.[36]

But Van Noy remained behind. The firefight continued, with Junior changing the ammo belts, concentrating ferociously on making the beach in front of him a kill zone.

At the secondary lines, his comrades saw grenades land repeatedly near his position. Finally, the firing waned, a few more grenades exploded on the beach. The long night of fighting with its hours of darkness was over. Deadly silence reigned on Scarlet Beach as the sun rose.

The Allied soldiers slowly moved down through the jungle to the beach. The first barge was sunk but still visible, just off the shore. The two other barges were burned-out wrecks on the shore. Thirty-nine Japanese dead lay near or in front of Van Noy's isolated gun position. Other Japanese bodies lay scattered all along the beach, some half-in, half-out of the water. Other bodies were bobbing in the surf.

Scarlet Beach had truly earned its name.

At the lone machine-gun position, they found the body of Nathan K. Van Noy Jr. His left leg had been completely blown off by a grenade. He had also received several shrapnel and bullet wounds. An ugly bullet hole centered in his forehead between his eyes suggested that he had been executed at close range, or that a Japanese survivor, stunned by Junior's ferocious fighting spirit, had fired a "make sure" final bullet.

But before he died, Junior had fired every round of ammunition he had.[37]

* * *

The entire Japanese landing party had been wiped out, but Private Van Noy was the only Allied fatality. Such a strangely lopsided fate is actually common in war. One could argue that Van Noy's death and his valor in killing dozens of Japanese invaders, actually saved lives—Allied lives.

A Western Union telegram, dated October 24, 1943, addressed to Mrs. Pauline H. Van Noy, 325 West, 2nd South, Preston, Idaho, read:

> Regret to inform you report received States your son Private Junior N Van Noy who was previously reported Slightly wounded twenty September returned to Duty twenty two September and is now reported killed in action on Seventeen October in the South West Pacific area the secretary of war extends his deepest sympathy. Letter to follow. The Adjutant General[38]

Today, a casualty notification officer would call personally on the bereaved family to break the terrible news with a human voice; but World War II sent telegrams—brief, impersonal statements of fact in fragmented sentences, fragmented like the lives they shattered upon delivery.[39] The overwhelming and enormous fact was Junior's death—the phrase "killed in action" erasing all of the repeated reassurances of Junior's letters. It stated that he had been wounded on September 20 and returned to duty on the 22nd; in fact, it was the 22nd when his unit reached Scarlet Beach, and he had shot down a Japanese Zero, was wounded in the process, but talked his way out of the aid station and back on duty.

Over the following days, weeks, and for months to come, Pauline Van Noy received dozens of consolation letters and telegrams from all over the country, especially after the article about Junior in *Yank Magazine* appeared three months after Junior's death. McLeod's description of his youth, his modesty, and his near innocence, coupled with his startling heroism, touched a chord in the American public.

But accolades also came from those who served with Junior Van Noy. Padre W. E. Holt, a minister of the Church of England and a chaplain in the Australian army, wrote to Pauline in May 1945, a year and a half after the action: "During the Huon Peninsula campaign in New Guinea, I had the sad duty of burying your gallant son. What can I now say to cheer and comfort your mother-heart and help you see the purposes of divine love shining through the darkness which this news must have brought?" He searched for consoling words: "There will be many who remember your lad with gratitude and pride. . . . If our Christian faith means anything, it doesn't much matter what happens to the cast off cloak of this physical body but somehow we do care for our remains (especially mothers who know what a new life costs)." Padre Holt's closing praise was not that of a religious leader but of a sympathetic and appreciative man: "Junior's chief characteristic was his irrepressible humour and his sunny smile."[40]

In addition to the Purple Heart, authorized before Junior's death but not in time for him to find out about it, he was nominated for the Medal of Honor. Major Harry M. Rising Jr., the commanding officer of the Shore Battalion of the 532nd Engineer Boat and Shore Regiment, wrote from New Guinea on March 10, 1944: "Pvt Van Noy's courage fills the men of the organization with pride at having been allowed to serve with him." After mentioning the news of Van Noy's nomination for the medal, Major Rising continued his letter to Pauline, "I wish to tell you how strongly we have been inspired, how much more determined we will be in trying to live up to the high ideals of bravery and sacrifice shown by Private Van Noy."[41] There is no greater compliment for a soldier than praise from his comrades in arms.

By February 1944, the Van Noy family learned that Junior had been awarded the Medal of Honor. The award ceremony took place in the Franklin Stake Tabernacle in Preston on March 17, 1944. Representing the president of the United States, the commander of the 9th Service Command headquartered at Fort Douglas in Salt Lake City, assigned Colonel A. E. Merrill, a reserve cavalry officer, to officiate and present the award to the family.[42]

The U.S. Army also christened a "port repair" ship, the first of its kind and type for the Army Corps of Engineers, after Van Noy, on May 20, 1944. The *Josephine Lawrence*, a 2,500 ton and twenty-five-year-old commercial freighter, was renamed the *Junior Van Noy*. Manned with a crew of Army soldiers and captained by an Army engineer, it sailed for Italy in the summer of 1944 to repair harbor facilities in Naples.[43] In the 1950s, the Army and the Corps of Engineers named the community library at Fort Belvoir, Virginia, the Van Noy Post Library.

* * *

In 1948, Junior's remains were returned to the United States and interred in the cemetery of his birthplace, Grace, Idaho. Later, a monument was erected at his grave. In Preston, his other home, another monument was dedicated to Nathan Van Noy and also to Private First Class Leonard C. Brostrom, who, like Van Noy, was posthumously awarded the Medal of Honor.

NATHAN ("JUNIOR") VAN NOY

Rank and organization: Private, U.S. Army, Headquarters Company, Shore Battalion, Engineer Boat and Shore Regiment. Place and date: Near Finschhafen, New Guinea, October 17, 1943. Entered service at: Preston, Idaho. Birth: August 9, 1925, Grace, Idaho. G.O. No.: 17, February 26, 1944.

Citation

For conspicuous gallantry and intrepidity above and beyond the call of duty in action with the enemy near Finschafen, [sic] New Guinea, on 17 October 1943. When wounded late in September, Pvt. Van Noy declined evacuation and continued on duty. On 17 October 1943 he was gunner in charge of a machinegun post only 5 yards from the water's edge when the alarm was given that 3 enemy barges loaded with troops were approaching the beach in the early morning darkness. One landing barge was sunk by Allied fire, but the other 2 beached 10 yards from Pvt. Van Noy's emplacement. Despite his exposed position, he poured a withering hail of fire into the debarking enemy troops. His loader was wounded by a grenade and evacuated. Pvt. Van Noy, also grievously wounded, remained at his post, ignoring calls of nearby soldiers urging him to withdraw, and continued to fire with deadly accuracy. He expended every round and was found, covered with wounds, dead beside his gun. In this action Pvt. Van Noy killed at least half of the 39 enemy taking part in the landing. His heroic tenacity at the price of his life not only saved the lives of many of his comrades, but enabled them to annihilate the attacking detachment.

Notes

1. John McLeod, "Bravery and Death on Scarlet Beach," *YANK Magazine: The Army Weekly*, December 31, 1943, 1–2.

2. Ibid.

3. Van Noy Family Collection. The Van Noy family, especially brother Spencer Van Noy compiled an album of papers, letters, certificates, and documents relative to Private Van Noy. They were preserved with friends of the family in Preston, Idaho. It includes family and official records, newspaper clippings, letters, and other material. Copies of this collection are also held by the Idaho State Military Museum in Boise, and the Saints at War Project, L. Tom Perry Special Collections and Manuscripts Division, Harold B. Lee Library, Brigham Young University, Provo, Utah; and at the Special Collections, David O. McKay Library, Brigham Young University-Idaho, Rexburg, Idaho.

4. Baptismal certificate, dated July 24, 1893, Pauline Justine Petersen, Aalborg Conference, Denmark; certificate of ordination Nathan Kilby Van Noy Jr., October 25, 1936, both in the Van Noy Family Collection.

5. There is little doubt in a small farming community of some 2,000 people that Leonard and Nathan knew each other. Preston and its high school are famous for another detail of popular culture. The film *Napoleon Dynamite* was filmed there, and many of the students in the film were actual Preston High School students.

6. Leo Huekelr, Letter to Spencer Van Noy, January [no day], 1944, Van Noy Family Collection.

7. William Manchester, *American Caesar: Douglas MacArthur 1880–1964*, 425.

8. Ibid.

9. Harry A. Gailey, *MacArthur's Victory: The War in New Guinea, 1943–1944*, 4–5.

10. Induction orders, February 9 and 17, 1943, Van Noy Family Collection.

11. Nathan Van Noy, Letter to Pauline Van Noy, March 23, 1943, Van Noy Family Collection.

12. Ibid.

13. Nathan Van Noy, Letter to Pauline Van Noy, [no date] 1943, 1 p., Van Noy Family Collection.

14. In 1919, Congress promoted General Pershing to the rank of General of the Armies, the grade equivalent of six-star general or field marshal. In 1976 Congress promoted George Washington to the same grade—with an earlier date of rank, of course.

15. Nathan Van Noy, Letter to Pauline Van Noy, [no date], 1943, 6 pp. Van Noy Family Collection.

16. Nathan Van Noy, Letter to Pauline Van Noy, March 23, 1943; Van Noy Family Collection.

17. Gailey, MacArthur's Victory, 10–12.

18. John Keegan, The Second World War, 300–301.

19. Gailey, MacArthur's Victory, 14–15; John Miller, Cartwheel: The Reduction of Rabual; The United States Army in World War II, 20–22.

20. Gailey, MacArthur's Victory, 48. LSTs were first conceived by the British in 1941 after the Dunkirk disaster in 1940. The United States established its own building programs in 1942.

21. Edward J. Drea, New Guinea: The U.S. Army Campaigns of World War II, 2.

22. Gailey, MacArthur's Victory, 41–46.

23. Ibid.

24. Miller, Cartwheel, 40–41.

25. Gailey, MacArthur's Victory, 60–61.

26. Ibid., 56–57.

27. Ibid., 62–63, 70.

28. Miller, Cartwheel, 217–18.

29. "MacArthur's Amphibs," The Military Engineer 36, no. 223 (May 1944): 148.

30. John Fucina, Letter to Pauline Van Noy, December 5, 1943, New Guinea, Van Noy Family Collection.

31. Adjutant General's Office, Ward Department, Letter to Mrs. Pauline Van Noy, October 27, 1943, Van Noy Family Collection.

32. Miller, Cartwheel, 220.

33. Gailey, MacArthur's Victory, 88–89; Reports of General MacArthur: Japanese Operations in the Southwest Pacific Area, 232.

34. Drea, New Guinea, 14.

35. McLeod, "Bravery and Death on Scarlet Beach," 2. There are some contradictions in various accounts of the action. Some have stated that the barges landed five yards from the machine-gun position, others say fifteen yards; some have other inconsistent facts. Also, later accounts have two Japanese "officers" carrying flamethrowers in the fight; officers did not normally carry flamethrowers in action, especially this type of operation.

36. Ibid., 2.

37. Ibid.

38. Adjutant General, telegram to Pauline H. Van Noy, October 24, 1943, Van Noy Family Collection.

39. Use of the telegram as the method of notifying families of casualties developed during the Spanish-American War but was definitely the process used during World War I and World War II. Sometimes in the case of a high ranking officer's death, multiple losses from the same family, or a large number of casualties from one community, an officer would deliver the news; but there were so many fatalities in World War II that the telegram was standard operating procedure.

40. W. E. Holt, Letter to Pauline Van Noy, May 20, 1945, Van Noy Family Collection.

41. Harry M. Rising, Letter to Mrs. Van Noy, March 10, 1944, Van Noy Family Collection.

42. Press Release, War Department, Bureau of Public Relations, March 16, 1944; Van Noy Family Collection. The invocation was offered by Phenoi H. Edgely, a local LDS leader and father of Richard C. Edgely, who would later be a prominent leader and General Authority in the Church.

43. Julia Shawell, "Army Engineers Go to Sea," Philadelphia Daily News, May 19, 1944, Van Noy Family Collection.

Lieutenant Colonel Edward Michael. Unless otherwise noted, the photographs in this chapter are from the U.S. Navy History Institute.

Chapter Four

LIEUTENANT EDWARD S. MICHAEL AND THE CREW OF "BERTIE LEE"

April 11, 1944, England

Turbulence caused by many gaping holes, damaged surfaces, and the wild wind buffeted the wounded bomber as it pitched, rolled, and yawed nearly out of control. The co-pilot did his best to manhandle the stricken B–17 Flying Fortress as it made the last of several passes over the obscure airfield on the English Channel. The co-pilot's wounded aircraft commander had fainted from loss of blood. The Royal Air Force airfield at Grimsby, England, built for fighters, not bombers, looked like a postage stamp compared to the bomber's home base. But RAF Grimsby, near Waltham, 175 miles northeast of London, was the first available field. During the last pass prior to the approach, the wounded pilot suddenly regained consciousness and, after a moment, resumed control of the aircraft, determined to land his bomber. After all, the *Bertie Lee*, named for his wife, was his aircraft, his responsibility.

The long, deadly mission was nearly over, after hours of attacks by German Luftwaffe fighters and flak[1]—antiaircraft fire. German fighter attacks had damaged the *Bertie Lee* before it could reach its target east of Berlin. Losing both airspeed and altitude, the aircraft commander turned the heavy bomber about before it could drop its load of forty-two, 100-pound incendiary bombs. One of the direct hits by a German fighter's 20mm round smashed into the bomb bay, igniting a small fire that eventually threatened to either engulf the bomber or cause it to explode in mid-air. It was a miracle that the aircraft was even airborne. And that had been hours ago.

The pilot, with the co-pilot's assistance, wrestled the bomber, trying to force it into its final approach. The rudder, the left wing, the elevators, and the trim tabs had all received hits from flak or German fighters. Another 20mm burst had struck the cockpit, destroying all of the instruments except the magnetic compass and two engine gauges. Hydraulic fluid was smeared across the windscreen, and it was nearly impossible to see out.

The British ground crew and especially the controllers in the small tower tried their best to raise the American bomber on the radio, on the standard emergency frequencies, but failed. The radio had been shot out.

Then the crippled bomber fired flares, signaling that it was in trouble. The tower responded with its own flares, confirming the emergency. The ground emergency crew sprang into action. Ambulances, firefighters on fire trucks, and many others sped to the flight line.

The pilot decided that his best option was to attempt a crash landing on a strip of grass next to one of the runways. But it was risky. He had no idea how the aircraft would handle, or if he could descend in a smooth controlled approach on a shallow glide path to his intended landing point. He did not know whether the rudder, elevators, trim tabs, flaps, and especially hydraulic-assisted controls would allow him to land smoothly or whether they would jam on final approach. That was only half of the story.

Not only were the controls sluggish, but the guns of the ball-turret on the belly of the fuselage were stuck, pointing directly down. The bomb-bay doors were jammed open. Worst of all, the landing gear would not lower, either mechanically or manually.

That is why the pilot elected to land on the turf and not on the concrete runway. It would have to be a belly landing.

Slowly the pilot made a standard-rate turn to final approach and carefully reduced power. This maneuver too was extremely tricky. The 20mm hit that had struck the instrument panel had also disabled the power controls on two engines. The super-charger levers on the other two engines were "inop." This landing would require a very delicate control touch and great skill.

Tensely the ground crew, tower controllers, and emergency personnel watched.

The British airfield commander, a group captain, wrote later:

> You could see that "Birdie [Bertie] Lee" had had a rough time as she circled the airfield at Grimsby. . . . Our Squadron were busy on their own account that afternoon—getting ready for night ops. . . . [We did] watch the "Birdie Lee's" gallant attempt at the almost impossible. At last she touched down so smoothly that she seemed to be skidding along on her bomb-doors for a few hundred yards before her weight told and she settled in the turf . . . a picture of a battered grace, and perfect, cold-blooded airmanship. Her props flashed angrily in the sunlight as they hit the grass and buckled back in a smother of dirt, and with hardly a sound the fortress came to a rest.[2]

The ambulance and other vehicles rushed to the smoldering aircraft as smoke and heat gushed from the engines and bomb bay. A flight doctor sprinted up to the aircraft and peered into the narrow, pipe-like fuselage, then called: "Where's the rest of the crew?" The pilot was already on a stretcher and being carried away. He called back: "They're gone! I ordered them to bail out. I never thought we would live to get back here." Then, after a moment's pause, he cried, "Oh God, what will I tell their families?"

For the next nine months, First Lieutenant Edward Michael would constantly think about his seven fellow crewmen who had bailed out. Were they alive? Were they prisoners of war?

* * *

The *Bertie Lee* after its last mission, never to fly again. The typed caption attached to these photos reads: "Damage sustained to aircraft on the last combat mission flown by Major Michael, which resulted in the award of the CMH." The vertical stabilizer and elevators sustained severe flak damage that caused them to be nearly jammed and inoperative.

The fuselage above the wing had a large hole caused by the fire in the bomb bay that nearly burned completely through the bomber.

The nose and plexi-glass took numerous flak and 20mm hits by German fighters.

The wind-screen was severely damaged by a 20mm hit from a German fighter, which also destroyed all the instruments on the panel.

Months passed before word arrived that six of his seven para-chuting crew members had survived the jump and were in German hands. Miraculously, Lt. Michael, his co-pilot Lieutenant Franklin Westberg from Albert Lea, Minnesota, and the bombardier, Lieu-tenant John Lieber from Flushing, Long Island, had nursed the bomber back to England. Lt. Michael was severely wounded in the right leg; after being hospitalized in England for weeks, he was sent home to the United States. For months, he harassed the Army Air Force personnel staff and eventually the Red Cross for information on his crew members. The last mystery involved Sergeant Jewell Phillips. Severely wounded, he had been the last to bail out. Had he died on the way down? Had he survive the jump only to die of his wounds later?

During Michael's hospital stay, he worried, prayed, and pressed for information. At first, because he was in recovery, he did not shave; after a few weeks with no information, Ed Michael decided that not shaving was how he could demonstrate to himself and others his resolve and hope for his crew members. As Samson de-rived strength from his long locks, Lt. Edward Michael would sym-bolically show his determination—by not shaving—that Sergeant Phillips would one day be accounted for.

As time passed, Lt. Michael learned that he had been nominat-ed to receive the Medal of Honor for his heroism and leadership on his twenty-sixth mission against Nazi Germany. In late November 1944, the nomination was confirmed. He would indeed receive the nation's highest award for valor. He still did not shave his chin ex-cept to shape his blond Van Dyke beard and mustache.[3]

For a time his superiors ignored the situation; but when the White House announced that President Franklin D. Roosevelt himself would present Lt. Michael with his Medal of Honor on January 10, 1945, Michael's officers ordered him to shave and pres-ent a proper military appearance before the nation's commander-in-chief.[4]

Ed Michael refused. Until he learned what had happened to Jewell Phillips, he would not shave.

Lieutenant Ed Michael
with a goatee.

January 10, the day of the presentation arrived. As Lt. Michael, his wife, Bertie Lee, and his parents prepared to leave their hotel for the White House, an army officer knocked on the door. He brought word that Sergeant Phillips was in a hospital in England. His wounds were so severe that the Germans had repatriated him to Sweden, and he reached to England through diplomatic channels.

Grinning from ear to ear, Lt. Edward Michael went into the bathroom and picked up his razor.[5]

* * *

When people think of the air war in Europe during World War II, they may have images of sleek P–51 Mustangs mixing it up in dogfights with German Messerschmitts and Focke Wulfes, or scenes from the old footage of aircraft in dogfights—gray and fuzzy, shooting, dodging, and slicing through the air. A few movies show lumbering but magnificent B–17s flying in perfect formations, dropping waves of bombs that fell gracefully on targets far below, with flames blossoming up from German factories, refineries, or cities. These cultural depictions show a mighty American war machine going forth in vast numbers, a virtual armada of bombers, fighters, and transport aircraft winging their way to victory. This glamorous depiction is true—but it is incomplete.

What is not commonly known is that thousands of American airmen died in the skies over France, Germany, England, and other parts of Europe, besides in the Pacific Theater. Thousands of aircraft were lost, to be replaced with even more airframes from American aircraft assembly factories. As the common soldier fought and lived in the muck of mud—struggling and dying by the yard across Africa, Italy, France, and then finally Germany—theirs was an awful labor of constant privation, danger, fear, and the unknown. But these valiant men normally entered the front once, perhaps twice during various campaigns. The incredible amphibious landings at Morocco, Sicily, Salerno, Anzio, and Normandy were frightening and life-changing experiences. But very few soldiers ever endured such a dreadful event again.[6]

In contrast, aircrews—pilots, radiomen, bombardiers, navigators, and gunners—may have slept between sheets in real beds every night, but every time they climbed aboard an aircraft to strike at Nazi Germany's power, it was as though they were hitting the beach and entering the combat area. To fly twenty or thirty missions over Germany and occupied Europe, each time evading hundreds of bursts of flak and then fighting off dozens of German fighters swarming like flies on a carcass, reaching the target area, dropping bombs and then, once again enduring both flak batteries and enemy fighters on the way home was a terrible aspect of air warfare. Each successful mission was a miracle for these men, celebrated afterwards with some happy hours of drinking, dancing, and girls. Then two days later, they woke up again before dawn, ate, received a mission briefing, and by sunlight embarked once again across the

English Channel to face flak and fighters. This was an incredibly stressful way to fight a war. Experts and veterans have puzzled for some time about how such a lifestyle is possible; some have hypothesized that some learned to cope in "light-switch" style: on or off, compartmentalizing their experience with no leakage from "on mission" to "off duty"—except, of course, for nightmares. American flyers may have had three "hots and a cot," but such moments of comfort ended every time they hit the flight-line. In an instant, a crippled or damaged aircraft meant the men had to parachute into enemy territory and, if they survived capture, then spend the remainder of the war in a prison camp.

During one mission on October 14, 1943, 320 heavy American bombers—B–17s and B–24s—were dispatched on a mission to Schweinfurt, Germany. The bombers carried more than 3,000 aircrew members. Two hundred ninety bombers made it to the target area and dropped their ordnance. Another thirty aircraft went down on the return to base; 594 men either died aboard their aircraft or survived to become prisoners of war. Thus, on one day, the U.S. 8th Air Force in England lost 20 percent of its men and aircraft sent aloft. In the annals of American military aviation history it is called "Black Thursday" to this day.[7]

The air war in Europe was an essential part of the Allied war effort to defeat Nazi Germany. Since the Battle of Britain in the summer of 1940, Great Britain had taken the war to German-occupied Europe in the air. Some day-time bombing missions were conducted early on, but soon it became obvious that it was more practical to conduct a night bombing campaign; besides, British resources of aircraft, aviators, bombs, and fuel were limited. It single-handedly fought the Axis powers of Italy and Germany for nearly two years.[8]

After the attack on Pearl Harbor in December 1941, Britain officially had the United States as its formidable ally. First beginning as a trickle in the summer of 1942, then a flood, hundreds of American aircraft arrived in England. Bomb groups and squadrons were formed, airfields manned, and missions commenced in July

1942. The great question soon was raised by Major General Ira Eaker, the first commander of the 8th Air Force: Could American military might stand the test of a daylight bombing campaign with all of its risks? It was up to General Eaker and his faithful Army airmen to prove the legitimacy of daylight bombing.[9]

The answer was yes, which is why, seventeen months later on April 11, 1944, Lt. Edward Michael, through daring, courage, and exceptional skill, saved two of his men and aircraft and later received the Medal of Honor. Some thirty years later, he became a member of the Church of Jesus Christ of Latter-day Saints. Ed Michael served his country, his family, and his new church with all his heart and soul until the day he died in 1994.

* * *

The family name in Polish was originally "Mikolayczyk," but that was too hard for Americans to say, so the first generation of immigrants adopted the name "Mikol" which was easier for the American tongue. Born May 2, 1918, in Chicago to Stanley Mikol and Lillian Harriet Konior Mikol, Edward was the second of three children, between two sisters, Loretta and Armella. They were very strong Roman Catholics, devout and faithful. In fact, the family had several members who became members of religious orders. Three of Edward's aunts became nuns, one eventually was a mother superior, and another was a teacher in Catholic schools for many years. Called both "Eddie" and "Skip," the future pilot grew up in a rough-and-tumble section of Chicago. There were ball games, card playing, wild drinking, and street fights nearly every day, and Skip became a tough city kid, street-wise and determined. He never caused any trouble with the law, attended mass every Sunday, served as an altar boy, and loved the Roman faith; but he hated paying money into the collection plate and swore he would never become a priest like some of his uncles and cousins. He was nevertheless a young man of faith.[10]

The family finally decided to adopt the Anglicized last name of "Michael." Skip was seven when his parents bought and moved into their first house, a small, humble dwelling. At age nine, Skip discovered his calling in life. He would watch airplanes "buzz" his house at low levels and land in fields and pastures near the city. He often went out to Glenview Naval Air Station where he spent hours watching the old biplanes land and take off. The desire to fly entered into his soul.

He entered his teen years with the Great Depression. Money was tight, and he caddied at nearby Bunker Hill Golf Course where he became friends with a wealthy businessman who owned his private aircraft. Skip saved his money for flying lessons. He graduated from Carl Schurz High School, but he would rather take flying lessons than attend college.[11]

In November 1940 at age twenty-two, Edward Michael took a drastic step. With war raging in Europe and the American isolationists hoping for peace and security, he joined the U.S. Army and applied for the aviation cadet program. He failed the admittance test by two points, a terrible disappointment. Instead, he was assigned as a mechanic on Army aircraft at Wheeler Airfield in the Hawaiian Islands. Wheeler Field was an old Army Air Corps field some thirty miles north of Pearl Harbor, Oahu.[12]

That's what Skip Michael was doing on the quiet Sunday morning of December 7, 1941, when Japanese carrier-based aircraft launched a surprise attack on American military bases and facilities on Oahu. Pearl Harbor and the Pacific Fleet were the main targets; however, dozens of aircraft attacked the Army posts of Hickam Airfield, Wheeler Airfield, and Schofield Barracks. Michael was assigned "KP"—kitchen police—that Sunday morning when he heard the drone of fighter bombers. He stood amazed as waves of Japanese aircraft flew overhead, dropping bombs near him. Machine-gun rounds struck the parade field where he was crossing to the flight line, and a rock chip hit him in the face.[13]

America was now in the greatest of all wars, a true global war. For Ed Michael, war brought the opportunity to attend flight

Air Cadet Edward Michael
in 1943.

school. He had no college, a circumstance that would haunt him
and thousands of officers later, especially those who elected to stay
in the service after the war. Ed received primary and advanced pilot
training at Douglas Airfield, Arizona, in October 1942, flying the
AT–6 Texan and other single-engine trainers.

Primary flight training was a difficult and challenging experience, requiring him to master the fundamentals of flight and aero-
dynamics, and to gain an expert's knowledge of a powerful machine
and its mechanical systems. After the required hours of supervised
instruction, students progressed to the exciting day when they flew
"solo," then continued to advance in skill and confidence. It was in
Douglas, Arizona, where he met and married Bertie Lee, for whom
he named his aircraft.

On April 12, 1943, Edward Michael graduated from flight
training and was commissioned a second lieutenant in the Army

Air Forces. He wanted to fly fighters, as did most pilot trainees, but the Army Air Forces needed bomber pilots. He received orders for a B–17 transition at Hobbs Field, New Mexico.[14]

*　*　*

In August 1934, the Army Air Corps, the forerunner of the Army Air Forces, announced a bid for a new bomber prototype to replace the outdated Martin B–10B. The requirements were, basically, a bomber that performed well at 10,000 feet MSL (Mean Sea Level), could reach a cruising airspeed of at least 200 mph, had a range of 2,000 miles, and could carry "a useful bomb-load," which was not defined precisely. The tactics and war plans of the 1930s called for a bomber that would fly reconnaissance and coastal defense missions to bomb enemy vessels or submarines. War planners did not envision another European war or a world war.

Most companies prepared and entered designs for twin-engine aircraft into the competition. The Boeing Company in Seattle, however, showcased a four-engine aircraft with a sturdy aerodynamic design, its famous blunt rounded wingtips, and a massive tail and rudder, called the "Cheyenne Tail" in later models. These were the most obvious characteristics of the Model 299, which had its first flight on July 28, 1935. The Air Corps officers were immensely impressed, not only because of its design, but because of its incredible performance and ability to carry nearly 5,000 pounds of ordnance. A reporter on hand for the test flight saw the many machine guns protruding from the airframe and casually called it a "flying fortress." The name stuck. The War Department ordered thirteen airframes of the model, now designated as the YB–17, in January 1936. By 1941, the Army Air Forces had just under two hundred B–17s in various models based in Hawaii, the Philippines, and the United States.[15]

The B–17 was the work-horse bomber of World War II. Some 12,000 airframes were manufactured in several different models. There were other fine bombers—the B–24 Liberator, B–25

Tail markings of a B–17G, denote the 305th Bombardment Group and the fuselage "WF" of the 364th Bomb Squadron. The *Bertie Lee* had the same markings. Computer graphic by Hyrum H. Fleek.

Mitchell, and the B–29 Superfortress, along with the British Lancaster, Wellington, and Handley-Page Halifax—yet the Flying Fortress caught both the imagination and soul of the American war effort. The bomber was simple, reliable, and efficient. It could endure a great deal of punishment and still remain aloft. The B–17G Model that would be christened the *Bertie Lee*, flown by Lieutenant Michael, was built in 1942, so its tail number began with "2": 2–37931. The B–17 had a cruising airspeed of 182 mph, a service ceiling of 36,500 feet, an unpressurized cabin, and a gross takeoff weight of 65,500, depending on conditions. It carried 2,450 gallons (14,400 pounds) of fuel, and was powered by four Wright R–1820–97 "Cyclone" engines that were super-charged radials (meaning that the cylinders were mounted in a circle). Each engine produced 1,200 shaft horsepower. The flight controls, landing gear, ball and top gun turrets, and several other systems were powered and operated by hydraulic and electrical systems.[16]

There was no heating system for the crew on missions with open waist gun windows, so at high altitudes the temperature could be 30° below zero, and touching metal with bare skin was a painful experience. The men wore heavy fleece-lined leather coats, trousers, and gloves that had electrical webbing laced throughout that provided heat. The famous "flak jacket" of later wars was first developed for bomber crews—a heavy leather garment lined with plate-armor, front and rear. Besides parachutes, flak jackets, and fleece-lined flight suits, the airmen also wore oxygen masks, life-preservers, sometimes "steel pot" helmets, and, underneath all the gear, pistols and other personal equipment. The seemingly glamorous B–17 was actually a hard way to fight a war.

The most important function of the B–17 was not the defense of the crew or the plane but dropping bombs on a target. Keeping personnel safe was a necessary prerequisite, but bombing runs were the sole purpose of the bomber and main mission of the men, squadrons, support functions, and the Army Air Forces. A key crewmember was the bombardier who squatted on a steel seat and bent over the famous and innovative Norden bombsight, a state-of-the-art device then and one of the best-guarded equipment secrets of World War II. The goal was to place 50 percent of the bomb-load within a 100-foot area—the mean target center—from altitudes above 20,000 feet, In reality, the bombers rarely dropped more than 50 percent within a quarter mile of the target center.[17]

The Norden was a sophisticated gadget with several sight glasses, electric gyros, and a stabilizing mechanism. It was linked to the flight controls by an autopilot that the pilot switched on, allowing the bombardier, who was in the most exposed station of the plane, to fly it through the bomb run. There were control measures that the navigator provided to the pilots and bombardier for references, such as the rally point, check points, the initial point, release point, and then the final course for the approach and bomb run. Then the bombardier took control. If a bomber was serving as flight lead aircraft, dozens if not hundreds of bombers followed the leader to the release point. These functions required intensive training, team-work, coordination, and expertise.[18]

* * *

Bertie Lee Michael returned to her family in Douglas, Arizona, when Lieutenant Ed Michael received orders to deploy overseas, arriving in England on November 3, 1943. At this point in the war, literally hundreds of airfields in England and Scotland supported the Allied air effort. Not only were thousands of bombers stationed at small airfields or bases throughout the United Kingdom, but there were also just as many fighter bases and airfields for transport aircraft. Including the British squadrons, England was an island honeycombed with airfields, aircraft, and airmen.

Ed Michael joined the 364th Bombardment Squadron at Chelveston, a small town north of London. A squadron had twelve aircraft and some 250 aircrew men and ground support personnel, commanded by a lieutenant colonel by authorization, but sometimes a major or even a captain as the war progressed. The 364th Bomb Squadron, along with three other bomb squadrons, formed the 305th Bombardment Group (Heavy). The "Can Do" 305th Bombardment Group, formed in Salt Lake City, Utah, on March 1, 1942, was one of the first B–17 groups to arrive in England in September 1942. The first group commander was a man who would sear his name into U.S. Air Force and Cold War history as the master architect and father of the Strategic Air Command: Lt. Col. Curtis LeMay. He later served as Air Force Chief of Staff and ran for vice president of the United States in 1968 with George Wallace of Georgia.[19]

Each bomb group was normally stationed at an assigned airfield. Thus, the groups were self-sustaining organizations with medical, maintenance, security, mess, transportation, clerical, and construction personnel besides the aircrews who flew the missions. Perhaps the real heroes of the Allied air war were the unglamorous ground support crews—especially the mechanics, the airframe, powerplant, and avionics specialists, the ordnance loaders, machine-gun armorers, electricians, and refuelers. After a mission, some aircraft returned that should have never flown again; but with incredible skill and determination, ground crews worked unceasingly to repair, rebuild, and prepare aircraft to be functional and airworthy by the next morning. These soldiers—mechanics, cooks, military police, supply, weathermen, ordnance men, and clerks—were the unsung heroes of the U.S. Army Air Forces during the war.

Michael, through fate or fortune, was billeted with another pilot and aircraft commander of the 364th Squadron, First Lieutenant William L. Lawley from Birmingham, Alabama. Lawley would receive the Medal of Honor for heroic actions on February 20, 1944. Thus, two future Medal of Honor recipients were roommates for several months and many missions.[20]

* * *

Soon after arriving in England, Ed Michael began flying missions with a crew of nine others. Three were officers: co-pilot, bombardier, and navigator. Six were enlisted men: the engineer, who doubled as the top turret gunner, two waist gunners, the ball turret gunner, the radio operator, and the finally the tail gunner. Thirteen M–2 .50 caliber Browning machine guns protruded from the aircraft like quills on a porcupine. Each gun had a basic load of some 200 rounds that came in nine-yard belts packed in each ammunition can. Four positions mounted "twin-fifties": the chin turret under the nose, on the B–17G model like the *Bertie Lee*; then twin guns for the top, ball, and tail positions. The only crew members who did not man guns were the two pilots.[21] This is why the B–17 was a powerfully armed aircraft—one the German Luftwaffe feared.

These gun positions were not used in a haphazard display of American fireworks and individual "cowboy" bravado. Each position had an area, a field of fire with interlocking and overlapping coverage with the other gunners, providing an umbrella of defense for each aircraft. Then, each aircraft provided coverage and protection against German fighters for the entire formation by squadron and bomb group. This was the other great strength of the B–17 when flying tight formations.[22] Around them swarmed the fast-moving Allied fighters: P–47 Thunderbolts, P–51 Mustangs, and P–38 Lightnings.

The 8th Air Force and all American flying units by 1943 had developed an incentive system of total missions flown. After reaching a certain number, the crew would be reassigned other duties in the United States: recruiting, pilot and aircrew training, or war bonds. The first criterion was twenty-five missions—which the famous *Memphis Belle* reached in May 1943.²³ Then in January 1944, the 8th Air Force received a new commander, Lt. Gen. James ("Jimmy") Doolittle, one of the most colorful American pilots and air force commanders in history. Before World War II, he had been a civilian airplane racer and stunt pilot with the reputation of being a dare-devil. While serving in the Army Air Corps, he was a flight training officer and leader. By 1941, Doolittle was a lieutenant colonel, qualified to fly the twin engine B–25 Mitchell medium bomber. He was chosen to command and lead the famous attack on Tokyo in April 1942, America's first offensive strike in the Pacific. His squadron of B–25s took off from the swaying deck of the aircraft carrier USS *Hornet* in terrible weather. He was later awarded the Medal of Honor.

One of the first decisions Gen. Doolittle made was to scrap the twenty-five-mission policy because the Allied air effort needed experienced aircrew members. Soon, a new formula was created for each man, taking into account number of missions, number of months in the Europe Theater of Operations (ETO), and other factors. This policy changed the horizon of expectations for aircrews and individuals. Michael's crew had to fly twenty-seven missions before they could return home. Later in 1944, the policy changed and increased the mission total even more.

On January 22, 1944, Lt. Michael received his first of four Air Medals, one for every five combat missions flown. The Air Medal is an attractive medal: a diving eagle suspended from an orange and purple ribbon.²⁴ The missions soon added up, week after week. Sometimes the winter weather was so harsh that missions were scrapped for several days. Ground crews used those times to make their damaged and overworked aircraft airworthy.

The Allied air campaign from late 1942 to 1944 had strategic objectives more than mere night and daylight bombing. At first the targets were mostly in France: German U-boat pens, docks, and repair facilities. Then in 1943 more missions were directed against German harbor cities, Bremen, Bremerhaven, Wilhelmshaven, and other northern cities that had military targets. The logical next step was to strike at the German aircraft industry.

From the very beginning, dozens of German fighter groups and hundreds of squadrons deployed across France and Germany were a critical factor. The German fighter aircraft—the Focke-Wulf 190 and Messerschmitt 109—were superb airframes packing 20mm cannons and several rapid-fire machine guns of lesser calibers. The German pilots at this time were tough, hardened, and experienced aviators. Many had scored hundreds of victories against allied fighters and bombers. These wolves and jackals of the air perfected the art of the hunt. With the help of ground-based radar, the *Jägdgeschwader* (fighter groups), or JGs, were directed against the lumbering, densely grouped Allied bomber formations. With the incredible firepower that the bombers controlled, the Germans soon learned that the area most vulnerable to an attack was straight on at the twelve o'clock position and from above. At closing speeds nearing 500 mph, the German hunters had only seconds to fire their deadly 20mm cannons; the bomber gunners had even less time to engage straight on with their .50 caliber Browning machine guns.

The Allied formations were usually organized by bombardment groups with three separate squadrons at high, middle, and low levels, forming squadron "combat boxes" of some ten or so aircraft with wing tips only a few dozen feet apart, yet they were staggered left or right, and high and low. These combat boxes were the best solution for defense against German *Jägdflieger* ("fighters") and their tactics. Yet once the bomber formations flew through the menacing fighters and neared their targets, they were easy targets for another German antiaircraft weapon: flak.

As the tightly formed bomber groups plodded over Germany, France, and the Low Countries, they were extremely vulnerable to German "barrage boxes." Again, the Germans had nearly perfected the art of the kill by grouping eight or so Flak 40 128mm rapid-firing antiaircraft guns in batteries. Some were mounted on platforms or high places to provide better fields of fire. In Germany, especially surrounding major industrialized cities such as

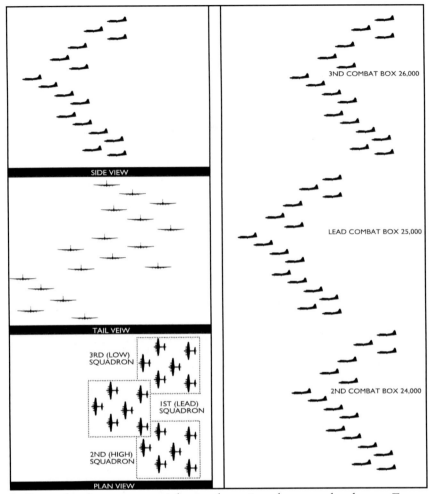

Left, combat box stagger; right combat wing-three combat boxes. Front, side, and top views of a typical squadron "combat box" depicting high, middle, and low elements. Each bomb group had this organization. Diagram by Hyrum H. Fleek.

Berlin, Hamburg, Dresden, and Bremerhaven, the Germans built 120-foot-high, concrete "flak towers" well above houses and buildings that afforded them a clear field of fire.[25] The Flak 40 had entered service in 1942 and, by this point in the war, was the most effective German antiaircraft gun. Each gun and mount weighed twelve tons, had a rate of fire of 20 rounds per minute, and could reach an altitude or range of 35,000 feet.[26]

The "barrage box" concentrated fire from several flak batteries into a tight "box" that the Germans plotted, based on knowing or deducing where the bomber formations would have to fly. The flak towers and "barrage boxes" near major bombing targets and other likely areas were part of the German defense scheme known as *Festung Europa* ("Fortress Europe"). The idea resembled duck hunting—aiming the shotgun into the flight path of the duck, waiting until the duck flew into the sights, and then firing. All the Germans had to do was wait for dozens of B–17s to fly into the barrage box. The combination of fighters and flak guns was lethal.[27]

* * *

Between Ed Michael's arrival in England on November 3, 1943, and April 11, 1944, his day of greatest challenge, the *Bertie Lee* flew bombing mission after bombing mission—twenty in all. The crew roster changed, due to illness or reassignment. "Mike," as some of his friends called him, honed his skills as a pilot, and his crew developed that brotherhood peculiar to warriors.

In early 1944, 8th Army Air Force planners developed a very aggressive plan later known as "Big Week." For several weeks, the weather over Europe was miserable; but then, beginning on February 20, the weather staff predicted a week of storm-free weather. The plan called for a "maximum effort," meaning that any craft that was airworthy and could carry a bomb would go up. At this time, the Army Air Forces were using the first onboard radar, the H2S/H2X, to help navigators pinpoint the target areas, though the tactic of BTO—"bombing through overcast"—was often used.[28]

The second day of "Big Week" was February 21, with 861 bombers taking to the skies. Hundreds of bombers in twenty-eight bomb groups, with dozens of squadrons from all three Air Divisions of the 8th Air Force winged their way to a dozen different targets in Germany. The Allied effort was particularly targeting aircraft factories in an effect to cripple Germany's vaunted Luftwaffe. Allied losses that day were sixteen bombers destroyed or lost, another 105 damaged, and twenty-four airmen killed. It was actually a light day for losses.[29] Some historians and others believe that "Big Week" was the turning point in the air war. Gen. Doolittle commented after the war: "It is generally conceded that the war in air against Germany was won during the phase of our operations between the beginning of February 1944 and D-Day. The rate of attrition of the Luftwaffe's pilots exceeded Germany's rate of replacement."[30]

Lt. Michael and the *Bertie Lee's* crew flew during "Big Week" and for two more months with no serious hits, no crew member wounded, and no disruptions of its assigned missions. On March 31, Lt. Michael was awarded his fourth Air Medal—twenty missions without a scratch or major incident. That would all change two weeks later.

* * *

April 11, 1944, Day of Days

The *Bertie Lee* crew began their morning mission routine at 0230 when the duty officer awakened them for breakfast at 0300. This was mission number twenty-six for eight of the ten crew members; with Gen. Doolittle's new "pro-rated" system they had one more mission before they would be rotated back to the United States. But as life, war, and fate would have it, the first snafu[31] occurred when two crew members missed breakfast, then didn't show up for the 0500 briefing.

Where were they?

Staff Sergeant Clarence Luce, the tail gunner, and Sergeant Jewell Phillips, engineer and top turret gunner, from Alto, Texas, were new, so recently assigned to the *Bertie Lee* that they were not billeted with the rest of the enlisted crew as per standard procedure. Another crew member had to find the duty sergeant, then find their barracks, and get them out of bed. This was Sergeant Phillips's first combat mission—and his last, though he did not know it. They reached the aircraft at 0645, unfed and hardly ready for the 0700 engine start and line-up. One of the crew members asked the pilot how long the mission would be, and when they would return to base.

"Seven o'clock this evening," Lt. Michael called through the intercom.

"Oh, no, don't say that!" returned the airman. "I got a date with the prettiest girl in England tonight, and the last bus leaves for town at six!"[32]

The two tardy sergeants were not the only new members of the crew. Second Lieutenant Meredity Calvert, the navigator, from Lincoln Park, Pennsylvania, was also on his first mission with the *Bertie Lee*. The officers, four of them, attended the 0400 mission briefing. The mission had been posted the night before and involved 828 aircraft drawn from the 8th Air Force with several targets in Germany. One of the missions was a ball-bearing factory in Stettin, some seventy miles east of Berlin on the Oder River. Along with the *Bertie Lee*, 126 other B–17s from various groups and squadrons would fly to Stettin to drop thousands of tons of bombs. The day's mission would eventually cost five aircraft lost, 406 damaged, nineteen airmen dead, thirty-one wounded, and 126 missing—presumably dead or captured. The Americans claimed seventy-three enemy aircraft destroyed and twenty-four probable kills.[33]

Most of the flight paths to Germany were over the North Sea, crossing landward only when necessary to avoid flak and fighters. Yet to fly beyond Berlin was indeed a difficult proposition which would require more fuel, a longer flight time, and a reduction of the ordnance they could carry. Inevitably, it would also expose their aircraft to more time over enemy territory with more concentrated flak batteries to evade. For Lt. Michael and his crew, this was the most dangerous mission yet, and it did not start well.

The flight altitude was 13,000 feet, rather low, with *Bertie Lee* assigned to the high squadron as the third ship in the staggered formation of several elements. This was the most vulnerable position—aviators called it "Purple Heart Corner"—because it was the closest ship in the formation for the *Jägdflieger* killers to attack. Over the North Sea, the crew tested their weapons; they were already above 10,000 feet so they were on supplemental oxygen and the ambient air temperature was at 10° F or less—not terribly cold.

Tail number 2–37931 lumbered along carrying ten American airmen, forty-two hundred-pound incendiary bombs, and the hope that after this mission and one more, seven of these men would return home to their families.

The huge aerial armada took various routes to its targets in Rostock, Politz, and Stettin. By the time the *Bertie Lee* crossed into Germany, the Allied fighters had already turned back because they reached their "bingo-time" a term for their fuel limit. The vulnerable bombers were flying with only their own guns for protection.

At 1045, enemy flak struck the left wing of the *Bertie Lee*, ripping a two-foot-wide gaping hole completely through the aluminum airfoil. Lt. Michael called to Fred Wilkins, a staff sergeant from Columbia Station, Ohio. He had the only clear view of the aircraft from underneath. Was any gas leaking from the wing tank? Wilkins called back the good news: no gas leak. Hundreds of gallons of valuable fuel were in that wing, so they had some good luck.

Minutes later, the crew saw a formation of B–24s fly over and ahead of their formation. Later in the far distance Michael and his co-pilot, Second Lieutenant Franklin Westberg, noticed some strange flashes on the distant horizon. They were not flak bursts. What they were witnessing were several B–17s in a formation three minutes ahead of them exploding from attacks by *Jägdgeschwader* 2, perhaps one of the most notorious and experienced fighter wings in the Luftwaffe. Its nickname was "Richthofen" after the famous World War I ace, Manfred von Richthofen, the Red Baron, who was credited with eighty kills before he was shot down in 1918. In a few minutes, these German hunters would strike *Bertie Lee* and the 305th Bombardment Group.[34]

The first fighter attack seemed to come out of nowhere.

"It seemed like all hell had broken loose," Michael wrote in a later account. An estimated 125 ME–109s and 150 FW–190s swarmed in like flies, mostly at twelve o'clock high; but after the first passes, the assault came from all directions. "Bombers and fighter planes were going down in flames," Michael recorded. "The enemy planes plunged toward the Fortresses in what seemed to be a suicide mission. Nothing like this had ever been encountered before by the crew of the 'Bertie Lee.' They [the Germans] flew directly through the bomber formations forcing them to give way or collide in mid-air."[35]

In the midst of the desperate fight, forward gun positions engaged a German fighter flying head on at *Bertie Lee*. "One enemy plane seemed to . . . level his ship off as one would level his rifle when drawing a bead on a target." Michael called over the intercom to the top turret gunner, Sergeant Phillips, "Get that plane!"

The top turret and also the "cheek" guns in the nose, manned by bombardier John Lieber and the navigator, Meredity Calvert, opened fire on the menacing fighter. Yellow and orange flames burst from the guns, both from the fighter and the bomber. Closer and closer, the two aircraft closed.

Then, the German killer burst into flames from underneath and reeled off into a steep dive. The crew of the *Bertie Lee* who saw the kill, hollered with delight. Other fighters were attacking also— diving, strafing, and firing as the gunners continued to return fire. The scene was like a bar brawl with aircraft instead of men.

Suddenly a blast rattled the aircraft, then another, followed by two more severe shocks. The bomber began to stagger as it flew along. Four direct hits from the German fighters' 20mm cannon had slammed into the bomber. The crew knew immediately that their B–17 was in trouble.

One blast destroyed the instrument panel and also lacerated Ed Michael's right thigh. The 20mm round had severed two throttle controls and cables on two engines and damaged the supercharger controls of the other two engines. The controls and gas and air mixture of all four engines would be difficult to manage the remainder of the flight. Blood pooled on the floor under Ed's seat.[36]

In moments the *Bertie Lee* began to lose altitude and airspeed. Michael and Frank Westberg did all they could to force the battered bomber back into formation—but it was no use. Slowly, the stricken aircraft fell out of the formation, well before reaching the target area. As Edward Michael was bleeding, and perhaps slowly dying, so was the *Bertie Lee*.[37]

The wind lashed through a gaping hole behind Westberg's head. Fortunately he had been wearing his steel helmet when the cannon round struck, or he may have been seriously wounded also. Then, suddenly, the aircraft began to roll and pitch wildly. German machine-gun fire had ripped through some of the flight control cables and linkages, besides wrecking the elevators, rudder, and trim taps on the elevators.

Then, violently the aircraft rolled over into a spin, dropping several thousand feet in only a few minutes. Michael and Westberg together wrestled the mammoth bomber to gain control against the forces of gravity, centrifugal force, velocity, and weight. Finally they managed to level off and fly the rattling aircraft along. Lt. Westberg later declared, "Lt. Michael was struggling with the controls, and I was helping out. . . . It took our combined weight and energy to get her flying level again. We lost about 3,000 feet, but did not lose the fighters that were following us down."[38]

The fighters began their gun runs again.

Then the most awful news came over the intercom: "Sir, the bombs are on fire."

The third of the four 20mm shells had hit the bomb bay, and some of the aircraft's forty incendiary bombs were ablaze.

Panic set in.

"Release the bombs!" Michael yelled over the intercom. He waited but felt no lift or shift as the heavy bombs dropped.

He called out again, "Release the bomb load!"

Again and again, he anxiously called. He did not know that the intercom between the pilot's station, bombardier, and navigator, was out.

The fire in the bomb bay was actually small at first, but at any moment the bombs could explode. When they did, the entire aircraft and its crew would disintegrate in an incendiary inferno. In great pain, Michael considered the options. If they bailed out over Germany, the entire crew of ten would be captured and interned in a prison camp for the remainder of the war. But could the heavily damaged bomber make it back to England? Lt. Ed Michael faced a dreadful decision—the first of several in the next few hours.

He decided the crew had to bail out.

With so many enemy fighters pouncing for the kill, he had to first evade these killers. Michael lowered the nose; and with Westberg's help, they dove into a bank of clouds to escape the German pursuers. They had turned back toward England, but their course and bearing were nearly impossible to determine. The navigator, Calvert, had lost his references and positions during the fighting, the evasive maneuvers, and the cloud cover. They were somewhere over northern Germany. Their last known position was Braunschweig, west of Berlin. Only two power instruments were operative—manifold pressure and one tachometer. The single flight instrument that had not been destroyed was the magnetic compass, not an especially reliable source for navigation.[39]

Onward flew the *Bertie Lee*, managing to evade German fighters as the bombs continued to burn.

Then Sergeant Phillips struggled up the catwalk past the smoldering bomb load and reached the cockpit. He stood in terror and agony, blood dripping down his face. A blast from the first 20mm salvo had struck and disabled the top turret gun that Phillips manned. Frank Westberg, in his statement for Michael's Medal of Honor nomination, wrote, "How the Engineer did not get killed, I do not know. That boy was in bad shape. He was bleeding about the head and his eye had been shot out of its socket. He held it in his hand, and was trying to feel his way around" the aircraft.[40]

Just then another blast smashed into the nose area of the crippled bomber. Bombardier John Lieber was thrown from his chin turret position backward into the navigator's position. In his hands, he held the firing handles for the twin .50 caliber machine guns; the handle cables had been sheared off by the blast. Lieber was shaken but not hurt.

The fire continued to burn in the bomb bay.

Michael yanked on the emergency bomb-release handle mounted near his seat. Nothing.

Michael called out the order: "Bail out!"

The crew began to strap on their parachutes and bail out. In a few moments, six white canopies puffed open as these men floated down to a year of captivity. The circling German *Jägdfliegers* held their fire, allowing the descending jumpers to clear the air space before they resumed their attacks. Not all aviators observed this old-fashioned act of chivalry, though technically the Geneva Convention protected airmen during their exit and descent from a downed aircraft.[41]

Wasting no time as the men bailed out and floated down, Michael banked the aircraft and flew directly into a cloud to lose the German killers.

It worked.

For several minutes and miles, the *Bertie Lee* sliced through a thick cover of cumulus clouds. With the flight instruments shot away—especially the artificial horizon (gyro) and turn-and-slip indicator, it was nearly impossible to know if the plane was flying straight and level. This maneuver bought them a few minutes' respite from fighters and flak.

The bomber broke out at 2,500 feet above ground altitude and flew on. The Germans were gone; but the bombs were still burning and the badly wounded Sergeant Phillips was still on board. He could not don his chute by himself or deploy it.

Ed Michael gave the controls to Westberg, clambered out of his seat, and despite the searing pain from his bleeding wound, hobbled back to Phillips, helped him strap on his parachute, and then positioned him at the lower belly hatch. He gave him one last look, realizing that he might never see this brave airman again. Then he pushed the wounded man into the swirling air and pulled the ripcord as Phillips, groaning with agony, fell down and away from the limping bomber.[42]

In the rear, avoiding the flames as best he could, Michael tried the manual bomb release himself several times.

Nothing.

He crawled back to the cockpit and told Frank Westberg to bail out. He would fly the aircraft, allowing Westberg to escape.

Westberg refused.

They argued.

Then Michael got out of his seat and opened the door to the cockpit to show Westberg the dangerous situation in the bomb bay. As he did, flames lapped up a few feet toward the door.

The sight changed Westberg's mind. They both decided to bail out. Westberg turned on the autopilot and they began to struggle into their parachutes.

Just then, a lone German fighter swooped down on the crippled bomber and fired its lethal 20mm cannon.

Bam! Bam! Bam!

Suddenly, to Michael and Westberg's utter surprise, the *Bertie Lee*'s nose gun fired back at the German.

The fighter made another pass; and the nose gun blasted dozens of .50 caliber rounds into the diving adversary. The German plane exploded in front of the lumbering bomber, spraying burning fuel and metal. Pieces of the fighter struck the right wing of the bomber.[43]

Michael immediately yelled, "Who is it?" and struggled into the navigator and bombardier's stations in the nose, down under the cockpit. There he saw Lieutenant Lieber, the bombardier, manning a "cheek" gun in the nose.

Michael was mad as hell. He demanded why Lieber had not bailed out.

Just as angry, Lieber showed Michael his parachute, shredded by enemy cannon fire. "My parachute's no good with a 20-millimeter shell hole in it," Lieber shouted above the noise.

Three men and only two serviceable parachutes. What to do?

"Take my chute," Michael pleaded. "For God's sake, jump. This plane is doomed."

"No, Mike, if we cannot both jump, we'll go down together."

Michael tossed his parachute on the deck and said, "All right, if that's the way you feel. But maybe this will change your mind. The bombs are on fire," he pointed to the bomb bay. "If you are planning on staying in this plane, get rid of those bombs if you have to kick them out."[44]

Westberg from the pilot's station yelled that Lieber could have his chute. Then the three argued about who would bail out. Michael cut through the wrangling by making the decision that the only option was to nurse the battered bomber back to England. He crawled back to his pilot seat.

Michael was still losing blood. His aircraft was crippled. It had weak engines, damaged flight controls, inoperative hydraulic and electrical systems, no instruments, no radio, no navigational aides, three men, two parachutes, and forty-two incendiary bombs in a burning bomb bay. It was a flying death-trap. The fire had burned a hole four feet long and two feet wide in the side of the fuselage. The airframe could snap in half at any minute.

Furthermore, they had no real idea where they were. They had been northeast of Berlin when they were first hit, then flew a 180° heading for some time during the fighter attack, then had turned back, flying a 350° heading as they maneuvered to avoid flak and fighters.[45]

After some effort, Lieber manually opened the bomb-bay doors and released the bombs that fell away to earth with smoke trailing after them.

Michael had just strapped himself back in his seat when he felt the lift from the dropping bombs. He looked at his watch. It was 1115. The *Bertie Lee* had been airborne four hours and had sustained the first hit at 1045—approximately thirty minutes. Amazingly, the bombs had been on fire for about twenty minutes but had not exploded.

They flew along over northern Germany, hoping to reach the safety of the North Sea, west of the Denmark Jutland peninsula

Then flak burst a few hundred yards ahead of them. Then came a closer burst. Flak hit the rudder and elevators once again. The pilots could feel it in the controls.

Michael and Westberg decided to drop to treetop level. In a few minutes, the *Bertie Lee* was winging its way about two hundred miles per hour only fifty feet above the trees and farm houses, barns, and German landscape. They saw a German soldier on the ground aim his rifle at the bomber and fire. After fifteen minutes at this low altitude, they climbed back to about 2,500 feet and flew safely along for about five minutes.

Then, once again a lone German fighter engaged them. Lieber crawled back along the cat-walk past the jammed-open bomb-bay doors. He fired the waist gun, making some hits on the German. Michael once again flew into clouds to evade the fighter.

It worked again.

The minutes stretched out agonizingly as the *Bertie Lee* descended to a low altitude to avoid more fighters and flak attacks. They flew so low that Michael and the others thought their wings might hit rooftops or trees. They saw people on the ground smiling and waving up at them. Were they over France? Holland? Belgium? They did not know. Some of civilians seemed to be pointing, and the aircrew interpreted these gestures as the direction to England.

In the far distance, the crew saw a coastline. They dared to hope that perhaps the worst was over. Lieber was trying to apply first aid to Michael, who was still losing blood. The floor of the cockpit was sticky and smeared with it.

It was just past noon, and the *Bertie Lee* was now over water, chugging slowly at a low level. The aircraft was not over the open sea. It was actually crossing near Zuider Zee, a large inlet of the Netherlands.[46] In the distance, the flyers saw two flak towers on the causeway a mile or two apart. The flak guns still had the bomber's range and opened fire.

Lt. Michael dared not take evasive action. The *Bertie Lee* was only about ten feet above the water. Accidentally dipping a wing into the water could cause the B–17 to cartwheel and crash. What occurred next was amazing. As the bomber approached the dyke, the flak guns fell silent. The antiaircraft guns were designed to engage targets at high altitudes. The Germans could not depress their guns enough to sight in on the low-flying stricken bomber.[47]

In minutes, the American metal bird flew out over the North Sea, and Michael coaxed the aircraft up to about 3,000 feet, giving them time to react in the event of engine failure or other problems. Later, Lt. Michael wrote in his personal account that he counted five separate miracles.[48] He and Frank Westberg also prayed together, though the co-pilot remarked he was not a believer.

Then for the third time, a lone German *Jägdflieger* attacked the weakened plane. Its 20mm cannon fire burst near the aircraft but missed. There were no clouds to hide in. Lieber had fired all the ammunition on board. The bomber was defenseless.

But after a couple of gun runs, the menacing hunter was gone. Vanished.

To a man, the three crew members always thought that it was either a miracle or that the German flyer felt sorry for the crippled B–17 and broke off the engagement.

By 1330 as they flew farther across the North Sea, they wrestled with the problem of navigation. Where were they? How many miles away was England? What if their course was too far north and completely missed Great Britain? Every minute or two, the two pilots looked at the "mag" compass. It became an obsession. And what about fuel? Would they have enough?

And could Lt. Michael make it? Somewhere over the North Sea, he slipped into unconsciousness. After hours of intense strain and pain, a half dozen attacks, the loss of his men, uncertainty over the aircraft's ability to fly, the safety of his last two crewmembers, and the loss of blood were taking a ferocious toll.

In the next hour, they spotted a British fighter and then a destroyer. Their hearts lifted.

The longer the *Bertie Lee* flew. the worse the weather became. The ceiling and visibility decreased, and Westberg had to descend to retain a visual reference with the horizon. At times they were only ten feet above the English Channel.

Finally, with the ceiling down to two hundred feet, Westberg and Lieber spotted the coast. For the next hour, the *Bertie Lee*, damaged so badly it would never fly again, crept closer to land. As the last miracle, Ed Michael regained consciousness and took control of the B–17 bomber. The battered bomber's landing gear would not lower, the windscreen was demolished due to flak hits; the rigging controls of the engines were badly mangled, the flight controls and hydraulics were nearly nonexistent, and the ball turret gun barrels and the bomb bay doors were stuck downward.

Such a dangerous situation would require phenomenal skill.

According to Michael's Medal of Honor citation, "Despite these apparently insurmountable obstacles, he landed the plane without mishap."[49]

* * *

Because of wartime security, Ed Michael's wife in Arizona and parents in Chicago learned no immediate details about this nearly fatal mission. On May 25, 1944, six weeks after this dangerous mission, the War Department sent Bertie Lee Michael a telegram at her home in Douglas, Arizona. It printed Ed Michael's rank, the date of the action. The crucial message was the line: SLIGHTLY SEVERELY WOUNDED IN ACTION IN THE EUROPE-AN AREA. "Severely" was crossed out.[50] It did not say where the action had occurred or where Ed Michael was.

Ed Michael also felt the frustrations of censorship and security during war. He was not allowed to write home any details; but from his hospital room, he thought of a clever way to send word to his family in Chicago. He wrote about the close call of "Skip," his own boyhood nickname, on April 17, 1944:

Dear Mom & Dad:

Well, I haven't heard from anyone back home as yet nor from any of the neighborhood boys that may be out here but I did hear about Skip from one of the boys who knows him very well.

You remember Skip don't you? He is the boy that is a B-17 pilot. Well, I hear that he was on his twenty-sixth mission and only a short way from his target which was deep into Germany when a large group of enemy fighters jumped them. His ship was hit hard with 20 millimeter hitting the bombs starting them afire, also hitting Skip in the right leg (it went right through his right thigh) and hitting his engines in several places. He ordered the whole crew to bail out, seven of them did, but Skip's bombardier couldn't jump because his parachute was shot to pieces. They managed to get to drop their bombs thus putting the fire out. They were attacked by fighters three different times while coming home alone and hit bad by more flak and small gun fire. They had to crash land and Skip was able to make a beautiful landing out of it. The three boys were Skip (pilot, co pilot and bombardier) but the plane was a wreck. It was only a miracle that they came back alive and in one piece—so they say. I am going to look him up the first chance I get—tell you more later.

Kisses to mom. I love you all.

Edward[51]

Now Bertie Lee and the Michael family at least knew that Ed was safe though wounded, but that soon he would be coming home. The war was over for him. Edward must have been delighted for that circumstance to a degree. But his heart ached for his seven crewmembers who were now listed as missing in action. Frank Westberg and John Lieber came to the hospital to visit Ed on occasion. They naturally talked about the mission and also their comrades.

All seven members who bailed out landed near Helmstedt, were soon captured and were interned in Luft Stalag 17B near Krems, Austria. For a year, these men endured the privation and hardships of prison life under sometimes brutal and austere conditions. Sergeant Phillips was repatriated through Sweden due to

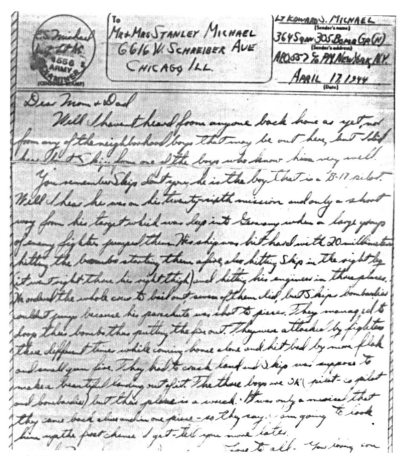

Ed Michael's handwritten letter to the Michael family about "Skip's" adventures.

his severe wounds. Eventually on May 3, 1945, American soldiers reached the camp and freed the five hundred remaining American airmen.[52]

Four months earlier on January 10, 1945, Bertie Lee Michael, Stanley and Lillian Michael, and Lieutenant John Lieber watched President Franklin D. Roosevelt present the Medal of Honor to Captain Edward Michael in the Oval Office. It was the last Medal of Honor ceremony at which President Roosevelt officiated. Frank Westberg and John Lieber had already been awarded the Silver Star Medal for their valor that day. All three officers had also received the Distinguished Flying Cross, the highest American award for valor in flight.[53]

* * *

Captain Edward Michael settled into a life-long career with the U.S. Air Force, totaling thirty-one years. He and Bertie moved to Love Field in Dallas, Texas, where Ed spent two years as a "ferry pilot," transporting B–17s from station to station, including from overseas bases back to the States. Though the great and dependable B–17 bomber had had less than ten years of service, the demands of war and peace were different. Within months of the end of hostilities, thousands of perfectly good fighters, bombers, and transport aircraft were taken to the "bone yard." Many service members felt the same way.

In 1947 the U.S. Air Force was created; and at this time, Ed was transferred to Hill Air Force Base in Utah. It was Ed Michael's first encounter with the Mormons of Utah as a community and culture. He made many temporary duty trips and also learned to fly other aircraft such as the reliable C–47 (the civilian DC–3), and then the new and exciting B–52 at McConnell Air Force Base outside Wichita, Kansas.

In 1950, the Korean War commenced. Later still, the USA became enmeshed with war in Vietnam. Michael's official documents cite the Air Force regulation that, as a recipient of the Medal of Honor, he was exempt from duty in a combat zone, although he served in other assignments.[54]

Bertie Lee and Ed divorced during these hectic years of many transfers, temporary assignments, and new aircraft training schools. They had a son, Gary Michael, and an adopted daughter, Nancy Lee Michael. Ed was promoted to major on January 14, 1955. One of his career challenges was that he lacked college credentials, unlike many older officers who had gone to college before World War II. Newer commissioned officers had acquired college degrees after the war, which was one of the requirements for a commissioned officer, especially in peace time. In 1957 while stationed in Utah as a recruiting officer assigned to Fort Douglas, he met Louise on a blind date. She was a devout LDS woman from Springville, Utah. They married on November 21, 1958, and together they began a wonderful marriage of nearly forty years. Religion was a major facet of their lives. Ed was Catholic, a believer, but not always a practitioner, whereas Louise was a faithful Latter-day Saint. Ed attended LDS services with Louise and also Catholic mass on occasion.

For the next twenty years, Ed and Louise lived and served in several places: Kelly AFB in Texas, and McConnell again. In 1959 they moved to Travis AFB near Sacramento, California; and though they served other tours elsewhere, they returned so frequently to Travis that it became their home station. The Michaels served in Lajes Air Base in the Azores, part of Portugal, in the mid-Atlantic. There they adopted Wendy, their only child.[55]

Back in the United States, Ed read the Book of Mormon and eventually took the missionary lessons. Louise knew that the decision about converting had to be his alone; she did not even sit in on the lessons, but she was thrilled when he told her, "I don't know how anyone can read this [Book of Mormon] and deny it that it was from God." In 1976, he was baptized into the LDS Church. Two years later, he and Louise were sealed in the Salt Lake Temple, and Wendy was sealed to them. Ed was comfortable with his religious decisions, and new life.

As a recipient of the Medal of Honor, Ed Michael had a certain degree of celebrity status among his Air Force comrades, friends, and even among the general public. On May 2, 1963, Ed attended a White House ceremony hosted by President John F. Kennedy for Medal of Honor recipients. Ed quipped, "It sure was nice that the president had this special birthday party for me." It was, indeed, Ed's birthday. Later the passenger terminal that Ed supervised at Lajes Air Base in the Azores was renovated and named after him. He loved the opportunity to meet other recipients at Medal of Honor Society reunions and ceremonies. He became friends with many fellow recipients, but he was especially close to Lt. Gen.

President John F. Kennedy greets Maj. Ed Michael at the White House, 1963.

Jimmy Doolittle, his former commander of the 8th Air Force in Europe. He also became fast friends with fellow Mormon Bernie Fisher. The friends often went fishing together, especially after Ed retired in 1971.

Being a war hero had its sour moments also. He did not like to speak to groups, but he loved to meet people and talk one to one, or, on occasion, to small groups.[56] While still on active duty, Ed came home one day extremely upset. Louise tried to understand what had happened, but Ed refused to open up. All he said was, "I will never wear this in public again!" He jerked the Medal of Honor ribbon from his rack of ribbons. He never explained what happened. Louise could only speculate. Had someone made an unkind comment? Had someone pestered Ed about the mission on that day in April 1944? Had someone sneered at his "special" status?[57]

Ed, Louise, and Wendy lived off base near Travis after he retired. Fishing, friends, family, church, and working around the house were his joys. Ed was thrilled to attend reunions with his former aircrew or other comrades, especially the fortieth anniversary of the flight day, in 1984. Co-pilot Frank Westberg and bombardier John Lieber joined Ed and Louise for the celebration; it was a touching occasion.[58]

At age seventy-six, Ed began to fail physically. He died in 1994 and was buried in Springville, Utah, Louise's hometown, a place where he had never lived. In July 1997, Louise Michael was invited to Lajes Air Base in the Azores as the guest of honor when the beautiful, renovated dining facility was rededicated in memory of Lt. Col. Edward Michael, USAF (retired), and recipient of the Medal of Honor.

Perhaps one of the best epitaphs for the memory of Ed Michael was one he wrote himself in 1992 when he applied for a new decoration created by Congress, the Pearl Harbor Commemorative Medal. In the "remarks" section of the form, he described in a few words his career in the military, including his service during the attack on December 7, 1941. Then he added: "In closing may I proudly say that I feel that the short time I served as a G.I. [enlisted man] still seems more rewarding (due to my being at Wheeler [Air Field] during that surprise attack) than all my other (31 yrs) put together."[59]

EDWARD S. MICHAEL

Rank and organization: First Lieutenant, U.S. Army Air Forces, 364th Bomber Squadron, 305th Bomber Group. Place and date: Over Germany, 11 April 1944. Entered service at: Chicago, Ill. Born: 2 May 1918, Chicago, Ill. G.O. No.: 5, 15 January 1945.

Citation

For conspicuous gallantry and intrepidity above and beyond the call of duty while serving as pilot of a B–17 aircraft on a heavy-bombardment mission to Germany, 11 April 1944. The group in which 1st Lt. Michael was flying was attacked by a swarm of fighters. His plane was singled out and the fighters pressed their attacks home recklessly, completely disregarding the Allied fighter escort and their own intense flak. His plane was riddled from nose to tail with exploding cannon shells and knocked out of formation, with a large number of fighters following it down, blasting it with cannon fire as it descended. A cannon shell exploded in the cockpit, wounded the copilot, wrecked the instruments, and blew out the side window. 1st Lt. Michael was seriously and painfully wounded in the right thigh. Hydraulic fluid filmed over the windshield making visibility impossible, and smoke filled the cockpit. The controls failed to respond and 3,000 feet were lost before he succeeded in leveling off. The radio operator informed him that the whole bomb bay was in flames as a result of the explosion of 3 cannon shells, which had ignited the incendiaries. With a full load of incendiaries in the bomb bay and a considerable gas load in the tanks, the danger of fire enveloping the plane and the tanks exploding seemed imminent. When the emergency release lever failed to function, 1st Lt. Michael at once gave the order to bail out and 7 of the crew left the plane. Seeing the bombardier firing the navigator's gun at the enemy planes, 1st Lt. Michael ordered him to bail out as the plane was liable to explode any minute. When the bombardier looked for his parachute he found that it had been riddled with 20mm. fragments and was useless. 1st Lt. Michael, seeing the ruined parachute, realized that if the plane was abandoned the bombardier would perish and decided that the only chance would be a crash landing. Completely disregarding his own painful and profusely bleeding wounds, but thinking only of the safety of the remaining crewmembers, he gallantly evaded the enemy, using violent evasive action despite the battered condition of his plane. After the plane had been under sustained enemy attack for fully 45 minutes, 1st Lt. Michael finally lost the persistent fighters in a cloud bank. Upon emerging, an accurate barrage of flak caused him to come down to treetop level where flak towers poured a continuous rain of fire on the plane. He continued into France, realizing that at any moment a crash landing might have to be attempted, but trying to get as far as possible to increase the escape possibilities if a safe landing could be achieved. 1st Lt. Michael flew the plane until he became exhausted from the loss of blood, which had formed on the floor in pools, and he lost consciousness. The copilot succeeded in reaching England and sighted an RAF field near the coast. 1st Lt. Michael finally regained consciousness and insisted upon taking over the controls to land the plane. The undercarriage was useless; the bomb bay doors were jammed open; the hydraulic system and altimeter were shot out. In addition, there was no airspeed indicator, the ball turret was jammed with the guns pointing downward, and the flaps would not respond. Despite these apparently insurmountable obstacles, he landed the plane without mishap.

Notes

1. Flak is short for *Flugzeugabwehrkanone*, literally, antiaircraft gun. Ian V. Hogg, *German Artillery of World War Two*, 22.

2. George K. Schubert, Officer Commanding RAF Station, Grimsby, Memorandum to Operations Officer, 364th Bomb Squadron, 305th Bombardment Group, USAAF, Chelveston, April 17, 1944, in Edward Michael, Official Military Records, Louise Michael Collection.

3. Ibid.

4. Ibid.

5. This passage is drawn from Edward Michael's personal account, "A Tale of Two Missions," n.d., Louise Michael Collection, photocopy in my possession courtesy of Louise Michael; Hal Bamford, "Last Mission for the Bertie Lee"; John L. Frisbee, "Gauntlet of Fire."

6. Richard G. Davis, *Bombing the European Axis Powers: A Historical Digest of the Combined Bomber Offensive, 1939–1945*, 42.

7. Roger A. Freeman, *The Mighty Eighth War Diary*, 126.

8. Davis, *Bombing the European Axis Powers*, 11, 20.

9. Ibid., 42.

10. Louise Michael, telephone interview by Sherman Fleek, September 19, 2009.

11. Ibid.

12. Ibid.

13. Ibid.

14. Edward Michael, Official Military Records. in Louise Michael Collection.

15. Frederick A. Johnsen, *B–17 Flying Fortress: The Symbol of Second World War Air Power*, 35–40.

16. Bill Gunston, *Aircraft of World War 2*, 23; Johnsen, *B–17 Flying Fortress*, 59.

17. Johnsen, *B–17 Flying Fortress*, 66–72.

18. Ibid., 70–74.

19. Martin Bowman, *B–17 Flying Fortress Units of the Eighth Air Force (Part 1)*, 14–15, 100.

20. Ibid., 76–77.

21. Johnsen, *B–17 Flying Fortress*, 58–59.

22. *Target: Germany, The Army Air Forces' Official Story of the VIII Bomber Command's First Year over Europe,* 115–16.

23. Bowman, *B–17 Flying Fortress Units,* 49.

24. Edward Michael, January 22, 1944, Official Military Records.

25. Johnsen, *B–17 Flying Fortress,* 90–92.

26. Hogg, *Antiaircraft Artillery,* 113–15.

27. *Target: Germany,* 34.

28. Bowman, *B–17 Flying Fortress Units,* 69–70; Roger A. Freeman, *The Mighty Eighth: Units, Men and Machines,* 108–10.

29. Freeman, *The Mighty Eighth,* 184.

30. Ibid., 214.

31. U.S. military slang for "situation normal: all f——d up."

32. Edward Michael, "A Tale of Two Missions," 3; and his "Lt. Michael's Own Story," 3. He did not identify Staff Sergeant Luce's hometown.

33. Freeman, *The Mighty Eighth War Diary,* 217.

34. Bowman, *B–17 Flying Fortress Units,* 9, 11–12.

35. Michael, "A Tale of Two Missions," 4; "Lt. Michael's Own Story," 5.

36. Michael, "A Tale of Two Missions," 4; "Lt. Michael's Own Story," 5.

37. Michael, "A Tale of Two Missions," 4; "Lt. Michael's Own Story," 5.

38. Lt. Franklin Westberg, Statement, June 5, 1944, Medal of Honor Nomination, in Edward Michael, Official Military Records.

39. Michael, "A Tale of Two Missions," 4; "Lt. Michael's Own Story," 5.

40. Westberg, Statement, June 5, 1944.

41. According to the Geneva Convention, to which Germany was a signatory, escaping airmen were protected from enemy gunfire both aloft and on the ground until they landed. Then they could be engaged. Airborne troops, however, were not afforded the same protections.

42. Michael, "A Tale of Two Missions," 6; "Lt. Michael's Own Story," 7.

43. Michael, "A Tale of Two Missions," 6.

44. Michael, "A Tale of Two Missions," 7 ; "Lt. Michael's Own Story," 7.

45. "Lt. Michael's Own Story," 8.

46. Michael, "A Tale of Two Missions," 9 ; "Lt. Michael's Own Story," 10

47. Michael, "A Tale of Two Missions," 9.

48. Michael, "A Tale of Two Missions," 8; "Lt. Michael's Own Story," 9.

49. Edward Michael, Medal of Honor Citation, G.O. 5, January 15 1945, Michael, Official Military Records. The order for the citation,

the best primary source, is housed at the Military History Institute at Carlisle Barracks, Pennsylvania.

50. War Department, telegram to Bertie Lee Michael, May 25, 1944; in Edward Michael, Official Military Records.

51. Edward Michael, Letter to Michael Family, April 17, 1944, Louise Michael Collection.

52. Arthur Koscino, Interviewed by Sherman Fleek, July 14, 2009. Koscino was an aircrew member and later a prisoner of war.

53. The Medal of Honor presented to airmen of the Army Air Forces was the 1904 Gillespie version used by the U.S. Army. The U.S. Air Force developed and sanctioned its own design of the Medal of Honor in 1963. In 1966, LDS recipient Bernard Fisher was the first Air Force person to receive the new-minted design.

54. AF Form 11, Michael Official Military Records; comment in item block 48, "Not to be asgd [assigned] in active combat area under provisions of AFR [Air Force Regulation] 35–30." Some recipients from World War II did, in fact, serve either in Korea or Vietnam. George Wahlen, Mormon recipient during World War II, also served in Vietnam. (See Chapter 6.)

55. Louise Michael, interview, September 19, 2009.

56. Ibid.

57. Ibid.

58. Ibid.

59. Edward Michael, Application for Pearl Harbor Commemorative Medal, February 25, 1992, Michael Official Military Records.

PFC Leonard C. Brostrom.

Chapter Five

PRIVATE FIRST CLASS LEONARD C. BROSTROM: SERVING GOD AND COUNTRY

For the generation of young LDS men who came of age during World War II, many were deprived of the opportunity to serve proselytizing missions. Some saw their wartime years as a type of missionary service, which it certainly was, because tens of thousands of people met LDS service members and learned of Mormon doctrines and teachings.

Of the nine LDS Medal of Honor recipients, only one served a full-time mission. Of the five who served in World War II, one was too old and well into his military career; one was not yet a member of the Church; two others were either too young or did not have the opportunity. Only one awardee served two years or more as a missionary: Leonard C. Brostrom.

Unlike the era after World War II and the Korean War, missionary service prior to this time was not stressed vigorously by Church leaders. Only a few thousand missionaries were called during the interwar period. In 1939, for example, 1,088 missionaries served in thirty-five missions world-wide.[1] Many missions in Europe closed after the German invasion of Poland and the commencement of another general European war. Some Americans, including Latter-day Saints, clung to an isolationist policy in hopes of remaining at peace. Most Americans went about their normal lives while anxiously watching events in Europe and Asia. When the missionaries of 1939 departed for their service, few would have forecast what greeted them when they returned home in 1941: war and military service.

But while war clouds billowed over Europe and the distant shock was already engulfing China, Leonard Brostrom from Preston, Idaho, was called to serve in the California Mission.

* * *

Unfortunately, the amount of extant information on Leonard Brostrom is extremely limited. All his immediate family are dead; he never married, and most people who knew him sixty years ago are also gone. Consequently, of the nine recipients, his life is the least documented.

* * *

The Brostroms were Norwegians who joined the LDS Church and eventually made their way to Utah and the Rocky Mountains. Leonard's parents lived in Preston, Idaho, a small community of mostly LDS people in southeastern Idaho. Leonard was born in Preston on November 23, 1919, the oldest son of Carl and Louise Brostrom. He was active in Church and school activities, including the Boy Scout program. Leonard had three brothers: Dale, Dean, and Stanley Brostrom.[2]

During his teenage years, the Depression of the 1930s deepened across the United States. Times were tough; money and jobs scarce. Perhaps the hardest hit were small farmers and rural communities where resources, government assistance, and charity were hard-pressed to help. Leonard graduated from Preston High School in the spring of 1938.[3] Coincidentally, as he was leaving high school,

Elder Leonard Brostrom,
LDS missionary.

a younger student, Nathan ("Junior") Van Noy was just beginning his years at Preston High School. Both would receive the Medal of Honor; both would die in the service of their country.

Despite these dire times, Leonard must have determined at an early age to serve an LDS mission. Since missionaries have always underwritten the costs of their missionary service, it is a tribute to his character to work, save, and collect sufficient funds to serve. Many young LDS men who wanted to serve missions during these difficult and trying years could not, mainly due to lack of resources or a good job. Perhaps family and friends assisted, and Leonard's own LDS ward may have helped defray the expenses; all this is lost to history. But it is reasonable to say that he and others sacrificed so he could serve.[4]

Elder Brostrom entered the mission field in the fall of 1939 and served in Oakland, California, and also Reno, Nevada, and perhaps other areas. At this time there was no set missionary program of discussions or lessons. The more experienced elders passed down to other missionaries their teaching techniques and lessons that were handed down to them by others or created by themselves. A few pamphlet series, such as the popular "Rays of Living Light" and the Book of Mormon itself could provide structure for systematic lessons. Mission presidents provided valuable instruction, inspiring words and sermons, but the missionaries, organized into companionships and districts were mostly on their own. Church members helped the missionaries in their area as they could, but it is doubtful that missionaries such as Elder Brostrom saw more then a few people accept their teachings and become members. The young elders also taught, assisted, and strengthened the members wherever they served besides proselytizing. Also, there was no standard term of service then. After more than two years, Elder Brostrom was honorably released and returned to Idaho in the spring of 1942. By that time the United States was already at war.[5]

Whether Leonard was drafted into military service or volunteered is unknown. His brothers Dale and Dean served in the U.S. Navy, and Stanley also served in World War II in the U.S. Army Air Forces and then finished a twenty-year career in the Air Force.[6] Leonard became a soldier in the U.S. Army, which is a good indication that he was drafted. Soon he was assigned to the 7th Infantry Division, which would be assigned to the Pacific Theater of War. Where he trained and other facts about his early military service are unknown except that he became an infantryman— a common foot soldier.

* * *

The U.S. Army in modern times is really three armies, or better said, three components of the same army. Technically, the Army of the United States created by the National Defense Act of 1920, has one active and two reserve components (not always referred to in this way in the 1940s). The Regular Army—the standing, professional force—was the foundation and core of the army. The National Guard of the United States, formerly the militia, was both a state and federal military force as sanctioned by the Constitution. Since Lexington and Concord, the militia had been primarily a force of citizen-soldiers, trained to augment the regular army when needed. During World War I, millions of men were drafted into military service and were organized into National Army regiments and divisions, which were separate from the Regular Army and National Guard units. During World War II, this same practice continued more or less; however some individuals, and even regiments, were intermixed. So, in a National Guard regiment of ten companies of some 3,000 men, some soldiers were draftees, most were guardsmen, and there were regular army officers and NCOs who usually served in command and primary staff positions. These arrangements were based on the needs of the Army and availability of men, trained leaders, and the demands of combat.

The U.S. Army assigned Private Brostrom to one of the oldest and most honored infantry regiments in American history, the 17th U.S. Infantry, a Regular Army unit. In 1942, the 17th Infantry was part of the 7th Infantry Division, the "Hour Glass" division, one of the original divisions of World War I.[7] The 7th Division, like many combat units, had been inactivated after the Great War. As the clouds of war darkened in 1939 and 1940, the War Department activated the 7th Division as a new unit, the 7th Motorized Division. The conflict in Europe introduced new concepts of war, new tactics, and new types of units. Some units were especially trained for specific tactics or operations: armor, airborne (parachute), mountain, desert, and amphibious warfare. In 1943, the motorized divisions were redesignated, and the 7th Infantry Division came into being. Thus, the Army had four types of divisions: airborne, armor, cavalry (motorized units, despite the traditional name), and infantry. All the divisions, except the airborne, had infantry, tank, and artillery battalions, besides engineer, signal, antiaircraft and support elements.

Along with the Regular Army 17th Infantry Regiment, the 7th Infantry Division had two National Guard regiments from California, the 159th and 184th Infantries. When these divisions were first organized in World War I, they were known as "square" divisions, because there were four regiments, two per brigade, and two brigades per division. However, in 1940 the War Department developed the "triangular" division of three regiments with no brigades. Another innovative concept was the first real attempt at a "combined arms" organization, called the "Regimental Combat Team," or RCT. The base or nucleus of the infantry regiment was augmented with slices of artillery, reconnaissance, antiaircraft, combat engineer, and other support units as mission and conditions required.[8]

* * *

The 7th Infantry Division's baptism of fire occurred on United States territory, not on foreign soil. Most Americans do not know that Japanese forces bombed and then landed in Alaska's Aleutian Island archipelago. In the spring of 1942, after successful invasions of Malaya, Borneo, New Guinea, and the large American prize of the Philippines, the Japanese planned yet another expansion against the weak and tottering Allies: Great Britain, Dutch and French colonies, Australia, New Zealand, and the United States. The Japanese Imperial High Command determined that it was time to draw the U.S. Pacific Fleet—fragile after its costly victory in the Battle of the Coral Sea—into open action and crush it with overwhelming forces. Thus, the stage was set for the climatic and decisive Battle of Midway in the first week of June 1942.[9]

A small Japanese surface force, the Northern Area Fleet, consisted of two small escort carriers, five cruisers, twelve destroyers, and four large troop transports. It was assigned to conduct a feint, a diversion to confuse and divide the limited America forces. The Japanese intended to threaten and even take the key Aleutian island of Dutch Harbor, luring American forces north while the main Japanese thrust focused on Midway and the destruction of the U.S. Pacific Fleet's last three remaining aircraft carriers.[10]

On June 3, 1942, the Japanese bombed the major American garrison of Dutch Harbor, then invaded and occupied the smaller islands of Attu and Kiska at the far west end of the archipelago. Americans could not tolerate enemy forces on their own soil; but they refused to be drawn into a major commitment in Alaska, instead concentrating on winning the great Battle of Midway, which proved to be the turning point in the long war in the Pacific Theater.

So it was almost a year before they dealt with the Aleutian sideshow. On May 11, 1943, U.S. Army forces made an amphibious assault against Attu led by the 7th Infantry Division. During the two-week campaign, the division lost some 600 men. Only twenty-eight Japanese out of the garrison of 2,400 surrendered. The rest died.[11] Two months later on August 15, the 7th Infantry Division invaded Kiska, supported by a Canadian brigade of some 5,500 men. When the forces hit the beach, they met no resistance. The Japanese had evacuated the 5,183-man garrison on July 28 without being detected.[12]

Whether Private Leonard Brostrom was in this campaign is not known exactly. It is likely that he served in both assaults, having been assigned to the 17th Infantry Regiment months earlier, unless he was ill or otherwise detached.

In September 1943, the 7th Division then went to Schofield Barracks in Hawaii for more training, rest, and reconstitution. They undertook a tough training program to prepare for the major actions in the western Pacific already on the planning boards.

* * *

The next target for the 7th Infantry Division was a place known by name to few until the thousands of soldiers and Marines landed there in February 1944: Kwajalein Atoll. The atoll was a formation of dozens of isles, nothing more than reefs in the shape of a huge backwards "C" curving across hundreds of miles. Kwajalein was part of the Marshall Island group and lay about midway between the Hawaiian Islands and the Philippines. To the north of the atoll chain, the 4th U.S. Marine Division would land on two small rocky crags, Roi and Namur. The 7th Division would invade Kwajalein itself. D-Day was February 1, 1944, when both elements hit the beaches. The worse fighting was on the main atoll of Kwajalein where Army forces met the stiffest resistance. The infantry landed on the western shores and fought eastward. After four days, the 7th Division reached the opposite shore. On February 6, the last enemy forces were eliminated or surrendered. The division lost 176 killed and 768 wounded.[13]

By the end of February 1944, the 7th Infantry Division was back in Hawaii. Not all units had the luxury of rotating off the battle line to such a pleasant place. Yet all of them knew that it was just a matter of time before they would ship out again. In fact, some elements of the division participated in the capture of Engebi in the Eniwetok Atoll on February 8, 1944.

Back in Hawaii in July 1944, the division stood for review for President Franklin Roosevelt and General Douglas MacArthur. These leaders were at Pearl Harbor for an important conference on war strategy and future operations that would clearly determine the course of the war. A controversy among senior American leaders about two avenues of advance toward Japan had risen and President Roosevelt himself, as commander in chief, settled the matter. The result was the 7th Infantry Division's invasion of the Philippine Islands and Private Leonard Brostrom's last action.

One of the interesting stories of personalities and leadership during World War II occurred when President Roosevelt came to Hawaii for this conference. For months the Joint Chiefs of Staff—Army and Navy, along with General Henry ("Hap") Arnold of the Army Air Forces—looked beyond the successes of New Guinea, the Marshall Islands, especially Tarawa, and the Solomon Islands, to the greatest challenge: invading mainland Japan. During the planning for this last major strategic move, the momentous question was whether to bypass the Philippines and invade Formosa, more to the north and closer to Japan, or go into the Philippines. The issue pitted two strong personalities at odds: General Douglas MacArthur against Admiral Ernest King, Chief of Naval Operations.

MacArthur, commander of the South West Pacific Area, was at his headquarters at Brisbane, Australia, when he received a summons to Pearl Harbor. He was told to report without his normal staff for a photo and public relations session with President Roosevelt. Once in Hawaii, his bitterness and anger about leaving his forces in Australia subsided when he realized the purpose was much more than a photo shoot. The president convened a council of war with MacArthur, Admiral Chester Nimitz, commander of the Pacific Ocean Areas, and Admiral William Leahy, the unofficial chairman of the Joint Chiefs of Staff.[14]

At this point, most of the senior American leaders had decided on the Philippine option; however, Admiral King, General Arnold, and some staff officers still pushed for Formosa. Arnold of the Army Air Forces wanted his new B–29 bombers based as close as possible to Japan, and Formosa was more suitable for aviation reasons.[15]

Admiral Nimitz led off with a complimentary briefing for Formosa as the target, but personally he favored the Philippines. After some time, it was MacArthur's turn. When President Roosevelt asked why the Philippines were so important, the general simply said, "Promises must be kept." For an hour, speaking without notes, he provided an eloquent argument why it was essential that the Allies take the Philippines. His two main arguments were that it was tactically dangerous to leave a garrison of some 280,000 veteran Japanese soldiers, many vessels, and hundreds of enemy aircraft astride the Allied line of advance and communications across the central Pacific. The second argument was a moral point in regard to American honor. The Allies could not bypass the Philippines where thousands of American, British, and Dutch soldiers and civilians were languishing in prison camps. It had stung MacArthur that, when he was ordered from the Philippines in April 1942, he had been promised that the Allies had already assembled a force ready to retake the islands. He soon learned that this was not true. Roosevelt and the others at the conference knew that the Philippine course of action was the soundest and most logical option.[16]

* * *

Private First Class Leonard Brostrom and F Company of the 17th Infantry, along with the rest of 7th Infantry Division, prepared for "A-Day" October 20, 1944—invading Leyte. Leyte was a prominent island of the Visayan Island group and was tactically attractive for many reasons but especially because of its location, harbor towns, and capabilities for follow-on forces.[17]

SAINTS OF VALOR

It also had some major drawbacks. Twenty thousand Japanese troops were entrenched there with tanks and artillery. These soldiers were part of the Japanese 14th Area Army, which had responsibility for the Philippines. Lt. Gen. Sosaku Suzuki commanded the 35th Army that defended the Visaya Island group, including Leyte and Mindanao. The American Sixth Army faced the Japanese 16th Division, which was under strength but still lethal.[18] The Japanese held five airfields with some 422 fighters and 337 bombers.[19] Even without the Japanese, the daunting terrain of knife-like ridges, jungles, and tropical diseases were major threats. Like most fights in the Pacific, the Japanese would use this vicious terrain against the invaders.

The invasion was divided between two main elements of the Sixth U.S. Army. The 6th U.S. Ranger Battalion would take two small islands near the approach of Leyte Gulf. Also the 21st Infantry, an independent Regimental Combat Team (RCT) would assault the southern tip of Leyte at Panaon Strait some seventy miles away. Three days later, the 7th Division, along with the 96th Infantry Division, a draftee outfit, made up the XXIV Corps. Its assignment was to strike near the coastal town of Dulag. The X Corps consisting of the 24th Infantry and 1st Cavalry Divisions was to land near Tacloban fifteen miles to the north. Eventually the two corps would advance inland, converge along the Leyte Valley, and move on to Carigara Bay. Along the southern valley was the Japanese 16th Division's two regiments, the 20th and 33rd, besides an independent tank company, a reconnaissance regiment, and support troops totaling about 21,700 men.[20]

Invading the Philippines meant that the Japanese fleet in the area would come forth to do battle. The Allies hoped and planned for this development—correctly, as it turned out. Eventually, the greatest naval battle in world history, Leyte Gulf, took place on October 23–25, 1944.[21]

* * *

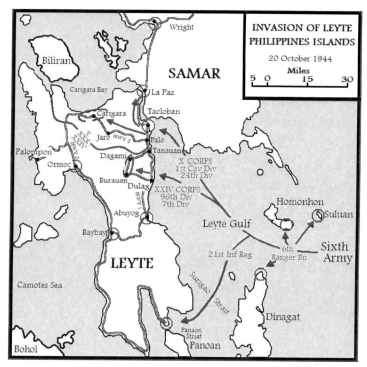

Invasion plan of Leyte. Cartography by Hyrum H. Fleek.

On October 17, 1944, the 6th Ranger Battalion invaded the outlying islands of Dinagat, Homonhon, and Suluan to secure the passage into the main area of Leyte Gulf. Three days later, on October 20, at 1000 hours as planned, the X Corps landed near Tacloban and the XXIV Corps assaulted the beach at Dulag. After securing a beachhead against little opposition, the two separate forces drove west toward the Leyte Valley. Maj. Gen. John R. Hodge commanded the XXIV Corps, of which the 7th Infantry Division was one of the assault units. A few hours after the assault, General Douglas MacArthur waded ashore in the vicinity of Tacloban with the 24th Infantry Division.[22] McArthur promised he would return to the Philippines and he had.

The Japanese resistance increased as the American units moved inland. The 7th Division captured Dulag, its first objective, forcing the Japanese back to a stronger position near Dagami; the U.S.

division's losses were 49 killed and 192 wounded. The next day the Americans took Dulag airfield and continued their advance over the following few days through swamps in scorching heat against stronger opposition. The 96th Division captured Catmon Hill in two days of hard fighting, while the adjacent 7th Division took the town of Burauen about ten miles inland. The enemy had built numerous concrete machine-gun emplacements. The GIs called them "pill boxes" because of their general shape.[23]

As the Army ground forces moved forward, the U.S Navy was engaging and fighting the Japanese fleet. The Battle of Leyte Gulf involved hundreds of ships—three Japanese and two American fleets.

Even though the Japanese fleet lay in shambles, the Japanese were still able to reinforce the defenders of Leyte with more troops from Mindanao and from as far away as Japan and China. The defense grew more desperate and savage every day as the battered American divisions slowly moved up the Leyte Valley toward the north shore.

* * *

October 28, 1944, Day of Days

The Japanese defensive tactics were clever and deadly. They did not always contest the beach itself but fought inland where the attackers could be ambushed, enticed into lethal cross-fires, trip on boobie-traps, and face overlapping fire from concrete bunkers. There were also "spider traps" where Japanese soldiers would suddenly pop up from hidden holes and tunnels with grenades and small-arms fire. Perhaps the most frightening weapon for both sides was the flamethrower. This type of combat was savage and very different than the fighting in Europe or North Africa against the Germans. American soldiers soon learned that the Japanese infantryman was a brutal, merciless, skillful, and a fanatical opponent.

PFC Brostrom and the 17th Infantry Regiment advanced west to Burauen which fell on October 24, 1944, along with its cluster of three airfields. Platoons and companies slowly moved north toward the next objective, Dagami, meeting more intensive resistance from the Japanese 16th Division.[24]

On the morning of October 28 at about 0700, the 2nd Battalion, 17th Infantry led the 7th Division's advance toward Dagami about 2,000 meters to the north. Intelligence estimates reported that 1,500 to 2,000 Japanese troops from the 20th and 32nd Infantry Regiments were defending the area, supported by the 16th Engineer Regiment, which had laid out the elaborate defensive scheme with many fixed positions.[25]

By 0730 the 2nd Battalion met heavy resistance near a damaged stone bridge over a stream that drained a 100 meter-wide swamp. F Company, PFC Brostrom's company, was wading through the waist-deep swamp toward a coconut grove on the far side when Japanese fire opened from several concrete gun positions. The mortar rounds rained down. Soon the 2nd Battalion commander, Lt. Col. William Moore, ordered E Company to reinforce both F and G Companies. The lead elements took more casualties. One of the advance scouts, Brostrom, was heavily engaged in the firefight. For hours, the battle seesawed in intensity.

The Americans tried to call up some M-4 Sherman tanks, but they could not negotiate the swampy land. On the far right end of the 17th regimental line was its 1st Battalion, locked in a savage fight with enemy forces. The Japanese defensive line extended farther to the west and turned south beyond the American lines. C Company was pinned down until three tanks that could traverse the drier ground arrived, engaged the heavy Japanese guns, and destroyed several of the concrete positions.[26]

By mid-afternoon, F Company was assaulting the last enemy-held positions in a mopping-up operation. American engineers had repaired a stone bridge and soon two M8 armored cars were brought up, providing more fire-power.

As the day began to wane, a few Japanese machine-gun emplacements and pill boxes remained intact, providing murderous fire. That is when PFC Brostrom went into action. Without or-

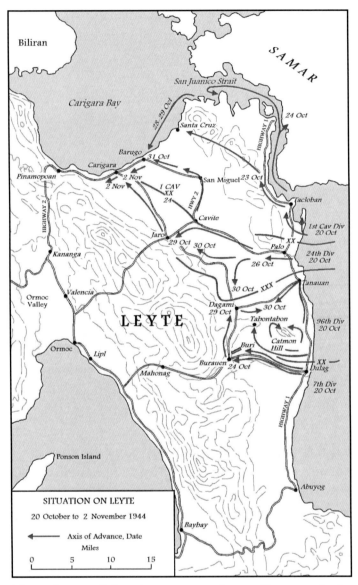

Tactical map of the advance across Leyte. Cartography by
Hyrum H. Fleek.

ders, he took the initiative and single-handedly charged an enemy
concrete defensive position, throwing hand grenades at the enemy and firing his M–1 Garand rifle. Brostrom immediately drew
heavy fire on himself away from the rest of his platoon and com-

pany. He was suddenly attacked by six enemy soldiers with fixed bayonets who popped up from trenches. He killed one with his rifle and forced the other five to flee from his fire. Brostrom was then severely wounded and knocked to the ground, but he rose and continued his lone attack. He hurled more grenades at the main enemy position. As he forced some of the enemy to withdraw, his fellow riflemen charged and engaged the fleeing enemy. Just as the enemy position was overrun by men of F Company, Brostrom collapsed, due to loss of blood from several serious wounds.[27]

Medics treated Leonard Brostrom; but as they were carrying him to the rear on a stretcher, he died from his wounds. Eventually his remains were returned to the United States and buried in Idaho.

* * *

More than a year later, Preston, Idaho, held a memorial service. By then the president of the United States had approved the awarding of the Medal of Honor to PFC Brostrom. On November 29, 1945, the Chamber of Commerce of Preston hosted the ceremony. Among the local participants, hymns, eulogies, and religious rituals, Elder Ezra Taft Benson of the Quorum of the Twelve Apostles was a guest speaker. General Robert M. Hardaway presented the Medal of Honor to Leonard's father, Carl Brostrom, representing the family. This was a fitting memorial by a community to a beloved son. Later, the city of Preston erected a monument in honor of PFC Brostrom and PVT Nathan ("Junior") Van Noy in the town cemetery, memorializing these two fallen heroes.[28]

The fleeting memory of a soldier, who fought proudly and bravely, survived in the form of a naval vessel. Christened the SS *Marine Eagle* in 1942, and built in Chester, Pennsylvania, the vessel made several trips to Europe during the war once the Allies had a foothold in Belgium and France. It also sailed to Antwerp in July 1945 just after the war ended. The ship was reassigned to the U.S. Army Transportation Service in 1948, renamed the *Private Leonard C. Brostrom*, and used for cargo operations to Japan, then

USNA *Private Leonard C. Brostrom* (T-AK-255). Photograph courtesy of Idaho Military Museum.

Korea, and later Vietnam. Once again under U.S. Navy control, this transport was decommissioned and transferred to the Maritime Administration for final disposition.

The USNS *Private Leonard C. Brostrom*, (T–AK–255), a large military cargo vessel, made its last voyage and arrived at the harbor dock in May 1980. After all the valuable gear, instruments, equipment, and furniture were removed, the ship was signed over to the salvage company in 1982 and sold for scrap. [29] Soon what was once a sturdy and dependable military freighter designed to carry tanks, would be nothing more than steel and debris, sorted, scrapped, melted down, and used for cars, washing machines, and parking meters.

In some ways the use and legacy of this ship is much like the service and memory of Leonard C. Brostrom: strong, dependable, relatively unknown, serving a vital function, and disappearing from memory, leaving no family, no papers, no personal legacy.

LEONARD C. BROSTROM

Rank and organization: Private First Class, U.S. Army, Company F, 17th Infantry, 7th Infantry Division. Place and date: Near Dagami, Leyte, Philippine Islands, October 28, 1944. Entered service at: Preston, Idaho. Birth: November 23, 1919, Preston, Idaho. G.O. No.: 104, November 15, 1945.

Citation

He was a rifleman with an assault platoon which ran into powerful resistance near Dagami, Leyte, Philippine Islands, on 28 October 1944. From pillboxes, trenches, and spider holes, so well camouflaged that they could be detected at no more than 20 yards, the enemy poured machine-gun and rifle fire, causing severe casualties in the platoon. Realizing that a key pillbox in the center of the strong point would have to be knocked out if the company were to advance, Pfc. Bostrom, without orders and completely ignoring his own safety, ran forward to attack the pillbox with grenades. He immediately became the prime target for all the riflemen in the area, as he rushed to the rear of the pillbox and tossed grenades through the entrance. Six enemy soldiers left a trench in a bayonet charge against the heroic American, but he killed 1 and drove the others off with rifle fire. As he threw more grenades from his completely exposed position, he was wounded several times in the abdomen and knocked to the ground. Although suffering intense pain and rapidly weakening from loss of blood, he slowly rose to his feet and once more hurled his deadly missiles at the pillbox. As he collapsed, the enemy began fleeing from the fortification and were killed by riflemen of his platoon. Pfc. Brostrom died while being carried from the battlefield, but his intrepidity and unhesitating willingness to sacrifice himself in a 1-man attack against overwhelming odds enabled his company to reorganize against attack, and annihilate the entire enemy position.

Notes

1. *2006 Church Almanac*, 655.

2. [Untitled article about Leonard Brostrom, No byline,] *Pass in Review: Idaho Military History Quarterly*, June 2004, 6.

3. Ibid.

4. Ibid.

5. Ibid.

6. Ibid, 6.

7. This division's nickname come from its shoulder patch, which looks like a red hour glass.

8. Richard W. Stewart, ed., *The United States Army in a Global Era, 1917–2003*, 119–20.

9. George L. MacGarrigle, *Aleutian Islands*, 4–5.

10. Stewart, *The United States Army in a Global Era, 1917–2003*, 96–97.

11. MacGarrigle, *Aleutian Islands*, 23.

12. Ibid.

13. Thomas Parrish, ed., *The Simon and Schuster Encyclopedia of World War II*, 353.

14. William Manchester, *American Caesar: Douglas MacArthur 1880–1964*, 425–26. The position of chairman of the Joint Chiefs of Staff had not been authorized by Congress, but the president appointed Leahy as an acting chairman through much of the war.

15. Ibid., 421.

16. H. Hamlin Cannon, *Leyte: The Return to the Philippines*, 4–5.

17. John Keegan, *The Second World War*, 554.

18. Charles R. Anderson, *Leyte*, 10.

19. Cannon, *Leyte*, 22.

20. Ibid., 23.

21. Keegan, *The Second World War*, 354–60.

22. Anderson, *Leyte*, 12.

23. Ibid., 15.

24. Ibid., 16.

25. Cannon, *Leyte*, 141.

26. Ibid., 142.

27. Ibid., 142–43.

28. PFC Leonard Carl Brostrom, Memorial Program, November 29, 1945.

29. Private Leonard C. Brostom, website of the Department of the Navy, Naval Historical Center, www.history.navy.mil/danfs/p12/private_leonard_c_brostrom.htm (accessed January 1, 2010).

Pharmacist's Mate Second Class George E. Wahlen. White House Medal of Honor ceremony, October 1945. Courtesy U.S. Navy Medical History Office, Washington, D.C.

Chapter Six

PHARMACIST'S MATE SECOND CLASS GEORGE E. WAHLEN: SAVING LIVES ON THE KILLING FIELD

January 1945

Tens of thousands of Americans—the vast majority of them Marines, Navy crewmen, and Army soldiers—boarded an armada of warships. They knew they were headed into harm's way: invading a Japanese-held island. After all, that was the strategy of the Pacific war: island hopping. With each island, the Allies, in this case the Americans, advanced ever closer to mainland Japan and hopefully the end of the war. In Europe, the Nazi empire was crumbling, and it was just a matter of time before the Third Reich would be history.

With all of the islands invaded and occupied, the goal was to create more airfields closer to Japan for the 20th Air Force, supporting the Central Pacific Ocean Area. Therefore, ordinary soldiers and Marines received no information about the name of the island, its size, the enemy forces involved, the battle plan, or its expected duration—until they had to know. All the men knew was that the

Japanese held well-fortified locations, and were heavily armed, professionally led, and fanatically determined to die for the Emperor. They were also dangerously lethal, waiting in their reinforced concrete bunkers and their deep cavernous tunnels, with enough ordnance for three empires. For the average Marine, it was not a pleasant proposition, especially after months and months of training. Seldom in history did combat soldiers enter a campaign with less information about their destination and mission. The planners called it Operation Detachment, a not-so-martial or interesting name for one of the great American military operations of all time. To this day, only historians and buffs know the code name. To those fought there, it was just two words: Iwo Jima.

The 2nd Battalion of the 26th Marine Regiment rode the waves aboard a troop transport still hundreds of miles from its final objective. The USS *Hocking* (APA–121, Transport Amphibious) was less than a year old. In fact nearly all of the 116 warships in the armada had been built after Pearl Harbor. On January 29, 1945, Lieutenant Colonel Joseph P. Sayers called a meeting for the entire 2nd Battalion—more than a thousand Marines. They had been at sea for three weeks and were still three weeks away from their landing or D-Day. At this point in the voyage, the men were anxious to not only know their objective but also get off the rolling steel tub. Standing before his men, most of whom had never experienced combat, Lt. Col. Sayers announced, "Gentlemen, I am here to disclose that our target is Iwo Jima." He removed the cover over a terrain model of the island. Hundreds of necks craned and thousands of eyes strained to see the three-dimensional model. Perhaps not one of them had ever heard the name before. Sayers and other officers then explained in rough outline the intelligence, the enemy's dispositions, the battalion's mission, and the general conduct of the invasion.[1]

Among the hundreds of men attending this pre-combat briefing, was Pharmacist Mate 2nd Class, George Edward Wahlen, a Navy corpsman, attached to F Company to provide medical treatment to its men. George Wahlen had been in the Navy nineteen months and had already been promoted once. He had been as-signed to the 26th Marine Regiment for about six months. This was Wahlen's first combat action, as it was the 5th Marine Divi-sion's first battle. George, a Mormon boy from near Ogden, Utah, was twenty years old.

Later, hours before the landing, George Wahlen who was not a habitually prayerful man at this time in his life, lay in his ham-mock and prayed earnestly for safety and protection for others; for himself, he prayed for the ability and strength to do his job. After he finished a calmness came to him, an inner strength that he had rarely experienced before in his life. He then drifted off into peace-ful rest.[2]

Just five weeks later, by the first week of March 1945, some 25,000 Americans of the 110,000 men who eventually came ashore would be casualties: 6,000 killed, and the remainder wounded in action. Some 60 percent of George's "Fox" company were casual-ties, including George himself. Even Lt. Colonel Sayers, the bat-talion commander, would be wounded on the fifth day, D-Day + 5. During two weeks of heavy and intense combat, Corpsman Wahlen treated scores of wounded men; he was wounded seri-ously in the face and in the shoulder and received several other smaller injuries from grenade fragments, killed a Japanese soldier with a grenade, and, after the most grievous day of battle, received a third wound so severe that he could no longer function. Final-ly, he agreed to be evacuated. For his courage and selfless service, George Wahlen received the Medal of Honor seven months later from the president of the United States.

* * *

Albert and Doris Wahlen lived in a small rented house in Og-den, Utah, for twelve years before they could save enough for the down payment on the $1,200 house on a ten-acre farm. It was unusual for ordinary Americans without wealth and connections to be able to buy a house in 1936 at the height of the Great Depression, but the Wahlens did. Albert Wahlen had lost his life's savings after the crash of 1929 when banks failed. From then on, he hid money at home. The fact that his family could buy a home gave twelve-year-old George Edward Wahlen a sense of security. George was born on August 8, 1924, and had twin younger brothers, Gene and Jack. The Wahlens were Mormon but had drifted from activity and did not follow the precepts of the faith, even while living in a predominantly LDS community.[3]

Young George grew up small and slight but determined. He was extremely competitive, especially in boxing and playing football at Weber High School. In November 1941, he left high school without completing his senior year and enrolled in an airplane mechanic course offered by Utah State Agricultural College in Logan. The card he played to convince his father to allow him to leave high school was the monthly stipend of $15—a lot of money for a seventeen-year-old.[4] Soon he was in beautiful, alpine Cache Valley, securing lodging and preparing for school.

A month later the Empire of Japan attacked Pearl Harbor and invaded Malaysia, the Philippines, and most of Indo-China. George's course began Monday, December 8, 1941, the same day the United States declared war on Japan. For the next six months, as American forces fought in the Pacific and prepared for major combat in the European theater, George learned important skills as an aircraft mechanic. In June 1942, he accepted a position with the U.S. Army Air Forces at Hill Army Air Field, ten miles south of Ogden.[5]

In June 1943, after a year at Hill Field and watching friends depart for war, George, who was nearly nineteen, went to Fort Douglas in Salt Lake City and volunteered. Because he was under twenty-one and had already registered for the draft, George merely put forth his name for voluntary military service. He underwent a battery of interviews at recruiting offices representing all the armed services ready to accept qualified volunteers. George opted for the Army Air Forces due to his aviation mechanical training, but he was denied an opening. He next turned to the Navy. On June 18, 1943, with American forces fighting in New Guinea and

New Britain, bombing Germany, and preparing to invade Sicily, George Wahlen said good-bye to his family and left Ogden for San Diego and Navy boot camp.[6]

* * *

The decision by the Joint Chiefs of Staff to invade Iwo Jima (Japanese for "Sulphur Island") was not controversial as the earlier decision to take the Philippines instead of Formosa had been. In the summer of 1944, General Douglas MacArthur won the political and strategic debate to strike at the Japanese in the Philippines, thwarting the Navy's desire to advance on Formosa. The plan to invade Iwo Jima was different. It was not based on a huge concentration of Japanese forces and aircraft in the Allies' rear as with the Philippines. The concept was simpler: The Army Air Forces needed airfields.[7]

Most of the new B–29 Superfortresses were based in the Mariana Island group some 1,500 miles from mainland Japan. It was a long haul even for the new long-range bomber. The distance was too great for American fighter escorts, so the bombers flew much of the route without protection. The 20th Air Force needed a base of operations for its shorter range but very versatile P–51 Mustang. Also, with three airfields on relative flat terrain, the island was suitable as an emergency alternate landing site for damaged bombers. The best candidate for a forward base was Iwo Jima. The Navy concurred, and the operational planning began in earnest in mid–1944. With twenty-one U.S. Army combat divisions already widely deployed throughout the Pacific, the logical candidates for the assault was the U.S. Marine Corps. Three of its six divisions would make the amphibious assault planned for late February 1945.[8]

The Marines would come from the Pacific Ocean Areas commanded by Admiral Chester Nimitz, and the overall amphibious commander would be Marine Lieutenant General Holland T. Smith. He was known by Marine and Army troops—especially by subordinate commanders who hated his guts—as "Howlin

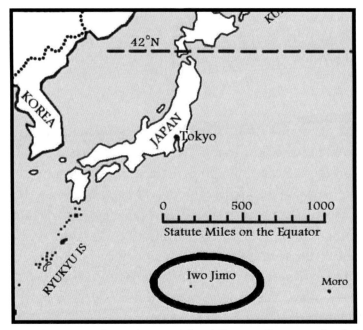

Iwo Jima in relation to mainland Japan. Cartography by
Hyrum H. Fleek.

Mad" Smith. Considered today by some as the "father of amphibious warfare," General Smith was a gruff, tough, and also strangely,
religious, old Marine. The Pacific Theater, especially the Pacific
Oceans Areas under Nimitz was truly a joint operation with Marine and Army divisions fighting and island-hopping together in
many operations; but the cooperation was not always harmonious.
"Howlin Mad" Smith's rancorous leadership style alienated Army
Major General Ralph Smith, commander of the 27th Infantry Division, a seasoned National Guard division of mostly New York
soldiers. The two Smiths hit an impasse on Saipan where Marine
Smith relieved Army Smith in July 1944. The Army staff and
generals in the Pacific Theater "howled" for the blood of "Howlin
Mad" Smith. A formal board of investigation later declared that
the mad Marine Smith was not justified in relieving Ralph Smith.
By this time, however, the war and "Howlin Mad" had moved on
to other enemies.[9]

As the planning continued, the realities of war again surfaced. The first major consideration is always the enemy—numbers, dispositions, type and amount of equipment, combat readiness, morale, quality of the officers and NCOs, and their training. Next is the terrain, the dirt one force hopes to wrest away from the other. Iwo Jima was basically a rock: a large volcanic rock with black sand, some trees but no forest, and a few springs of "putrid" water. Shaped like a pork chop, the island was just over ten miles in length and half that at its widest point. Its dominant feature was Mount Suribachi in the southwest rising 550 feet above the Pacific. A series of smaller hills and ridgelines lay to the north. Between the two areas of high ground on the flat central plain were three airfields, heavily damaged by American bombing raids but the prize of the operation.[10] Historian and World War II navy veteran Robert Newcomb summarized the operational plan: The Navy "would cut off the Japanese sea and air forces, transport the troops, and put them ashore; the Marines would take the island, the Army would garrison it and the Air Force would use it."[11] This was truly a joint operation.

* * *

For four weeks at San Diego, George Wahlen endured the discipline and regimentation of basic training, though he confessed he had trouble marching, "having two left feet." He often found himself in "extra training" after the duty day marching on the "grinder" or parade field. Still hoping to be an aircraft mechanic, he soon learned that he was assigned to be a medical corpsman. He pled with an officer to allow him to become an aviation mechanic. The officer recommended that he go to the medical training school at Balboa Park where perhaps they could make an exception for him. A warrant officer at the medical school told Wahlen if he did well in the medical course, then perhaps the Navy could assign him to an aviation squadron as a mechanic. After eight weeks and a great effort, George graduated near the top of his class of some 500 men, but again his desire to work on aircraft was rebuffed.

He found himself in a ward at the hospital treating patients and dealing with an ornery head nurse. One day after a confrontation, the nurse threatened to send him to a Marine unit; he replied, "Sister, you're not sending me anywhere," and then he forthwith requested a transfer to a Marine infantry regiment as a corpsman. The next day he departed for Camp Elliott, California, and duty with the Marine Corps.[12]

The medical training George received at Balboa Park was limited, almost primitive compared to modern military field medicine. He learned how to give immunizations, make simple sutures, dress wounds, set simple factures, and identify and treat some diseases. With the Marines, the training also included treating wounded men under simulated combat conditions. Assigned to an rifle company George marched, bivouacked, and endured rain, storms, and blistering sun with all the leather-necks under his care.[13]

After eight weeks, he transferred to Camp Pendleton in January 1944 and underwent more realistic unit training with a new combat unit, the 5th Marine Division. Officially activated on January 21, 1944, the 5th Division would have its baptism of fire on Iwo Jima a year later. Here George and some 15,000 Marines would join together in platoons, companies, battalions, and regiments, form the bonds of warriors, and develop unit *esprit de corps*.

Wahlen became a corpsman in the 2nd Battalion of the 26th Regiment, which Marines refer to as "the 26th Marines," and so on. The 26th Marines was one of three infantry regiments organic to the 5th Division, the 26th, 27th, and 28th Marines, besides the 13th Artillery Regiment, and also tank, transportation, and engineer battalions. It also included support units: medical, signal, tractor, laundry, and even a dog platoon.[14] A Marine regiment, commanded by a colonel, was authorized to have 4,608 officers and men according to the standard Table of Organization and Equipment (T&OE) during the war. With three regiments and all the combat and combat support units, a division numbered

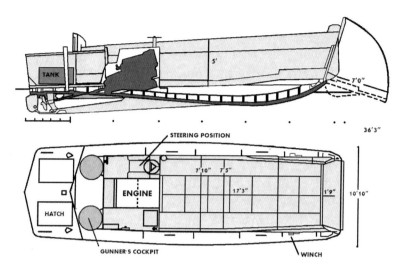

Technical diagram of a LCVP (Landing Craft Vehicle Personnel), more commonly known as the "Higgins boat." Drawing by Hyrum H. Fleek.

16,503 officers and men. The TO&E also established the authorized number and type of weapons and types, vehicles, rifles, flame throwers, tents, helmets, and even holding cots.[15]

To carry a full regiment to a beachhead, the Navy had to employ more than a hundred landing craft. The typical staging and marshalling plan, as in all invasions, was based on the number of landing forces, or "waves" that assaulted sectors of beaches designated as Green, Red 1, Red 2, Yellow, and so on. The landing craft, whatever their size and capacity, would often make several runs, delivering different "waves" to their assigned landing sectors. Time-charts, embarkation schedules, designated lanes, and rally areas—all organized with the number of landing craft—were planned just like a bus schedule. Among the flotilla was the Landing Craft Control (LCC), which acted much like a modern air traffic controller. Later on the beaches were "beachmasters," who were normally Navy enlisted men. They had the critical task of maintaining order and discipline despite the chaos and death. They were like traffic cops at a demolition derby. The goal was to keep the beaches clear, push the forces from squad to battalion inland, and move off the beach to clear the way for the next "wave." Soon traffic would be moving both directions. As new troops and provisions landed on the beach, the wounded would be transported off the beach to the waiting ships.[16]

In July 1944, the untested 5th Marine Division and Pharmacist Mate 3rd Class George Wahlen shipped out for Hawaii. Eventually, he was assigned to "Fox" Company, 2nd Battalion of the 26th Marines, or F/2/26.

The Marines at Camp Tarawa on Hawaii, the Big Island, trained rigorously, maintained their equipment, and anticipated the day when they would go into battle on the now-famous "D-Day." They had learned a great deal about amphibious warfare, but they did not know where they were going or what the next island was in the grand plan of the war. Lack of such a small item of information caused additional anxiety.

The Marines practiced loading their equipment aboard transport ships, and then disembarking into rolling landing craft according to plans and schedules. They would cross the line of departure (LD) to approach the beach in proper order. The Marines had to learn how to deploy and fight on various types of landing craft, whether a larger LCI (Landing Craft Infantry) without ramps but equipped with gang-planks; or the ubiquitous Higgins boats or LCVPs, the most common craft in the American arsenal. Some Marines also approached the beaches on tracked vehicles or AMTRACs.

In the gigantic logistical effort of a vast global war, it is difficult to believe that a food fight occurred among the Allies and the separate theaters of war over a certain type of amphibious vessel. The large, slow, but durable LST (Landing Ship Tank) influenced planning throughout the war. The bulky LST was ocean-going, had an enormous load capacity, and could drive itself up onto a beach where it would off-load hundreds of troops, vast amounts of stores, and dozens of vehicles. Perhaps small compared to an aircraft carrier or a mighty battleship, nevertheless, the LST was the backbone of amphibious warfare in both Europe and the Pacific.

Once the beachheads were secure, LSTs would bring in the heavier equipment such as more tanks, bulldozers, larger trucks, and also harbor materials. Designated by Navy as a "ship" because its length was greater than 200 feet, the standard LST was 320 feet long, had a displacement of 4,000 tons and could cruise at 12 knots speed, or 15 mph. These ships could carry nearly twenty medium tanks and berth more than 200 men.[17] The LST was so essential to the war effort that, on several occasions, entire invasions were cancelled or rescheduled due to their availability. One of these delays was Operation Overlord, the famous Normandy landing in northern France, which created a second "western" front in Europe. It had to be postponed to June 1944. In southern France, "Operation Anvil," an invasion by the U.S. Army and a few French commandos also had to be postponed due to the lack of enough LSTs. The ambitious landing along the sunny and picturesque French Riviera had been scheduled to occur simultaneously with the Normandy invasion. But there were not enough craft, especially LSTs, to support both landings in Europe simultaneously.[18] Renamed "Operation Dragoon," it finally hit the southern French coast on August 15, 1944.[19] The same situation prevailed in the Pacific. In July 1944, the landings on Guam and Saipan required a smaller number of LSTs, but still the total number available could not support multiple major amphibious landings in both theaters, the Pacific and Europe.[20]

Allied leaders and planners were so frustrated at times that a frantic push to manufacture and launch more LSTs became a major industrial incentive. Even at the highest levels, leaders were baffled that "the plans of two great empires like Britain and United States should be so much hamstrung and limited," British Prime Minister Winston Churchill lamented in April 1944, by an "absurd shortage of L.S.T.'s."[21]

The LSTs were shuttled back and forth from the Atlantic to the Pacific throughout the war. Iwo Jima put some 30,000 troops

LSTs on Iwo Jima beachhead. Photo courtesy of the National
Archives, Washington, D.C.

ashore the first day, mostly Marines. "Dragoon" the invasion of
southern France, landed 80,000 men. Operation Overlord, the
grand Normandy invasion, put 154,000 Allied soldiers in France
by nightfall.[22]

* * *

Corpsmen like Wahlen were called "Doc" by the men. A medical corpsman had to gain the loyalty and trust of the men in his
unit in order to perform his duties. If the men felt in any way that
"Doc" was not proficient and willing to function in combat, then
he would fail in his duties. One way a corpsman could gain the
tough Marines' confidence was to endure all the rigorous demands
of combat training. The more George trained and interacted with
the men, the more they relied upon and trusted him.

The many weeks of training, amphibious assaults on Hawaiian beaches, forced marches across volcanic fields, and maneuver-

ing through thick jungle terrain made the Marines of the 26th combat-ready. During one particularly difficult march, Wahlen's platoon sergeant, a tough gunnery sergeant, taunted him about being a corpsman and a sailor. Marines have traditionally ridiculed sailors, sometimes in jest and sometimes in earnest. After hours of "joking" that George was in danger of falling out, being weak, or not being manly enough to march with the Marines, it was the large, husky gunnery sergeant who began to fall behind. George, still with power and stamina, walked up to the struggling Marine and asked with mock innocence, "Do you want me to take your pack and rifle for you?" The older man, pricked in his pride, grunted, "No damn corpsman's ever going to take my pack and rifle."

After months of challenging training, the 5th Division left the port of Hilo on January 4, 1945. In six weeks, after stops at Eniwetok and Saipan, the convoy steamed toward the Bonin-Volcanic Island group and their objective of Iwo Jima.[23]

What awaited the Marines were some 21,000 well-trained tough and entrenched Japanese soldiers and sailors with hundreds of large guns, artillery, and a demanding warrior code handed down from generation to generation: the pride and determination of the samurai.

* * *

Iwo Jima had few resources and was not, in itself, a prized possession. Fresh water had to be shipped in, and there was nearly no top soil. Before the Japanese troops had arrived, the native Iwa Jimans, numbering about a thousand people, herded goats, fished, and grew vegetables in pockets of soil.

But Iwo Jima's location made it valuable. By the summer of 1944, the Japanese high command realized that it was only a matter of time before the Allies began invading homeland territories. Japan had lost much of its naval aircraft and surface fleet over the last three years and had not been able to replace them quickly. The Japanese war effort was reaching its own culminating point.

Realists in Tokyo and in the officer corps knew that the inevitable could be delayed no more than a year at best, and probably less. Even some of the junior officers, including one stationed on Iwo Jima saw the end approaching:

> Seeing that it was impossible to conduct our air, sea and ground operations on Iwo Jima toward ultimate victory, it was decided that in order to gain time necessary for the preparation of the Homeland defense, our forces should rely solely upon the established defensive equipment in that area, checking the enemy by delaying tactics. . . . It was a most depressing thought that we had no available means left for the exploitation of the strategical [sic] opportunities which might from time to time occur in the course of these operations.[24]

The meaning behind this polite language of "delaying tactics" was a starker reality. The Imperial Japanese forces on Iwo Jima had one mission: to die in place and kill as many Americans as possible in the process. Prior to the invasion of the Bonin-Volcanic Islands, the Japanese had been defending occupied places like New Guinea, Saipan, Tarawa, Guam, and the Philippines—not sovereign Japan soil. But Iwo Jima was viewed as part of the Japanese homeland.

The Japanese Thirty-first Army under General Hideyoshi Obata was responsible for defending the island chains near the mainland of Japan. There were fewer than 3,000 naval troops on Iwo Jima in the spring of 1944. Army troops began to arrive in April; and by August, nearly 21,000 navy and army troops were preparing for the American onslaught. In these hectic days for the crumbling Empire of Japan, the Army general staff made a wise move to appoint an outstanding officer to lead the suicidal effort to defend the small, indefensible rock island. Lt. General Tadamichi Kuribayashi, a career officer in the Japanese Army with thirty years of experience, assumed command in June 1944 just as the U.S. Navy made one of its bombings raids on the airfields and destroyed most of the land-based Type 0 Zeke ("Zero") fighters. Kuribayashi was an honorable warrior—educated, cultured, and well traveled. He spoke English and had served for two years in the

United States as a military attaché. When war came in 1941, he wrote presciently to his wife: "The United States is the last country in the world that Japan should fight. Its industrial potentiality is huge and fabulous, and the people are energetic and versatile. One must never underestimate the American's fighting ability."[25]

Although he knew that defending Iwo Jima was a doomed mission, he worked, led, and prepared his men and resources as if his only goal was victory. With vigor and vision, Kuribayashi immediately unified the chain of command and settled the long-standing quarrels between the former army and navy commanders; he sent a sickly and pessimistic naval officer back to Japan and replaced with him a more energetic senior naval officer, Rear Admiral Toshinosuke Ichimaru. Kuribayashi also sent away all of the civilians. His soldiers dug wells and established distilleries to assure a pure water supply.[26]

Kuribayashi's defensive strategy concentrated on fortifying the inland terrain. Iwo Jima was particularly suitable for this tactic because of Suribachi's steep escarpment in the south and the more gradual, sloping hills in the north. These dominating terrain features were perfect for direct-fire weapons systems whose assigned fields of fire would create engagement areas, or kill zones. As the Americans came ashore with little cover on the dark, deep sand, especially on the eastern shores, they would soon encounter a vicious defense. The fire plan was also a defense in-depth with a series of interconnecting and mutually supporting defensive positions. The plan was a cross-fire with heavy guns, artillery used in a direct fire role, mortars, automatic weapons, and even antiaircraft guns. The defensive plan was simple, lethal, and brilliant. Creating this defensive system took every available resource.[27]

Most of the soldiers were part of the 109th Infantry Division, commanded by Kuribayashi himself with the major subordinate units of the Independent Mixed Brigade and the 145th Infantry Regiment, besides several service support and artillery battalions. (The Independent Mixed Brigade is the Japanese equivalent of an American Separate Brigade with combined arm units, infantry, armor, artillery, and so on.) Soon caves turned into labyrinths of tunnels—literally miles of underground passageways, storerooms, and quarters. Lacking tanks or armored vehicles, the Japanese cannibalized all the weapons they could and deployed them in the defensive scheme. Eventually they installed six 6-inch (225mm) coast artillery guns, 41 dual mounted AA guns, and 70 larger caliber machine guns positioned in various gun emplacements. They built 316 concrete bunkers or blockhouses. Nearly a hundred other artillery pieces of various calibers were deployed in the open and could be mobile if necessary. In addition, Kuribayashi had a dozen heavy Type 98 Spigot mortars 320mm, dozens of 81mm mortars, several hundred crew-served machine guns, other automatic weapons, the Type 99, 7.7mm bolt-action rifle issued to every soldier, and other weapons. There were also hundreds of individual and squad fighting positions.[28]

* * *

There is an old adage among military professionals, especially since World War II that no battle plan or operations order survives the first rounds fired.

The staff develops the plans, and the commander approves them. The invasion plan for Operation Detachment was made by majors and lieutenant colonels on the staff of the Fleet Marine Force (FMF). Its various iterations over several months were then reviewed by colonels, the chief of staff, and the commander, who approved it. The invasion was more than just the 70,000 Marines and a few thousand Army soldiers going ashore over several days. An operation of this magnitude involved some 800 ships and landing craft, manned by 100,000 sailors, and mountains of provisions, ammunition, rations, and fuel—enough for 30 days.[29]

The preliminary planning for the invasion and occupation of the Bonin Volcanic Islands began in September 1943. The Joint War Plans committee recommended the operation in July 1944 in Washington, D.C., and the Joint Chiefs of Staff approved it on

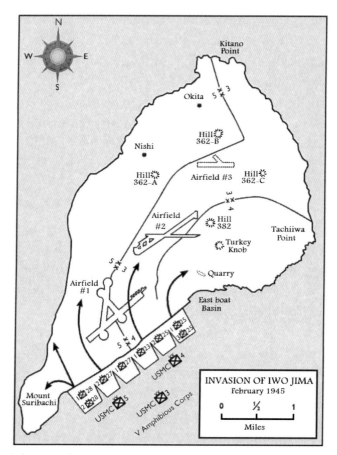

The assault on Iwo Jima. Tactical scheme of maneuver through D+5; the 26th Marines landed where the 2/27th Marines went ashore. Cartography by Hyrum H. Fleek.

August 12, 1944. With the campaign through the Central Pacific Ocean Area and the seizure of the Marianas in July, the need for a more forward base of operations had become even more acute. The assets available for Operation Detachment were enormous.[30] Admiral Raymond Spruance, the victor of Midway in June 1942, was senior commander; Vice Admiral Richmond K. Turner was the Joint Expeditionary Force Commander; Lt. General "Howlin Mad" Smith was commanding general of the Expeditionary Force; and Major General Harry Schmidt, USMC, was commander of the landing force. Under Admirals Spruance's and Turner's control were 116 capital ships—sixteen aircraft carriers with hundreds of carrier-based aircraft, eight battleships, and all the landing craft and support vessels necessary.[31]

Eventually, many types of plans were developed to cover transportation, fire support, landing, traffic control (to and on the designated beaches), designating reserves, implementation of command and control measures, and even medical evacuation planning. The last plan was simple: a craft approaching the beaches would off-load its cargo, and then return to sea with the wounded. This was a major joint operation, where Navy and Army Air Force bombers had the mission to conduct preparatory bombing of Iwo Jima, destroy all the enemy aircraft on the ground, demolish as many gun emplacements as possible, and cut off reinforcements by land or sea. By the end of 1944, all the Japanese aircraft had either escaped or were destroyed; the three airfields were wrecks; and most of the identifiable defensive positions were neutralized. By the time Task Force 58 under Admiral Turner arrived off-shore to prepare for the amphibious assault, the Japanese forces on Iwo Jima were isolated, surrounded, and without any air or naval support at all.[32]

The final tactical plan was assigned to the V Amphibious Corps (VAC), a subordinate element of the Expeditionary Force under Mad Smith. The tactical plan would direct the actions of the three combat divisions and provide guidance for the first few days of the invasion. After the third or fourth day of combat, the initial operations order would be amended by "on/order" missions or "fragmentary orders" or FRAGOs. The scheme of maneuver was simple, the classical and doctrinal "two up and one back" formation. In this case, two divisions would simultaneously assault on line (the 5th Division on the left, the 4th Division on the right) with one division (the 3rd) in reserve. The divisions and regiments did not land with their full complement; they followed the VAC scheme, two forward, one in reserve; therefore only eight of the eighteen battalions landed with the division force. Still, it required sixty-eight landing craft to carry some 13,000 men in the first wave ashore.[33]

The 26th Marines, including George Wahlen's 2nd Battalion, were the 5th Division's tactical reserve. The first contact with the Japanese occurred at D-2, or two days before D-Day, on February 17, 1945, when 21 LCI (G) Landing Craft Infantry (Gun) (commonly called "gunboats") charged toward the beachhead from 2,500 yards away. They provided covering fire for the 100 "swimmers" or frogmen of the Underwater Demolition Teams, two swimmers per team, whose mission was to find and clear underwater obstacles, conduct reconnaissance of the submerged approaches to the beaches, and brief the beachmasters later.[34]

During the charge of the gunboats on D–2, General Kuribayashi made the mistake of thinking that this was the real invasion, so he ordered some of the hidden guns to open fire, thereby giving away their positions. Several LCI (G) were hit. A few dozen Americans were killed or wounded; one swimmer died in the operation. Then followed the barrage of naval gunfire for two days to "soften" the beach for the assault waves. It appears that this preliminary fire had little effect on the Japanese defenses.[35]

* * *

D–Day, February 19, 1945

A Landing Craft Vehicle Personnel, LCVP, the famous "Higgins boat," pitched up and down and also listed left and right in the natural swells of the Pacific waters. Hundreds of yards from the beach, the waters were in commotion from the wakes of hundreds of ships, craft, and vessels of many types and sizes. Much of the island and the landing beaches were partially obscured by the smoke and haze of artillery fire. Gunfire, heavy artillery, and mortars made a distant rumble across the churning waves. But the roar of the LCVP's huge inboard motor was the loudest and most constant noise.

Packed like sardines, up to thirty-six fully equipped Marines tried to keep their balance as the craft rolled and pitched, crossing

LCVP loaded with a full complement of troops. Photo courtesy
of the National Archives, Washington, D.C.

wakes and cut through or rolled over breakers. The waves splashed
aboard, drenching the men with cold salty water, perhaps calming
some but frightening others. Just because they were Marines and
had served at sea did not mean that they had sea legs for this small
craft exercise. Furthermore, they were now under fire. Some were
seasick. Others were nauseated from anxiety. All of them were
afraid although they refused to admit it. Iwo Jima was the first
combat experience for some 60 percent of the men of 5th Division.

The men of the 2/26th had eaten a large hot breakfast aboard
the USS *Hocking* very early in the morning. Now it was late in the
afternoon, and the regiment was going ashore by battalions and
companies. Part of the reserve of the 5th Marine Division, the 2nd
Battalion embarked in several dozen craft. Soon they approached
the line of departure in column formation. Then the craft, on order from the seaborne control craft formed into assault lines. The
5th Division had been assigned three beaches: Green, Red 1, and
Red 2.[36]

* * *

A huge geyser of water splashed a dozen yards away, the over-powering concussion making it obvious that an artillery round had hit nearby. Earlier, "everybody was looking over the edge and being real concerned about what was going on," George Wahlen remembered after the war. But after this first near-hit, "everybody stayed down. . . . It kind of gave you a feeling: We're really in a war now. It was a shocking experience." He and thousands of others had watched the "softening up" process from their relatively safe position a couple of miles off the beach. Haze and smoke continued to cloud the small island except for glimpses of Suribachi's heights. They could not hear the gunfire on the island. But now they were in it.[37]

Pharmacist's Mate George Wahlen with his detachment of F Company was soon on the beach. Initially he and Fox Company were pinned down a few dozen yards inland, but soon they maneuvered off the cluttered and congested beach. George noted the surprising number of dead. That night the men slept as best as they could despite the noise and fear. They were wet, cold, and hungry. Tracers, mortar, and artillery flashed throughout the night. "I might have dozed a couple of times," Wahlen recalled, "One time I was about half dozed off and I [felt] something hit in my hole. It shocked me; I thought it was a grenade. I looked for it but couldn't find anything." The next morning he saw that a huge piece of shrapnel "had landed in my hole and just missed me."[38]

Though George's company did not experience any casualties on D-Day, some 600 Marines were dead and some 2,000 were wounded. It was perhaps the bloodiest day in Marine Corps history.[39] Among the dead was a Marine legend, Gunnery Sergeant John Basilone, known as "Manila John" because he had served in the Army before the war in the Philippines. He had been awarded the Medal of Honor for actions and valor in October 1942 on Guadalcanal when he repelled a Japanese attack with two machine guns and a pistol. He was the first Marine in the war to receive the

medal and was also offered a direct commission, which he refused
because he preferred to serve among average Marines in combat.
He received his wish. He made it to the beach and was approaching airfield #1 with the 1/27th Marines, when a mortar exploded
near him. It killed "Manila John" and four others.[40]

Fortune, fate, or luck preserved F Company the first day, D–Day.
That fortune soon changed.

The 2nd Battalion's mission was to move inland toward its first
objective, the southern area around airfield #1. The Marines dug
in and threw up a hasty defense, pausing in their advance. During this temporary lull, Second Lieutenant James W. Cassidy,
George's platoon leader, was "trooping the line" when a Japanese
sniper hit him in the chest near his heart, a dreadful wound in any
war. "He was the first casualty I treated. He was semi-conscious
and we got him evacuated right away," George later remembered.
Corpsman Wahlen fought diligently to stop the bleeding and keep
the young officer from going into shock. All the while he stayed
low and kept under cover so he would not also become a target
to the sniper as enemy fire whizzed overhead. Wahlen applied
the common Carlisle bandage, a pad of sterile white gauze with
four green linen tails to tie it in place. It was first developed by the
Army's medical research staff at Carlisle Barracks, Pennsylvania.
As the action continued, Wahlen dragged Cassidy down a slope
where litter teams carried him to the rear. He was evacuated to the
ship where he died.[41]

By nightfall, George's unit was near the end of the runaway
of airfield #1. The next day, February 21, D+2, they slowly advanced to support the 27th Marines, which was headed toward
the western shore of the island. The 2/26th had to conduct one of
the difficult maneuvers in war, a passage of lines between friendly
forces, also called a battle handoff. The 2/26th Marines assumed
control of the area of operations of the 3/27th west of the airfield.
Then the battalion continued to advance and soon encountered
resistance from Japanese cleverly hidden in "spider traps" and well-
camouflaged blinds. It was a cruel and deadly form of combat. En-

emy soldiers would rise and fire, hurl hand grenades, and engage with machine guns from just yards away.[42] The defenders at this early stage in the battle could not absorb heavy casualties in large counterattacks; however, the Japanese conducted limited spoiling attacks to harass the advancing Americans. In fact, Japanese navy swimmers came ashore on the western beach trying to infiltrate through the 5th Division flank. This unsuccessful maneuver caused an exaggerated intelligence report that a major Japanese landing was taking place.[43]

Gunnery Sergeant Joseph Malone had taken command of George Wahlen's 2nd Platoon after Lieutenant Cassidy's wounding. As in all such actions, when officers are lost, the NCOs take over; leadership is at every level during war. On D+3, February 22, the 2nd Battalion received a serious artillery and mortar attack in the late afternoon, followed by a local counterattack that pushed back the Marine outposts and forward positions. The 26th Marines sustained many casualties as it reestablished its lines and repelled the Japanese attack. During this action, Sergeant Malone led the platoon up a small hill where a projectile exploded at his feet, throwing him through the air. Wahlen, just yards away, quickly made his way under fire to Malone. The scene was awful. Malone's right leg had been blown off above the knee. He had lost some fingers on his hand, and his face was a mess—bloody and ghastly. Malone's uniform was still smoking from the powder burns. Wahlen "put a tourniquet on his leg," then applied "a battle dressing on his face. Within minutes a stretcher team came behind us and they evacuated him back to the beach." Joe Malone survived his wounds and Wahlen saw him later in Guam when they both were patients in a rear hospital.[44]

The next day, February 23, 1945, the 28th Marines raised two separate flags on the summit of Mount Suribachi, a moment captured in an immortal photo by Joe Rosenthal that became possibly the most famous photograph of the war and the inspiration for a bronze statue erected in Arlington, Virginia. It has become the most powerful symbol of the U.S. Marine Corps.

* * *

February 26, 1945, A Day of Days

The nature of combat on Iwo Jima and the engagements that
George Wahlen experienced were distinctive when compared to
the other LDS Medal of Honor recipients. The criteria the Navy
officials used to consider Wahlen's actions covered nearly a two-
week period and were not based on one action or the events of one
day. In fact, Wahlen's valor and unflagging service during these
two days of February 26–27 were such that the Navy awarded
him a Navy Cross for each separate action. The Navy Cross is the
second highest decoration for courage in the sea services. Therefore the narration of his Medal of Honor exploits covers these two
main actions or periods and several lesser actions in between.

The 5th Division held the line oriented mostly north and east
of about 1,200 yards frontage. The 2nd Battalion held the center;
the 3rd Battalion was on the right and had a salient to the south,
while the 2/27th Marines' position was on the left, running all the
way to the western beaches. Between their landing on February
19 and February 25, Fox Company had had several days of intense combat and also a couple days in the rear for recovery and reconstitution. In those days of combat, the Marines had witnessed
some horrendous scenes. Lt. Col. Sayers, the commander of the
2nd Battalion had been wounded. Major Amedeo Rea, the executive officer, assumed command.[45] George had seen two Japanese
soldiers burned alive with flamethrowers. Among other wounded,
he had treated both his platoon leader and platoon sergeant, both
severely wounded. The former died; the latter was maimed for life.

But despite the heavy fighting, the most demanding combat
still awaited the 26th Marines. The Americans were entering the
killing zones established by Kuribayashi's defensive planning. The
defense was increasingly stubborn, the enemy more numerous, the
casualties greater.

On February 26 American battleships and cruisers provided nearly pinpoint gunfire to eliminate fixed enemy gun positions. By 1000 hours, Fox Company under the command of Captain Frank Caldwell moved forward to relieve E Company across a contested "no man's land" of several hundred yards that lay before the cliffs northwest of airfield #2. They were honeycombed with tunnels and spider holes. Machine guns occupied emplacements with hidden entrances and blinds. The enemy had deadly fields of artillery fire to cut the Marines down as they advanced. The Japanese 26th Tank Regiment had camouflaged several medium tanks among the caves and gullies of the cliffs to support the overall fire plan. The commander of the tank regiment was a celebrity of sorts. Cavalry officer Lt. Colonel "Baron" Takeichi Nishi had won a Gold Medal in the 1932 Olympic Games at Los Angeles in one of the equestrian events. Lt. Colonel Nishi knew it was useless to employ the tanks as a rolling force, so they became stationary gun platforms with revolving turrets. The 2nd Battalion's main objective was to capture and occupy these low hills, known as Hill 362A.[46]

The battalion made steady progress toward the hills, especially after the heavy bombardment from off-shore early in the morning. Soon they encountered heavy small arms and mortar fire and had to beat off numerous small Japanese suicide attacks from caves and hidden positions. As George made his way across the increasingly lethal area, he realized that several Marines had been wounded—more than a dozen. Under fire, Wahlen crawled to the first Marine, down with a serious thigh wound that had severed his femoral artery. Blood was spouting like a geyser as George stuffed a dressing into the wound, applied a pressure bandage, and moved on to the next man. The next Marine's leg had been blown completely off. George cinched up a tourniquet to stop the blood loss. On he went until he had treated a half dozen wounded men. Then unexpectedly he came across a fellow corpsman, Eddie Monjaras, who had sustained a savage abdominal slash through which his intestines were protruding. George kept a grip on his emotions, bandaged the gaping wound, and gave Monjaras morphine with an injector syrette. Eddie was eventually evacuated, but he did not survive.[47] Morphine syrettes were small disposable injectors of the powerful pain-killer. After use, they were attached to a wounded man's uniform so that, at a glance, the number of syrettes used was known. This precaution prevented overdoses.

Wahlen treated some fourteen or fifteen wounded men as Monday, February 26, crawled by. He was often exposed to heavy small arms fire and mortar attacks. Yet, unflinchingly he did his job, saved lives, provided medical care, and did his best to instill confidence and peace in these horribly wounded men. Finally, George's medical supplies were exhausted. So was he. It was late afternoon. He crawled into a shell hole and nearly collapsed from the strain and the terrible scenes he had witnessed. The battle continued to rage around him as M–4 Sherman tanks arrived from B Company, 5th Tank Battalion, to reinforce the assault on the hills and cave complexes. Though the 26th Marines took a lot of casualties, they inflicted many times more upon the defenders.[48]

Later that day, Fox Company received orders to withdraw and reconstitute a few hundred yards off the front line. As Wahlen crawled down a slope with others of his company, he heard and felt a thud. He knew immediately what it was. "I caught the concussion right in the face," he explained. "It about half knocked me unconscious. I had grenade fragments in my face and I could feel the blood." In fact, his right eye had been pierced by a fragment and swelled up so rapidly that he could not see out of it at first. As best he could, even though he was out of sterile supplies, George dressed his own wound. Then, he heard cries from some wounded soldiers nearby. He crawled toward them, disregarding the blasts from several grenades that landed nearby.

Peering ahead with his left eye, he saw the location of the Japanese soldier who was lobbing the grenades. George was armed only with a .45 caliber automatic pistol and called to some Marines to toss him a grenade. They threw him several unarmed grenades. "So I grabbed one and started to crawl up the hill toward the place the grenades were coming from," he stated.[49] "As I was crawling up

I was catching grenade fragments in the back of my legs and my butt," but he kept going until he was right under the spider hole from which a Japanese soldier would rise up, throw a couple of grenades, and then dodge back down. "As I got up to the side of it [the hole] I went to pull the pin out of the grenade but the ring came off and the pin stayed in," George recalled. "As I lay there, I was getting machine gun fire from farther up the hill. I can't understand why I was so calm under those circumstances, but I took my K-bar knife out and straightened out that pin. I then pulled the pin out and looked over at the hole where the grenades were coming from." He could see the Japanese soldier just a few feet away, "so I let the spoon flip off, counted to 3 and just lobbed it right at his feet." The grenade exploded almost the instant it hit the ground and killed the soldier, but inflicted yet another concussion on Wahlen. This was the only time that George killed an enemy soldier.[50]

Wahlen then returned to the wounded Marine he had treated earlier and dragged him down the hill until stretcher-bearers arrived to take him to an aid station in the rear. Wahlen then crawled back to the raging battle area to find his own platoon. He came across some wounded in a shell crater along with a fellow corpsman from his unit, Pharmacist's Mate 3rd Class George Long. Farther away, wounded Marines were calling from a ravine. Wahlen immediately headed out toward them, followed a few moments later by a reluctant Long. They bandaged and administered aid until they were out of supplies. Then the two medics argued over who should expose himself and cross the deadly "no-man's land" to retrieve more medical kits.

"Well, I'm senior, and I'm telling you go back," Wahlen demanded.

Long said, "If you're senior, then you go back."

According to Wahlen's later account, "we discussed that for awhile and finally I went back to get some supplies."[51]

He made it safely to the rear of Fox Company. As he restocked his medical kit with dressings and morphine, Captain Caldwell saw his bandaged and bleeding face, and his other lighter wounds. He wanted to evacuate Wahlen to a hospital ship off shore. George Wahlen refused and returned to the line.[52]

By the end of Monday, February 26, 1945, George Wahlen had treated some twenty casualties, had suffered a serious eye injury and several lesser wounds, and had killed a Japanese soldier. Fox Company's casualties were eighteen killed and forty-nine wounded.[53]

* * *

The next day, Tuesday, February 27, F Company withdrew and became the regimental reserve for the next few days. At last they could meet their two main needs of food and sleep. Though off the line and not exposed to direct fire, they were still vulnerable to artillery and mortar fire, small, localized enemy attacks, and the awful dread of returning to the fight. A unit reconstitutes under such conditions, replacing men and equipment, cleaning, and repairing weapons, often making up for items in short supply by creative scrounging.

Medical personnel are often tasked to assist in the necessary but unwelcome duty of "graves registration" and the final disposition of remains. Even before the last bullets are fired, bodies are identified for burial, often being buried in a temporary cemetery. It is a thankless task.

George had his wounds treated. Many small fragments were removed from his legs, back, and butt. His right eye looked awful, but he could at least see out of it again. He found shelter in a cramped shell crater and took some much-needed sleep. He was very stiff from the great labor and in pain from his injuries. Later, the 2nd Battalion and F Company returned to the fight.

In every battle, some entity—a unit, a commander, a type of weapon, or a piece of terrain—becomes key. At this stage of the fight for Iwo Jima, the 5th Division's sector was on the western side of the island. A series of hills near the abandoned village of

Nishi became "key terrain." A key terrain is a small but critical factor in a local battle or battle area. The force that controls it usually has the advantage and wins. High ground is almost always key terrain, and this was true with Hill 362A, the same hill that the 2/26th had been advancing toward for several days.

On February 27, the 5th Division continued its slow probing advance up the western shore where it encountered heavy resistance from the dominant Hill 362A and supporting resistance from the surrounding series of hills. It was tough going, mostly for the 3/27th Marines. By midday on February 28, the 2/26th, including George Wahlen, moved forward to relieve the battered battalion of the 27th Marines.[54]

The original tactical plan was for the 3/27th to cross the LD (line of departure) at 0815 to flank the eastern slopes, while the 2/27th supported it on the left across a flat plain extending to the shore. Almost immediately, the two battalions smashed into a fearful fight. By noon the advance had ground to halt. Thus, the 2/26th, the regimental reserve, moved up to reinforce the combat battalions. These battalions conducted a battle hand-off, which took hours. The 2/26th then assumed the heaviest burden of battle. This isolated part of the battle soon became one of the bloodiest phases and areas of the entire campaign. Wahlen's 2/26th did not effectively assume control of the forward edge of the battle areas (FEBA), until after midnight. They had soon established forward outposts and were preparing for an attack come daylight.[55]

Wednesday, March 1, brought a change of plans. The 3/27th was ordered to stay in place in a defensive position, while the 2/26th angled westward (left) to assault the long, low ridge line that extended from Hill 362A. Along the western shore, LCI (G) gunboats scurried up and down the coast to give the artillery observers aboard better vantage points from which to observe and call for fire on the Japanese positions. The 5th Division now held a thousand-yard frontage from the shore toward the 3rd Division on its right. By the end of the day, March 1, these Marines had captured twelve prisoners and killed an estimated 3,200 in the division's area of responsibility (AOR). The division thus far had suffered 48 officers and 952 men killed and more than 3,000 wounded.[56]

At 0800 on March 2, Dog and Fox Companies advanced to fill in the gap or seam that had opened up between the two battalions. One of the worst tactical situations in war is to have one's "seam split," leaving a space between two units. A great tactical objective, of course, is to split the enemy's seam, then conduct a penetration and roll up the enemy's flanks. Thus, F Company moved out to fill the gap before the Japanese could see this weakness and take advantage of it.[57]

George was assisting some wounded Marines when he came to his next patient, a Marine who weighed some 200 pounds. Wahlen, who was much smaller, was struggling to drag the man to safety when an artillery round went off behind them. Wahlen was thrown to the ground and nearly knocked unconscious. He lay there dazed and shaken for a few minutes. As soon as he collected his senses, he realized that his left arm seemed paralyzed and numb. He must have been wounded by the shell. He later said the shock was "like I'd been hit with a sledge hammer the way it knocked me flat. It had taken a big chunk of flesh out [of] my shoulder."[58] After a few more minutes of recovery time, he crawled to where a Marine was taking cover. George talked him through the process of cleaning the wound with sulfanilamide and then applying a dressing.

On Friday, March 3, the Marines finally seized control of Hill 362A. The advance continued. Ahead lay Hill 362B, which had the same elevation as 362A. It was part of the new objective, Nishi Ridge—actually a series of hills near airfield #3. This airstrip had not been completely finished and was the last cohesive element of the Japanese defense. The 26th and 28th Marine Regiments advanced online toward the Nishi Ridge at 0745. It was D+12 and George Wahlen's last day of combat.

* * *

March 3, 1945, the Final Day of Days

George was in awful shape. He had received several painful but non-debilitating injuries and two serious injuries, one to his eye and one to his left shoulder. Still, he refused to be evacuated to a hospital ship and moved forward with his company as it assaulted Nishi Ridge and Hill 362B. The resistance was weakening across the division frontage, but General Kuribayashi's kill zones were still holding up, making each inch of ground desperately disputed territory. George treated several wounded Marines that morning.[59]

Once over the ridgeline, the 26th Marines had to cross a rugged plain. The Japanese fire intensified. Soon the two forward battalions of these two regiments entered an inferno. They struggled forward as the afternoon waned, pushing the determined enemy back slowly. The battle fought by the 26th Marines has almost become legendary. The official Marine history recorded, "By far the most spectacular fighting and resultant gains were made in the zone of the advance of the 26th Marines."[60]

As the lines and units advanced to the north, Wahlen was hobbling as best he could. A Marine sergeant ordered him to help find a wounded Marine. George set out and came across three Marines in a shell crater. He was just approaching them when suddenly the familiar whistle and whiz of an incoming artillery round sounded. Probably none of them heard it, but the blast of the explosion was deafening and powerful; George was thrown to the ground, stunned. After a few moments of recovery, he crawled up to the crater's edge and saw a ghastly scene. The shell had landed directly in the crater. One of the Marines was only a mass of tissue, flesh, bowels, and some fragmented bones. The second Marine had both legs blown off, and the third had one leg blown off. Both were gushing blood. Wahlen started to climb down into the hole when he collapsed. He then felt a piercing pain in his right leg and foot. He looked down to see that his boot was blown off. His entire lower leg was a bleeding mess. He guessed that he had broken bones in his foot, although it seemed to be intact.[61]

George summoned up his powers, crawled down into the blood-sodden crater, and tightened tourniquets on the stumps of the two Marines who were still alive. A couple of other naval corpsmen happened by and rapidly took over treating the two Marines. George powdered his foot and leg with sulfanilamide, then applied dressings, pushing past his own pain and weakness to do so. His final self-treatment was to inject morphine, which soon worked its magic.[62]

The war continued around Wahlen as stretcher-bearers arrived to remove the wounded. While he was waiting, he heard a cry of pain a short distance up a small slope near him. Wahlen rolled over and began crawling toward the desperate cries of, "Corpsman! Corpsman!" Dragging his wounded leg, he crawled over some fifty yards of rough ground and reached the wounded Marine. Both of his legs were broken, and he was in tremendous pain. They were exposed to enemy fire from small arms and mortars. Despite the morphine, George knew that their only option was to crawl down the slope and find cover. He gave the Marine a syrette of morphine, but both of them were in agony, as they dragged themselves back on their elbows, inch by inch. Unbelievably, they both reached a large crater in which they could take cover. Litter-bearers made their way to them, and took the Marine with the broken legs away.[63]

Another set of stretcher-bearers came for Wahlen. As they hauled him away, snipers opened fire on them. The bearers dropped the litter and took cover. George, who hit the ground hard, lay still for a moment, then began to crawl—not toward cover, but toward the Japanese sniper. His plan was to shoot the enemy with his .45 caliber pistol. Fortunately, other Marine sharpshooters quickly took out the sniper and other enemies who had the range of this slope before Wahlen had crawled more than a few feet.

The bearers took him up again and carried him off the field. The battalion aid station was several hundred yards in the rear; and even though George was a small man, the exhausted bearers struggled to reach it. Medical staff treated him, discovered that his leg was broken, splinted it, dressed his other wounds, and injected more morphine. An hour later he was aboard a truck en route to the beach, flinching in pain with every jolt. He rested for the night in a field hospital on a cot and was evacuated the next day to a hospital ship.[64]

Wahlen had come full circle. Twelve days earlier he had landed at the beach and now he was leaving, bloodied, battered, but alive. The war for George Wahlen, Navy corpsman, was over.

* * *

Wahlen was treated in military hospitals, first in Guam, than at Pearl Harbor, and eventually in California. By a quirk of fate, he met some of the Marines he had treated in combat, especially his former platoon sergeant, Joseph Malone. At one point, Joe told George with little eloquence but great sincerity, "Doc, I understand you really did well there. I appreciate all you've done for me." George experienced serious problems with his broken leg. The wounds were not healing. He underwent surgery a couple of times to improve the blood circulation to his leg. His foot was in intense pain, necessitating changes of the cast in an effort to ease the pain.

After some time in an Oakland hospital, he was transferred to one near San Diego for specialized treatment. Portions of his leg and foot turned black from the lack of circulation. His doctors were baffled as the pain and circulation problems continued to plague him. He underwent more operations. Fortunately, this round of surgeries was successful. Soon he began to recover, and his skin color returned to normal.[65]

While convalescing, George Wahlen began smoking to relieve his nerves and to break the boredom of hospital life. Ironically, considering its concern for health, the Red Cross supplied cigarettes free. The habit he acquired was a burden for decades to come. In August 1945, after five months of treatment, surgeries, plaster casts, and many doctors and tough Navy nurses, he received convalescent leave and departed for Utah. He enjoyed seeing his family again, and his recuperation continued. About mid-month came the news of the atomic bombs dropped on Hiroshima and Naga-saki, followed by the surrender of Japan. Like many, George was overjoyed. He went to downtown Ogden's 25th Street and joined in the joyous, wild drinking and celebration that lasted all night.[66]

When he returned to the hospital in California, the com-mander called George into his office to congratulate him. He had been awarded the Navy Cross—the highest decoration in the U.S. Navy and second in rank only the Medal of Honor. The citation outlined his incredible valor over many days of combat but focused on February 26 and March 3, especially. In an unusual move, he received two Navy Cross awards, the second being the Gold Star affixed to the first award. The award recommendation was signed by Lt. Gen. Holland ("Howlin Mad") Smith, USMC.[67]

Biographer Gary Toyn explained that Wahlen's superiors rec-ommended him for a separate award based on each of those two days. They were later combined into one citation, but still, two awards were granted. Later, however, the chain of command deter-mined that George Wahlen's courage, sacrifice, and absolute dis-regard for his own life so he could treat and save others, deserved the Medal of Honor. So the Navy Cross awards were "upgraded" for consideration for the Medal of Honor. Through bureaucratic maneuvering, the Navy rescinded or revoked the Navy Crosses in favor of the formal approval of the Medal of Honor. An inter-esting detail in this bureaucratic snafu is that, although the Navy Crosses do not appear on Wahlen's official records, he retained physical possession of both the medal and citations, because the Navy never asked for their return.[68]

After more treatment and improvement, George was anxious to leave the military and return home. Then he received orders to report to the Naval Barracks in Washington, D.C., on October 3, 1945. No reason was given; but he dutifully followed orders, flying to New York City, then taking a train to Washington. An officer at the Naval Barracks informed him that, in two days, he would receive the Medal of Honor from President Harry S. Tru-

President Harry S. Truman congratulating George Wahlen
at the Medal of Honor ceremony, October 3, 1945. Courtesy
U.S. Navy Medical History Office.

man himself. Along with thirteen other recipients, Pharmacist's
Mate Second Class George Wahlen received the Medal of Honor
in a White House ceremony.

Two months later in December 1945, Wahlen received his
honorable discharge and left the U.S. Navy.

* * *

At home in Utah, George faced the same challenges as other returning veterans: settling into a routine again. Since he was also a home-town hero, many people, high and low, sought him out to attend events, speak at special occasions, and represent groups. Naturally shy, he consistently declined. George hated to speak publicly. All his life he shunned the spotlight and public acclaim. His wounds continued to bother him, but he soon took a job as a truck driver.

When he met seventeen-year-old Melba Holley on a blind date, he was not too shy to know she was the girl for him. He began spending more time at her home in Ogden with her faithful Mormon family. Melba's father, John, was concerned that George, though a nominal member, had slipped away from activity years earlier and particularly worried about George's smoking. It was a source of contention between the two men. George and Melba decided to marry; but because she was underage, she required her parents' permission. George gritted his teeth and went after the acceptance of her father who finally relented. They were married on August 16, 1946, and had five children, three daughters and two sons.[69]

George enrolled at Weber State College in the fall of 1946 and two years later had an associate's degree in business. His job in a mail service company paid well but consumed his family time. Then a friend recommended the advantages of a career in the U.S. Army. Although it seems counterintuitive for someone who had survived the kind of war George had endured, he enlisted in November 1948. He was an Army recruiter in Ogden until March 1950, then was transferred to Fort Huachuca in Arizona to work in the medical service.

During the Korean conflict, he received orders in 1952 for deployment but was deferred to Japan instead where he was the Noncommissioned Officer in Charge (NCOIC) of a dispensary with major responsibilities on the medical staff. All during his professional career, he seldom mentioned that he was a recipient of the Medal of Honor.[70]

In 1957, the Wahlens moved to Fort Ord, California, and George was promoted to master sergeant. George excelled in his profession and was recommended for promotion to first sergeant, but he did not meet the minimum time in service requirements. Soon some officers recommended that he pursue a "direct commission" to first lieutenant. There was the normal bureaucratic hassle, but soon George received news that his application had been approved by the Department of the Army. On July 15, 1959, he received his commission as a first lieutenant in the Medical Service Corps. He underwent his officer basic course at Fort Sam Houston, Texas, and learned the fundamentals of hospital and patient administration, and supply procedures, among many other technical skills.[71]

George served an unaccompanied tour (without family) in Korea in 1963. After fifteen months, he was assigned to Hawaii, where his family joined him. His commanding officer allowed him eight months' furlough to finish his bachelor's degree. George attended classes at the Church College of Hawaii (the LDS-owned four-year college in Laie) and graduated cum laude at age forty. In 1967, Captain Wahlen deployed to Vietnam and was stationed near Saigon as a personnel officer in a large medical command. Because of his Medal of Honor status, he was exempt from combat duty in the field. George worked long, exhausting hours on the medical staff under very trying conditions.

He also began taking stock of his life and what he wanted for his family. Religious urgings came to him. He had begun regularly attending LDS services at Fort Ord; but in Vietnam, he had more time to reflect on the future. One of the great obstacles to full activity in the Church was his twenty-year addiction to smoking. He had tried to quit several times in the past. Then, as he recorded, "I didn't have my wife or family asking me to quit, but I just decided to quit on my own." He struggled but "once I got that commitment in my head, I just quit, and I never wanted to smoke again after that."[72]

George was a major when he retired in August 1969, after twenty-three years of military service. The Wahlens returned to Utah, and George eventually took a position with the Veterans Administration where he worked for the next fourteen years, retiring in 1983 at age fifty-nine. The Wahlens were sealed in the LDS temple. George was happy to serve in Church callings and regularly attended the Ogden Temple.

In retirement George was active in community projects, especially with veterans' groups, where he was a strong proponent of the veterans' cemetery near Camp Williams, a reserve installation south of Salt Lake City. In 1997, he was a guest of honor at the cemetery's dedication. During the 2002 Winter Olympics in Salt Lake City, George was honored to carry the Olympic torch for a segment of the route. In December 2003, President George W. Bush signed legislation for the veterans' hospital in Salt Lake City to be memorialized as the George E. Wahlen Department of Veterans Affairs Medical Center. The next year on Veterans Day, November 10, 2004, the hospital was officially dedicated.[73]

George Edward Wahlen died in June 5, 2009, just short of his eighty-fifth birthday.

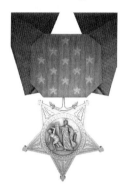

GEORGE EDWARD WAHLEN

Rank and organization: Pharmacist's Mate Second Class, U.S. Navy, serving with 2d Battalion, 26th Marines, 5th Marine Division. Place and date: Iwo Jima, Volcano Islands group, March 3, 1945. Entered service at: Utah. Born: August 8, 1924, Ogden, Utah.

Citation

For conspicuous gallantry and intrepidity at the risk of his life above and beyond the call of duty while serving with the 2d Battalion, 26th Marines, 5th Marine Division, during action against enemy Japanese forces on Iwo Jima in the Volcano group on 3 March 1945. Painfully wounded in the bitter action on 26 February, Wahlen remained on the battlefield, advancing well forward of the frontlines to aid a wounded Marine and carrying him back to safety despite a terrific concentration of fire. Tireless in his ministrations, he consistently disregarded all danger to attend his fighting comrades as they fell under the devastating rain of shrapnel and bullets, and rendered prompt assistance to various elements of his combat group as required. When an adjacent platoon suffered heavy casualties, he defied the continuous pounding of heavy mortars and deadly fire of enemy rifles to care for the wounded, working rapidly in an area swept by constant fire and treating 14 casualties before returning to his own platoon. Wounded again on 2 March, he gallantly refused evacuation, moving out with his company the following day in a furious assault across 600 yards of open terrain and repeatedly rendering medical aid while exposed to the blasting fury of powerful Japanese guns. Stouthearted and indomitable, he persevered in his determined efforts as his unit waged fierce battle and, unable to walk after sustaining a third agonizing wound, resolutely crawled 50 yards to administer first aid to still another fallen fighter. By his dauntless fortitude and valor, Wahlen served as a constant inspiration and contributed vitally to the high morale of his company during critical phases of this strategically important engagement. His heroic spirit of self-sacrifice in the face of overwhelming enemy fire upheld the highest traditions of the U.S. Naval Service.

Notes

1. Gary W. Toyn, *The Quiet Hero: The Untold Medal of Honor Story of George E. Wahlen at the Battle of Iwo Jima*, 58–59.
2. Ibid., 61–62.
3. Ibid., 20–21.
4. Ibid., 23.
5. Ibid., 24, 63.
6. George Wahlen, Oral History, October 30, 1996, interviewed by Jan Herman, 1.
7. Richard Wheeler, *Iwo*, 7.
8. Thomas Parrish, ed., *The Simon and Schuster Encyclopedia of World War II*, 643–49.
9. Ibid., 575–76. The incident of Maj. Gen. Ralph Smith's relief to this day rankles in the memory of World War II veterans and official histories of the U.S. Army in the Pacific.
10. George W. Garand and Truman R. Strobridge, *History of the U.S. Marine Corps Operations in World War II: Western Pacific Operations*, Vol. 4, 444–47.
11. Robert F. Newcomb, *Iwo Jima*, 26.
12. Wahlen, Oral History, 2.

13. Ibid., 2.

14. Gordon Rottman, *U.S. Marine Corps Pacific Theater of Operations 1944–45*.

15. Garand and Strobridge, *History of the U.S. Marine Corps Operations in World War II*, 766, 780.

16. Newcomb, *Iwo Jima*, 111–12.

17. Stephen E. Ambrose, *D–Day, June 6, 1944: The Climactic Battle of World War II*, 43.

18. Jeffrey J. Clarke, *Southern France*, 4–5; John Keegan, *The Second World War*, 376–77.

19. Ibid., 229–36.

20. Robert W. Coakley and Richard M. Leighton, *Global Logistics and Strategy, 1943–1945: United States Army in World War II*, 229–36.

21. Richard W. Stewart, ed., *The United States Army in a Global Era, 1917–2003*, 126.

22. Stewart, *The United States Army in a Global Era, 1917–2003*, 144–51.

23. Toyn, *The Quiet Hero*, 50.

24. Garand and Strobridge, *History of the U.S. Marine Corps Operations in World War II*, 450.

25. Ibid., 451.

26. Newcomb, *Iwo Jima*, 10–12.

27. Garand and Strobridge, *History of the U.S. Marine Corps Operations in World War II*, 458.

28. United States Pacific Fleet and Pacific Ocean Areas, "Operation Detachment (Iwo Jima)," October 7, 1944, U.S. War Plans, 1939–1945, 199–201; Newcomb, *Iwo Jima*, 68.

29. Garand and Strobridge, *History of the U.S. Marine Corps Operations in World War II*, 460–67.

30. Ibid., 462–64.

31. Newcomb, *Iwo Jima*, 27.

32. Garand and Strobridge, *History of the U.S. Marine Corps Operations in World War II*, 457–59.

33. Ibid., 469–72.

34. Newcomb, *Iwo Jima*, 76–77.

35. Ibid., 76–77, 91–92.

36. Garand and Strobridge, *History of the U.S. Marine Corps Operations in World War II*, 469, 472.

37. Wahlen, Oral History, 5.

38. Ibid., 6.

39. Newcomb, *Iwo Jima*, 132.

40. Ibid., 106; Wheeler, *Iwo*, 81–82.

41. Wahlen, Oral History, 6; Toyn, *The Quiet Hero*, 97–98.

42. Garand and Strobridge, *History of the U.S. Marine Corps Operations in World War II*, 460–61.

43. Ibid., 460.

44. Toyn, *The Quiet Hero*, 102; Wahlen, Oral History, 6.

45. Newcomb, *Iwo Jima*, 172.

46. Garand and Strobridge, *History of the U.S. Marine Corps Operations in World War II*, 617–19.

47. Toyn, *The Quiet Hero*, 129.

48. Garand and Strobridge, *History of the U.S. Marine Corps Operations in World War II*, 618.

49. Wahlen, Oral History, 8.

50. Ibid., 8–9.

51. Ibid., 6–7.

52. Ibid., 9.

53. Toyn, *The Quiet Hero*, 140.

54. Garand and Strobridge, *History of the U.S. Marine Corps Operations in World War II*, 622–24.

55. Ibid., 624–25.

56. Ibid., 625–26.

57. Ibid., 627.

58. Wahlen, Oral History, 8.

59. Garand and Strobridge, *History of the U.S. Marine Corps Operations in World War II*, 630.

60. Ibid.

61. Toyn, *The Quiet Hero*, 169–70; Wahlen, Oral History, 9.

62. Ibid., 170–71.

63. Toyn, *The Quiet Hero*, 171–72; Wahlen, Oral History, 9.

64. Wahlen, Oral History, 9.

65. Toyn, *The Quiet Hero*, 177–80.

66. Ibid., 184.

67. Ibid., 184–85.
68. Ibid., 207–13.
69. Ibid., 195–96.
70. Ibid., 197–98.
71. Ibid., 199–201.
72. Ibid., 201–2.
73. Ibid., 203–4.

PART 3
THE COLD WAR

AN INTRODUCTION TO
KOREA AND VIETNAM:
HOT SPOTS IN A COLD WAR

I f ever there was a misnamed or poorly titled label for a war or
a series of confrontations, it is the "Cold War." Shortly after
the termination of the global and catastrophic World War II,
world-makers and politicos had to find a suitable name for the rising
conflict between the West and the Soviet Union, where conventional nation-state wars were not envisioned in the new world of nuclear
weapons. The architects of the world had to create a title for a series
of political/diplomatic—but hopefully not military—clashes in the
future. In the nuclear age, the grand world masters could not con-
ceive of great armies pounding each other again. Rather, it was a new
world of "duck and cover," bomb shelters, guided missiles arching to
their targets, and nuclear mass annihilation. The title "Cold War"
expressed the doctrine of trying to contain the forces of the enemy
by firm resolve, collective political pressure, defensive posture, con-
tainment, appeasement if necessary, but only as a last resort, nuclear
deterrent and its potential of retaliation.

In spite of the goal of avoiding direct conflict, between 1947
and the early 1990s, the United States, the Soviet Union, their
satellites, and other nations fought conventional wars during the
Cold War. Millions of people perished, cities were leveled, entire

populations either decimated or relocated, and the amount of suffering matched that of other conflicts. Nearly 100,000 Americans died in the Cold War.

President Harry Truman's slogan of "police action" as matter of policy and as a substitute for war (or victory or both) lasted only through his presidency. Few accepted Truman's relabeling then, especially the million Americans who served in Korea where his "police action" cost some 38,000 American lives. With the birth of modern limited war, President Truman's irrational concept of war led to appeasement in Korea, which in turn hatched the second, even bloodier "cold" war in Vietnam from which another 58,000 Americans never returned home. Eight million Americans served in Vietnam and witnessed the bitterness and futility of another limited war. Commanders and soldiers had to endure Washington's extreme political overreaching from the Yalu River in Korea to the rice paddies of the Mekong Delta in Vietnam in near, "real time."

The Korean War, 1950–53

Known as the "forgotten war" today, a title that seems unfair, especially to those who served, the Korean War was actually a major conflict. The people of the Korean peninsula suffered through hundreds of years of invasion and occupation from several belligerents; and the latest—the Japanese incursion in 1908—was the worst. After World War II, the Korean land and people were divided at the 38th Parallel, to disarm and repatriate Japanese forces. Two separate regimes quickly emerged. In late 1949 the United States did not include South Korea as a nation protected under its sphere of influence.

This vulnerability was an open invitation; and on June 25, 1950, the Democratic People's Republic of Korea (North) invaded the Republic of South Korea (ROK), with the obvious goal of imposing Communist rule over the complete peninsula. U.S. reaction was swift but ineffective. The U.S. occupation forces in Japan had become weak, untrained, and under-resourced. The entire U.S.

armed forces relied too much on the concept of air power and its growing nuclear arsenal, giving readiness and well-maintained resources for conventional ground forces readiness a lesser priority.

The Korean War became the first conflict where the new United Nations became the broker and warlord that established military unity under a United Nations Command to stop aggression. The original mandate was to repel the invaders from the South and reestablish the *status quo antebellum* along the 38th Parallel. The commander of the U.S. Far East Command was General of the Army Douglas MacArthur, one of the great commanders of World War II and theater commander in the Pacific. No one knew the Pacific and Far East as well as MacArthur who oversaw the reconstruction and occupation of Japan. The focus on military affairs, reconstruction, and occupation duties in the Japan caused the few U.S. units and soldiers stationed there to be unprepared and untrained for combat operations. Furthermore, the military budget and resources had been severely reduced after the costly world war.[1]

Under General MacArthur, American forces, with U.N. troops soon to follow, quickly airlifted men and equipment to Korea where they witnessed the panic of the defeated South Korean army. The Americans themselves were overwhelmed by the horde from the North and were pushed back south along the Korean peninsula. Their defeat was due to the poor level of American combat readiness. But eventually the Allies established a defensive perimeter in the southeastern corner of the peninsula, especially as more reinforcements arrived. The defense of the port city of Pusan is now legend in military history as, by the end of August 1950, the lines stabilized into the famous "Pusan Perimeter." The month earlier, MacArthur was also named commander of the U.N. forces.

By August 1950, MacArthur decided upon a bold plan to take the initiative away from the Communist aggressors. In September, American Marines conducted a near-perfect and extremely dangerous amphibious landing at Inch'on on the west coast of Korea, well behind enemy lines. Their objectives were to quickly advance east and recapture the South Korean capital of Seoul, thus cutting off North Korea forces.[2]

MacArthur's brilliant success led to a change in war aims and policy in Washington. The defeat and retreat of the North Korean army was the opportunity for the U.N. forces to march north and reunite the entire peninsula under the not-so-democratic South Korean government. Thus, Truman and the United Nations changed the purpose of intervention and authorized a campaign to drive the North Koreans back all the way to Yalu River, the border between Korea and China. Communist China retaliated by warning that, if the Allied forces invaded the north, China would intervene. The Chinese "Red" Army immediately and skillfully sent tens of thousands of men across the border by October 1950. In November, its field armies counterattacked with some 300,000 men. As Inch'on was one of the most brilliant victories in American military history, the Chinese invasion was perhaps one of America's worst intelligence fiascos in history.[3]

The Americans and their U.N. allies were thrown back south of the original border. By December 1950, President Truman returned to the "non-war" policy of a "police action." He then prescribed strict limitations on MacArthur and his commanders. It took until April 1951 before the Allies stopped the Chinese rush southward and established a defensive line nearly along the original border of the 38th Parallel. Truman would not allow aerial interdiction bombing of targets in China nor authorize the conducting of large counterattacks even when tactical opportunities were optimum. Truman also did not allow a naval blockade of Chinese ports. Few of MacArthur's requests to permit the bombing of Chinese logistical bases in North Korea were granted. Frustrated and angry, MacArthur began challenging President Truman's policy publicly. His own slogan was very clear: "There is no substitute for victory." The American principle of having a civilian president as commander in chief of the armed forces meant that Truman was forced to relieve MacArthur of his command, replacing him with General Matthew B. Ridgeway.[4]

The battlefield lines stabilized, and soon the war become a Korean version of the Western Front stalemate of World War I in France. Over the next two years, the Allies fought a limited war of patrolling, small unit actions, firefights, and limited bombing for retaliation only. There was no tactical gain while enduring Korea's scorching summers and bitterly cold winters. It was a terrible way to fight a war with "no-fire," "no-artillery," and "no-fly-over" zones and limitations on bombing enemy-held positions. The inevitable result was that the war settled into an unnatural stalemate where any action above battalion level required permission from headquarters in Japan, Washington, or from President Truman himself. Finally, after two years of negotiation, an armistice was agreed upon, and Korea returned to a *status quo antebellum*. Thus, President Truman is the father of modern, limited war, and its ugly irresolvable shadow hung over every American conflict until the 2003 invasion of and total victory against Iraq.[5]

The Vietnam War, 1955–75

Vietnam was also a controversial, limited war. Few Americans except for military historians can describe its military actions, campaigns, and the war's course over time, perhaps because it was even more complex than Korea. Those born a generation or two later know only of the division it caused on the home front, the protests, the social tumult, and the polarization that the very word "Vietnam" stills conjures up today. Again, unfairly, the anti-war movement and wild years of social upheaval have all but silenced the American military victory. Most people remember only that, after nearly a decade of direct combat, South Vietnam was overrun by Communist North Vietnam in 1975. The haunting image of Huey helicopters lifting off and "pulling pitch" from the U.S. Embassy roof in Saigon as dozens of freedom-seeking civilians tried in vain to board is with us still.[6]

A lively debate continues, however, because the United States and the Republic of South Vietnam did indeed militarily stop and defeat Communist North Vietnam by late 1972. The parties entered into an armistice and peace treaty in Paris in January 1973. The last American military forces then departed, but soon the north once again began reinforcing its forces in the south. By the spring of 1975, the situation was ripe for a full-scale invasion. For two years, the U.S. Congress did little to support and supply South Vietnam as it had promised.[7] The north knew this and thus prepared for the final triumph. Yes, the nation of South Vietnam went under Communist rule, but can this be explained as a military failure? And did the United States lose the war?

Vietnam has been a target of political and military conquest for more than a thousand years by the Chinese, the Mongols, the Chinese again, and then European interests—mainly the French, who arrived in the nineteenth century. World War II saw Vietnam invaded by Japanese troops. For centuries, complicated by these wars, the Vietnamese people themselves struggled to establish their own distinct culture and destiny. In 1946, the Viet Minh led by Ho Chi Minh began its long, painful, and bloody road to independence and the establishment of a united, Marxist-Communist state. After several years of limited but bloody guerilla war, the French were defeated in 1954. Gradually other nations influenced by Cold War concerns entered the fray to assist the nascent and corrupt Republic of South Vietnam, which made no real attempt to establish a democracy. The main player in this deadly game of military and political escalation was the United States.[8]

Advisors, money, resources, arms, training, and equipment were the first installments supplied in the 1950s. They increased gradually until President John F. Kennedy reluctantly poured more and more advisors into this jungle war of insurgent and guerilla battles. His successor, Lyndon B. Johnson, committed ground combat troops in earnest. The first were U.S. Marines in 1965. Then direct intervention followed, based on a pretext of containing aggression after the North Vietnamese gunboats attacked U.S. warships in the Bay of Tonkin a year earlier in 1964. Soon, larger units, airfields, a major command structure, and facilities grew. The war escalated, the enemy body count multiplied, and so did American casualties. Though it was a war without conventional fronts, lines, and rear areas, the Allied forces—more than a dozen countries were involved on the U.S. side—fought back against the guerilla and partisan Viet Cong. Major battles occurred in cities, jungles, or mountain highlands with conventional engagements against regular North Vietnamese Army troops (NVA). Over the course of the war, large battles whose names are barely remembered raged in Ia Drang, A Shau Valley, Khe Sanh, Hue, and Hamburger Hill—just to name a few. These battles involved artillery, close air support, tanks, and some maneuver warfare on the ground. There was the river war of the "brown water" Navy. Special Forces came into maturity as a lethal option, assisting in the never-ending "pacification" programs to win the hearts and minds of the locals.[9]

The image of Vietnam is the helicopter—UH-1 "Hueys" flying into "landing zones" to move infantry and provisions into the battle. Much of the war was small-unit actions, patrols, airmobile operations, and the defense of certain villages and base camps. Air power was critical to the entire war effort, providing close air support for ground operations, carpet bombing, and logistical support. The U.S. Air Force and the Navy bombed the north beginning with Rolling Thunder of 1966–67, which ebbed and flowed as politics shifted, and military realities changed, sometimes based on fluctuating popular support at home.

More and more combat troops, bases, and an immense logistical support machine grew; the body counts on both sides also grew. The people who suffered the most were the farmers, villagers, families, and citizens of Vietnam, north and south, as entire villages and cities were destroyed. Soldiers entered villages to obtain information, take prisoners, and capture arms and equipment. But they also tried to provide medical treatment, food, and assistance when possible. Increasingly, the people's situation became unbearable.[10]

In 1968, the war resistance at home and the Tet Offensive in Vietnam spelled doom for President Johnson. With little warning, a massive and well-coordinated North Vietnamese offensive with hundreds of local attacks raged across most of South Vietnam starting at the Tet "new-year" observance in February 1968. The Americans and South Vietnamese Army responded quickly and successfully, decisively stopping and destroying the offensive. The media coverage in the United States, however, generated acrimonious and uninformed commentaries presenting the Tet Offensive as the turning point in the war and as a defeat. American political will wilted. A decisive victory seemed impossible. U.S. strategy shifted by 1969 with new national and military leaders.

The new policy, coined by newly elected Richard M. Nixon, was the "Vietnamization of the War," meaning to train, equip, and assist the South Vietnamese to fight and win their own war. More bombing campaigns continued off and on, some progress on the ground with the people bore fruit, and then the U.S. withdrawal began in earnest by 1970. Both sides were exhausted by the war of attrition. The successes of pacification programs and democracy were thin, and the local populace was also exhausted. The bombing, patrolling, and killing flared up one last time in the spring "Easter Offensive" of 1972. The combined NVA and Viet Cong assault was routed once again, this time mostly by the South Vietnamese. The Easter Offensive failed mainly because the north's logistics and command structure collapsed. The last major bombing offensive of the fall and winter of 1972 was enough to finally force the Communist North to the negotiation table.[11]

Thus, the American involvement ended in January 1973 with a peace signed in France. Then for two years the Communist aggressors rearmed and prepared. The war's last invasion in 1975 triumphed. After thirty years of war, Vietnam was united under one regime—a Communist dictatorship.

* * *

Both Korea and Vietnam were actually civil wars: contests between a people and a culture divided by politics, region, external forces, and ideology. That does not mean that other nations and allies should not have been involved. As demonstrated in historical hindsight, civil wars are the worst of all wars. Yet Americans were there; those who served remember those who sacrificed and honor the dead and near-dead. Other Americans remember the social turmoil, the vast mistrust of the government, and the bitter divisiveness of the era. They don't often remember the service.

Yet when armies clash and soldiers fight, valor is one result.

Latter-day Saints served, fought, and died in these two Asian civil wars. The LDS Church supported the war efforts; in fact, missionary service during Vietnam was curtailed sharply to allow more LDS men to serve through the draft and as volunteers. Three Mormons received the Medal of Honor: one in Korea and two in Vietnam. Two lived to see their valor honored; one, the youngest of the three, did not. One of these Medal honorees is still alive at this writing. Their particular stories are amazing moments during two hot wars in the Cold War era.

Notes

1. Richard W. Stewart, ed., *The United States Army in a Global Era, 1917-2003*, Vol. 2 of *American Military History*, 205, 220.

2. Perhaps the best one-volume study of the Korean War is T. R. Fehrenbach, *This Kind of War*.

3. Carter Malkasian, *The Korean War: 1950-1953*, 28-36.

4. William Manchester, *American Caesar: Douglas MacArthur*, 768-72.

5. Stewart, *The United States Army in a Global Era*, 236.

6. Ibid., 363.

7. Ibid., 363-65.

8. One of the finest and most comprehensive histories is *Vietnam at War: The History, 1946-1975* by the late Phillip B. Davidson, a three-star general who served as Military Assistance Command-Vietnam intelligence chief under General Westmoreland.

9. Alan R. Millet and Peter Maslowski, *For the Common Defense: A Military History of the United States of America*, 584-89.

10. Stewart, *The United States Army in a Global Era*, 341-45.

11. Davidson, *Vietnam at War*, 450-72.

Sergeant David B. Bleak. Courtesy of Idaho Military Museum, Boise.

Chapter Seven

SERGEANT DAVID BRUCE BLEAK: A COMMON MAN AND GENTLE GIANT

Six months had transpired since the combat action in the vicinity of Minari-gol, Korea, on June 14, 1952. Sergeant David Bleak, a medic serving in Japan who had been wounded that day, was ordered to report to the hospital orderly room. He did not know the reason. He thought he was in trouble; rarely did junior NCOs visit a colonel, the hospital commander, unless there was a problem. When he arrived, his commanding officer informed him that he had been awarded the Medal of Honor. Sergeant Bleak, a normally quiet and very unassuming man, was shocked speechless. It was December 1952.

Eleven months later on October 27, 1953, President Dwight D. Eisenhower presented America's highest decoration to the gentle giant and hero.[1]

* * *

Tamar Young Bleak was always proud of her sons, all seven of them. She had taught them in her Primary class in their LDS

255

ward in Idaho. She was a USO three-star mother in one war and a four-star in another. William Jr., the eldest, served in the Army in North Africa, Sicily, and then France during World War II. Newton was an Army ranger who fought in the Philippines. Richard served in the Army in the South Pacific, making her a three-star mother. A fourth son, Joseph, enlisted in the Army in 1947 and was later discharged without serving in combat.

When the Korean War began, Richard was already in the Army and had been shipped off to Korea. Eighteen-year-old David Bruce Bleak enlisted in the Army in November 1950. James enlisted in the Navy in 1951 and served aboard the USS *Hawkins* in Korean waters. Samuel, the youngest, joined the Army and the paratroopers in March 1953, just as hostilities waned. Thus, Tamar was a four-star mother during the Korean War. Perhaps they were all following the example of William Bleak, their father, who had served in France during World War I.[2]

All seven sons served and survived.

The Bleaks were simple people—hard-working, common folk, salt of the earth types. They lived, worked, loved, and died, quietly passing to the next generation their modest roles and sterling values. They were of pioneer stock, their lineage tracing back to John Young Jr., the older brother of Brigham Young, the great Mormon pioneer leader. Tamar was born in Huntington, Utah, and moved to Idaho with her family at age twenty-two. William Bleak met Tamar in Lincoln, a small town east of Idaho Falls, just after his safe return from France. They married and settled on a farm five miles south of Idaho Falls. Later, they farmed a tract of land east near the Bonneville and Bingham county lines and raised their seven sons and two daughters.[3]

David, the sixth son and seventh child, was born in Idaho Falls at the local hospital on February 27, 1932. He grew up farming, attending school, and living a normal life during a difficult time. David was a child of the Great Depression. The times, money, jobs, and opportunities were tough and tight. David was baptized a member of the LDS Church on April 5, 1941, just past his ninth birthday. For many years, the Bleak children's Primary teacher was their mother. David was ordained into the Aaronic Priesthood and attended Shelley Second Ward, Shelley Stake. There is no record that David advanced to the higher, Melchizedek Priesthood. In fact, for all of his adult life, David Bleak was not a participant in Church activities, though he was never antagonistic toward his LDS heritage.[4]

By the time David was eighteen, he was six feet three inches tall and weighed at least 250 pounds. He quit high school at sixteen to work odd jobs on ranches and with the railroad. He enlisted in the U.S. Army on November 1, 1950, five months after the North Koreans crossed the 38th parallel and invaded South Korea. David felt compelled to join the Army because of his family's military heritage.

Private Bleak reported to Camp Cooke, California, present-day Vandenberg Air Force Base. Camp Cooke was an old World War I training camp, named after a professional career officer affiliated with Mormon history. West Point graduate and Civil War general Philip St. George Cooke commanded the famous Mormon Battalion during the Mexican War. During 1950 as the United States mobilized for this new, foreign war, Camp Cooke was a reception station for all three components of the Army: the Regular Army, National Guard, and Army Reserve. Units had soldiers who represented all three components: regulars, draftees, and guardsmen. Bleak's serial number was RA (Regular Army) 19344416; and though he was a regular, he was assigned to the 40th Infantry Division of the California Army National Guard.[5]

* * *

Because of the suddenness of the North Korean attack in June 1950, the United States was unprepared for combat. Five years after World War II, where America fielded its finest and largest military force to date, the combat readiness, training, modernization, and even quality of soldiers had declined. Because of the advent of the atomic age and especially nuclear weapons, the Truman administration, Congress, and the new Department of Defense had neglected conventional ground forces, focusing much more attention on the new U.S. Air Force and systems for delivering atomic weapons. As a result, the state of readiness of conventional forces had deteriorated to a shameful level. Units, especially in Japan, were decimated by personnel losses and turnover, equipment and vehicles were in shambles, and training was a joke because of lack of resources.[6] The state of military affairs especially during the Truman years cost American lives in the long run.[7]

North Korea's invasion of South Korea occurred when the U.S. Army, especially in Japan, was in terrible straits. For nearly five years, General Douglas MacArthur had been rebuilding Japan from his limited military budget but with little assistance from Congress; Truman and his advisors were more concerned with Europe and the Marshall Plan.[8]

MacArthur reacted as quickly as possible after the North Korean invasion, sending understrength and untrained units from Japan to Korea to meet the Communist meat-grinder. The months of July and August 1950 were perhaps among the most disastrous military campaigns of American history. Entire units—battalions, regiments, and thousands of brave men—were sacrificed due to the speed and scope of the northern invasion. However, after two months, the United States had gained air superiority; and by throwing more and more soldiers against the steamroller, a hasty defensive perimeter was finally established in late August around the port city of Pusan. The famous "Pusan Perimeter" provided the breathing time the United States and the United Nations needed to organize and strengthen the defense.[9]

In the United States, training, recruiting, and mobilizing occurred at a feverish pitch. At Camp Cooke, the 40th Infantry Division was stuck with the responsibility of fielding, training, and equipping itself with little assistance from the Regular Army training commands. The 40th Division had been organized during World War I but did not see combat in that war. During World

War II, the 40th served in the Pacific and fought in the Philippines, most notably making an amphibious assault at Luzon.

On September 1, 1950, the division received orders to mobilize, and some 9,400 citizen soldiers from California and Nevada reported for duty in their hometown armories. Nine thousand men is a lot of men, but it was only half of the 18,600 soldiers authorized in a combat infantry division. As new recruits, draftees, and regular soldiers arrived, the 40th had to scramble together both a basic training program and also advanced training programs for specialized skills. Division leaders developed a twenty-eight-day training cycle to prepare their soldiers for combat. In the four months between October 1950 and February 1951, 14,273 new recruits reported for training. One of them was David Bleak from Idaho Falls.[10]

* * *

David Bleak wanted to be a tanker, an armor crewman, but when he started basic training in California, he was selected to be a medic. "I'd put in for tanks or artillery. . . . I wanted something big to shoot, it was fun," he recalled years later. "The sergeant looked at me and said, 'Well, you look like a medic to me.' So that's where I wound up." Thus his desire to become a combat line soldier ended, but he would indeed see combat.[11]

At Camp Cooke, Bleak underwent both basic training and medic training. The medical portion was not very high quality. It was the bare basics, designed to meet immediate demands. Fifty years later, Dave described his training in an oral history interview:

> INTERVIEWER: What was the method of teaching you had to treat soldiers?
>
> BLEAK: Kind of primitive I guess you'd call it now. We'd take a lecture, and then we didn't have dummies or anything like that, so we'd take somebody, lay him on the ground, and [unclear] on him, and then he has this, this, this, what do you do about it? We had, well it was about half and half medical and half and half taking care

of injured people, injured soldiers. They stressed a lot of the disease control, and the actual physical control, if you want to call it.

INTERVIEWER: Did . . . they take you into any of the medical clinics that were there at Camp Cooke, and actually let you actually treat soldiers on sick call or anything like that?

BLEAK: No, no, not there. When we were going overseas I spent three nights, for about five hours a night, giving shots to the soldiers, everybody going over. I spent about five hours, well 15 hours of giving shots.[12]

Soon Bleak was assigned to the 233rd Infantry Regiment, a California National Guard unit with draftees and guardsmen. The 223rd had previously been the California 7th Volunteer Regiment, organized in 1874 as a militia regiment. During World War I, it became the 160th Infantry, then in 1946, the 233rd Infantry of the National Guard. Bleak became a member of the Medical Company, an organic element of the regiment. The 40th Infantry Division shipped out for Japan in December 1951 aboard the USS *General M. C. Meigs*, a World War II era troop transport named after a famous Civil War quartermaster general for the North.[13]

The California division, when deployed to Japan in January and February 1951, was hardly a California unit any longer. Fewer than half were guardsmen from the Golden State. Stationed in Yokohama in the shadow of Mount Fuji, the raw division trained and received some new equipment. Eventually the Regular Army training cadre in Japan evaluated the division and deemed it combat ready in late 1951. Interestingly, the Army leaders decided that the 40th Division was to "relieve in place" another division— meaning that this National Guard division was to move into position, assume control of the fighting sectors, and use the equipment, tanks, trucks, and artillery of the departing 24th Infantry Division. The 24th Infantry Division, a Regular Army unit, had been one of the first combat units to engage in combat in Korea in July 1950. This was an unusual military move. Unfortunately, these orders meant that replacements assumed control of war-worn and ragged weapons systems, while leaving in Japan their relatively new and serviceable tanks, guns, jeeps, and trucks.[14]

* * *

What Bleak and his fellow soldiers witnessed when they arrived in Korea at the forward lines was the equivalent of the Western Front of 1915–18: trenches in a war of attrition. Korea was a stalemate of static lines and limited tactical expectations. Now it was a war of small unit actions. Units would capture a hundred meters and take a hill one day, then lose two hills and three hundred meters the next week. Meanwhile, peace conferences dragged on among the belligerent parties.

After three major offensives since November 1950, the Chinese People's Volunteers, CPV, was finally stopped in May and June 1951. The Communists knew they could not drive the United Nations forces from Korea so they sought a delaying tactic—peace talks at Panmunjom, a small village near Kaesong. For months, after the U.N. forces had pushed back and defeated two Chinese field armies, a stabilized front developed just north of the original 38° parallel line as the truce conference commenced among the four main belligerents: the United States, North Korea, South Korea, and China.[15] Historian Carter Malkasian has interpreted this new type of war: "After 1945, the advent of nuclear weapons and the increasing power of conventional weapons made total war prohibitively dangerous."[16] This may be the thinking of many even today, but the reality of such a doctrine only guaranteed *status quo antebellum* and mocked MacArthur's slogan, "There is no substitute for victory."

The main missions were: staying alive, maintaining a defense, and patrolling to gain information and intelligence on the enemy's dispositions and actions by capturing enemy soldiers. The Chinese were doing the same from their side. Occasionally, platoons and perhaps companies would engage to fend off the enemy's probing. Sometimes, headquarters ordered battalion-level missions to eliminate a pesky problem caused by an over-ambitious, local enemy commander. Sometimes it was necessary to adjust the front lines to make the war more pleasant for all. The quality that reminded the soldiers that they were at war was the ever-mounting casualties.[17]

Meanwhile the greatest power on earth, the United States, part of the United Nations, watched helplessly as a steady stream of Chinese supplies, ammunition, and men funneled across the Yalu River from Communist China into North Korea unopposed. Thus, the enemy freely and easily waltzed more men and matériel into the conflict, unchecked and unbloodied. The need to attack Chinese staging areas was a major issue with MacArthur, but Truman denied him permission. MacArthur crossed the line with his commander in chief by challenging official policy, negotiating with Nationalist Chinese in Formosa, and issuing statements of protest in the press. This insubordination forced Truman to relieve Mac-Arthur of his command in April 1951.[18] This was the war that David Bleak and the 40th Infantry Division entered in January and February 1952.

The transfer from the 24th Division to the 40th was a slow but mostly successful process. Simultaneously, the National Guard 45th Infantry Division of Oklahoma and New Mexico relieved the 1st Cavalry Division in place. Thus, two National Guard divisions took over more of the American effort in the war.[19]

Once in Korea, Corporal David Bleak was soon promoted to sergeant. He served in the Medical Company but was attached to G Company of the 2nd Battalion. Each infantry company had four medics to treat some 200 men. Each battalion had an aide station where an army doctor was in charge along with an executive officer from the Medical Service Corps who was to oversee the medical administrative actions for the entire battalion. The field medics and battalion aid station personnel treated the wounded immediately. Their mission was to save lives. The more seriously wounded were sent to the medical clearing company where they were screened and either treated and returned to duty or sent to the rear. The medical clearing company had X-ray, dental, and

Sergeant Bleak, far left, and fellow medics. Note pistol and holster on Bleak's right hip. Courtesy of Idaho Military Museum, Boise.

ambulance elements to support the medical treatment. The final medical unit was the Mobile Army Surgical Hospital (MASH), which could conduct most surgical procedures, stabilizing the most seriously injured soldiers. They were then transported to Japan for further treatment, then on to the United States.

As a medic, Sergeant Bleak was equipped with minimal medical supplies.[20] Like George Wahlen (see chap. 6), he had Carlisle bandages for normal bullet wounds, larger pads for chest and abdomen wounds, and morphine syrettes.

For months, David Bleak endured the boredom of stagnant warfare spliced with moments of terror while serving on the front lines of Korea. He treated some wounded soldiers, but he dealt more frequently with trench foot, colds, and routine ailments. Bleak, because of his size, was in charge of the litter-bearers, consisting of four-man Korean national teams per company.

Soon after his arrival, his sector endured a two-and-a-half-day artillery and mortar barrage during which a fellow medic was killed in a firefight. The terrain of steep hills and narrow valleys, broiling in summer and frigid in winter, marked the "no-man's-land" between the two lines, sometimes only a half mile apart. Bleak, an Idaho boy, knew about mountains. He later commented, "It only takes you about a week" to get in condition. "Then you can crawl up and down mountains all day long. . . . You can get tough and into it pretty fast."[21]

One of the terrible qualities of the Korean War was that the Chinese and North Koreans were not signatories to the Geneva Convention. Thus, they did not recognize the noncombatant status of medics. As a result, medics had to be especially careful. They did not wear armbands and helmets marked with the internationally identifiable Red Cross. Even a medical aid bag was too conspicuous. David stuffed the large pockets in his field jacket and his fatigue trousers with bandages and medicine. Most medics carried firearms, in violation of the Geneva Convention.[22] Sergeant Bleak carried an M-1 carbine, a .45 caliber automatic pistol, and clipped a couple of fragmentation grenades on his canvas web gear.

* * *

June 14, 1952, Day of Days

The North Koreans and Chinese were tough enemies, conditioned to adverse weather, scanty supplies, and rigid discipline. The U.N. forces were mostly South Korean or ROK (Republic of Korea) and Americans along the forward edge of the battle area (FEBA) facing this formidable foe. The Chinese were a "come as you are army," meaning that the Communist overlords hardly had the resources to oppose a modern force. A full third of the CPV soldiers crossed the Yalu River in October and November 1950 armed with only a few hand grenades and carrying rations for only a few days. The officers told their men to take the weapons from their fallen comrades as they moved forward. Many of their rifles were obsolete Russian arms, and thousands carried captured Japanese rifles, especially the Type 38 rifle, a long-barreled bolt action of 6.7mm caliber with a 30-inch-long bayonet. Rifle and bayonet made for a long and sometimes unwieldy weapon.

The lack of modern weapons and ample rations did not deter these tough, battle-hardened soldiers. Some carried wooden hand grenades because there were not enough steel fragmentation and concussion grenades available. Many had fought the Japanese for a dozen years in Manchuria and then in their own civil war against Chinese Nationalist forces. Now they were battling western forces among the hills of Korea.[23]

* * *

It started out as just another regular mission. The daily grind consisted of sending patrols into "no-man's-land" to disrupt the enemy's routine and capture some prisoners for interrogation. Every day across the entire width of Korea, a few dozen such missions occurred. The word would come down from regiment, battalion, or company headquarters for a patrol to round up a prisoner or two, observe any changes in the lines and enemy positions, and return with minimal loss. If they were lucky, they did. The patrol came from the Intelligence and Reconnaissance Platoon of the battalion's headquarters company. Sergeant Bleak volunteered to accompany the patrol and provide medical assistance.[24]

"We left the line of departure at 0245 on June 14, 1952," recalled Private First Class Willie G. Gay from Emporia, Virginia, "and crossed several enemy occupied fingers" of tall, steep ridges along the sector of operations of the 233rd Infantry Regiment. The patrol quietly ascended a hill in the vicinity of Minari-gol, a small hamlet of poor peasants in the war-ravaged countryside. Soon the patrol encountered enemy resistance, "As we neared the top of the hill, a hand grenade thrown by the enemy glanced off the helmet of one of our men. Sergeant Bleak, with total disregard for his personal safety," Gay remembered, "threw his body on top of the struck soldier and ascribed [absorbed] the full force of the concussion."[25]

The grenade exploded; but amazingly, neither Bleak nor the soldier he covered with his own body was harmed.

Years later, Bleak stated, "You got to remember that their grenades, quite a few of them were made of wood, so if you could get down low, the blast itself . . . wasn't going to really hurt you."[26] Yet the concussion was deafening. Now the fight became fierce as a dozen Americans found themselves on top of the Chinese lines. A couple of the men were lightly wounded. Bleak quickly moved to reach them, exposing himself to enemy fire. Then in a sudden rush, he jumped into a trench, startled three Chinese soldiers, and, amazingly, attacked them. According to his Medal of Honor citation, PFC Gay, and Bleak himself, he killed two of them with his bare hands, then stabbed the third with his trench knife.[27] Even in his oral interview, he did not explain how he killed these two Chinese soldiers with his bare hands. This was combat at its most primitive level, literally hand-to-hand.

Amid the din, noise, and confusion of this local firefight, the Americans continued up the hill and captured a prisoner under the veil of darkness. They quickly reorganized, then began to descend the hill toward friendly lines on the opposite hill. As they did so, more enemies opened up with small arms fire from a trench line about seventy meters away.[28]

One of the shots hit Bleak in the leg. He looked down and saw that the round had hit the flesh but missed the bone. It was hardly bleeding, so he did not even take time to bandage it. He continued down the slope with his patrol, limping but keeping up.[29]

Soon machine-gun fire and mortars pinned down the patrol, wounding three more Americans. After a few minutes, Bleak ran across the open hillside to reach soldiers while his patrol covered him with fire. In the darkness, the flashes of gunfire illuminated the summer night. Shadows and silhouettes moved back and forth in the confusion and chaos of battle.

According to PFC Gay, "disregarding his own wounds, and accepting aide [sic] from no one, [Sergeant Bleak] picked up one of the wounded men and carried [him] down the hill."[30]

The straight, dark, dead tree in the foreground points toward the ridge and hillside area where the action took place. Courtesy of Idaho Military Museum, Boise.

As the patrol crept down the hill, two Chinese soldiers rose out of the darkness and charged Bleak with their long unwieldy rifles and awkward bayonets. Quickly, Bleak dropped his wounded comrade and, like a matador dodging a bull, sidestepped their bayonets. In a burst of brute strength, he grabbed the two Chinese by their heads and smashed them together. Whether he killed them or merely stunned them has never been determined. Bleak did not wait to find out.[31]

* * *

The patrol reentered friendly lines with its prisoner and the wounded. The men were thrilled that they had survived the small intense action of a few hours; also, they could hardly believe what they had witnessed. Finally, Sergeant Bleak reported to the aid station where he saw a friend from his home state of Idaho, Earl Horne, who bandaged his wound. Then off he went to the field hospital.[32]

When he arrived at the hospital, the surgeons discovered that Bleak's wound was more serious than his self-diagnosis. The bullet

had severed a nerve. He was evacuated to a MASH unit, then to
Japan. During this time, when Bleak read the after-action report
describing his heroic action, he shrugged it off: "I really don't remember doing anything it said there. Things were kind of hot and
fast at the time."[33] After surgery in Japan, David Bleak returned to
the United States, landing in Seattle. He was hospitalized in Colorado Springs and Camp Carson in Colorado. From Colorado,
Bleak finally went home to Idaho on leave and saw his family for
a month.[34]

After a pleasant visit home, David went to Fort Sam Houston,
the future home of the Army Medical Corps. He was both an out-
patient and also a member of the medical school cadre, training
soldiers and especially new Army doctors in the basics of military
skills in marksmanship, marching, and physical training. At this
time, he volunteered to return to the Far East. He was willing to
return overseas, because as Bleak said later, "I didn't think much
of Texas."[35]

Arriving in Japan in January 1953, Sergeant Bleak was assigned to a hospital staff and then to the 25th Infantry Division.[36]
He considered returning to Korea but decided not to sign the
waiver that was required. Then one day he was called into his commander's office and learned he been nominated for the Medal of
Honor. Bleak was shocked, "Why me?" he humbly recalled. "Why
not the rest of them [his comrades]? Everybody was doing things
I received the award for."[37]

* * *

In the summer of 1953, David Bleak, now promoted to staff
sergeant, returned to the United States and was assigned to Fort
Lewis, Washington. By this time, the fighting war in Korea had finally come to an end. After two years of negotiations at Panmunjon,
a truce was signed on July 27, 1953—three years and one month
after the North Korean People's Army had invaded South Korea.
The final sticking point for months was the status of Communist

Staff Sergeant David Bleak, third from left, and other Medal of Honor recipients with President Dwight Eisenhower.

prisoners of war. Tens of thousands of POWs wanted to defect to South Korea. The Communist overlords refused. Finally, an international commission supervised the screening of prisoners and their return. Some 25,000 North Koreans stayed in South Korea. This cease-fire agreement was not a peace but merely a truce, an armistice to stop the fighting. It still remains in effect today.[38]

On October 1, 1953, after exactly two years and eleven months of service, Staff Sergeant David Bleak was discharged from the Army and returned to his family in Shelley, Idaho. Weeks later, on October 27, though a civilian, Bleak wore his Army Class A uniform and received the Medal of Honor from President Dwight Eisenhower in a ceremony at the White House. When President Eisenhower presented the award to Bleak, he had trouble connecting the catch of the neck ribbon; he commented to Bleak, "My God, you got a big neck."[39] He was only partly right. What David had was a big heart.

David's only regret was that his father had died in December 1952 and could not be present to see his son receive this highest of all military honors.

Citizen Bleak returned to Idaho and a normal life after the war, with his military service behind him and with a degree of national popularity ahead of him. He wanted to become a farmer and rancher, raise a family, and ignore the fame that his valor had brought him. He lived in various places over the next few years in Idaho and Wyoming, working as a ranch hand, a meat cutter, and a truck driver. In 1960, at age twenty-eight, he married Lois Marilyn Pickett. Soon they settled in south-central Idaho, north of the Snake River Valley in what is known as the Lost River Valley. By 1966, the Bleaks owned a diary farm in Moore, near Arco. With no education above high school, which he did not finish, David took a job as a janitor at the National Reactor Testing Station northeast of Idaho Falls. He and Lois raised their family of three boys and one girl. For the next thirty years, he gained more experience and skills until his last position was a manager and hot cell technician.[40]

David Bleak tried to lead a normal life as an average American, farming, ranching, working in the reactor station and then retiring quietly. Several honors and opportunities came his way. He served in veterans, trade, and local farm associations for many years, making friends.[41] Bleak was also invited to the presidential inaugurations of John F. Kennedy in 1961 and Richard M. Nixon in 1969. In 1995, the Fort Sill, Oklahoma, troop clinic that was built at a cost of $82 million was dedicated in his honor.[42] In 2000 he returned with several other Korean War Medal of Honor awardees to the battlefields of the past and met some of their Communist opponents.

The most recent edition of the Army's field manual on *Military Leadership*, FM 6–22 issued in 2006, highlights the initiative and courage of Sergeant Bleak as an example for all soldiers of the values that a combat leader should possess.

Some unforeseen honors came his way late in life and after his death in April 2006 at the age of seventy-four. On the fifty-fifth anniversary of Bleak's courageous actions in Korea, Lois Bleak donated David's Medal of Honor and other items to the Idaho Military Historical Society in Boise during a small but moving ceremony. That same day, Idaho Governor C. L. ("Butch") Otter declared by proclamation, June 14, 2007 as "Sergeant David Bruce Bleak Day."

General Eric Shinseki, former Army Chief of Staff and Secretary of Veterans Affairs at the time, made these comments about Bleak in 2009, "Sergeant Bleak distinguished himself by conspicuous gallantry and indomitable courage above and beyond the call of duty as a combat medic." Shinseki continued with his remarks to the Association of the United States Army, by alluding to his own status as a wounded soldier in combat, "I've been carried out of combat twice on the backs of American Soldiers—Soldiers like Sergeant Bleak."[43]

David B. Bleak

Rank and organization: Sergeant, U.S. Army, Medical Company 223d Infantry Regiment, 40th Infantry Division. Place and date: Vicinity of Minari-gol, Korea, 14 June 1952. Entered service at: Shelley, Idaho. Born: 27 February 1932, Idaho Falls, Idaho. G.O. No.: 83, 2 November 1953.

Citation

Sgt. Bleak, a member of the medical company, distinguished himself by conspicuous gallantry and indomitable courage above and beyond the call of duty in action against the enemy. As a medical aidman, he volunteered to accompany a reconnaissance patrol committed to engage the enemy and capture a prisoner for interrogation. Forging up the rugged slope of the key terrain, the group was subjected to intense automatic weapons and small arms fire and suffered several casualties. After administering to the wounded, he continued to advance with the patrol. Nearing the military crest of the hill, while attempting to cross the fire-swept area to attend the wounded, he came under hostile fire from a small group of the enemy concealed in a trench. Entering the trench he closed with the enemy, killed 2 with bare hands and a third with his trench knife. Moving from the emplacement, he saw a concussion grenade fall in front of a companion and, quickly shifting his position, shielded the man from the impact of the blast. Later, while ministering to the wounded, he was struck by a hostile bullet but, despite the wound, he undertook to evacuate a wounded comrade. As he moved down the hill with his heavy burden, he was attacked by 2 enemy soldiers with fixed bayonets. Closing with the aggressors, he grabbed them and smacked their heads together, then carried his helpless comrade down the hill to safety. Sgt. Bleak's dauntless courage and intrepid actions reflect utmost credit upon himself and are in keeping with the honored traditions of the military service.

Notes

1. "Korean War Medal of Honor Winner David Bleak," Associated Press, 1995, undated and unidentified newspaper clipping, Bleak Collection, Idaho Military Museum, Boise; hereafter cited as Bleak Collection.

2. "Idaho Hero Comes from Fighting Family," July 3, 1953, *Salt Lake Tribune*, 6.

3. Ibid.; "Hero's Brother Also Gets Army Praises," undated and unidentified newspaper clipping, Bleak Collection.

4. David Bleak, LDS baptism and membership ordinance record, LDS Family History Library; "Army Medical Aidman from Idaho Awarded Medal of Honor," Press release No. 595–53, June 1953, Department of Defense, Office of Public Information.

5. "Army Medical Aidman from Idaho Awarded Medal of Honor."

6. Richard W. Stewart, ed., *The United States Army in a Global Era, 1917–2003*, Vol. 2 of American Military History, 210–12.

7. Ibid., 200–201; T. R. Fehrenbach, *This Kind of War*, 92–93.

8. Stewart, *The United States Army in a Global Era*, 205–6.

9. Fehrenbach, *This Kind of War*, 157–62.

10. Michael Doubler, *I Am the Guard: A History of the Army National Guard, 1636–2000*, 235.

11. [Untitled article about David Bleak; no byline], *Pass in Review: Newsletter of the Idaho Military Historical Society*, June 2007, 6.

12. David Bleak, Oral History, August 26, 2005, 1.

13. "Army Medical Aidman from Idaho Awarded Medal of Honor"; Bleak, Oral History, 2; Naval Historical Center, USS *General M.C. Meigs*, (AP–116).

14. Doubler, *I Am the Guard*, 236.

15. Fehrenbach, *This Kind of War*, 500–502.

16. Carter Malkasian, *The Korean War: 1950–1953*, 8.

17. Fehrenbach, *This Kind of War*, 527–29.

18. Stewart, *The United States Army in a Global Era*, 238–39.

19. Doubler, *I Am the Guard*, 236–37.

20. Bleak, Oral History, 6.

21. [Untitled article about David Bruce Bleak, no byline], *Pass in Review*, June 2007, 6.

22. Bleak, Oral History, 6–7.

23. Malkasian, *The Korean War*, 30–34.

24. Andrew J. Brittle, *Years of Stalemate: July 1951–July 1953*, 21.

25. "Army Medical Aidman from Idaho Awarded Medal of Honor."

26. Bleak, Oral History, 7.

27. "Army Medical Aidman from Idaho Awarded Medal of Honor."

28. Bleak, Oral History, 7.

29. Ibid.

30. "Army Medical Aidman from Idaho Awarded Medal of Honor."

31. Bleak, Oral History, 7; "Army Medical Aidman from Idaho Awarded Medal of Honor." This version of the action is based on PFC Gay's account and Bleak's oral history; they differ slightly from the Medal of Honor citation.

32. Bleak, Oral History, 7.

33. [Untitled article about David Bruce Bleak; no byline], *Pass in Review*, June 2007, 7.

34. Bleak, Oral History, 8.

35. [Untitled article about David Bruce Bleak; no byline], *Pass in Review*, June 2007, 7.

36. Bleak, Oral History, 8–9.

37. [No first name] Prinalgin, Associated Press, "Korean War Medal of Honor Winner David Bleak," April 1995. Bleak Collection.

38. Malkasian, *The Korean War*, 83–86.

39. Bleak, Oral History, 9.

40. [Untitled article about David Bruce Bleak; no byline], *Pass in Review*, June 2007, 8.

41. Ibid.

42. "Army Honors ANL-W retiree for Gallantry," *Argonne Week*, May 1, 1995.

43. Eric K. Shinseki, Secretary of Veterans Affairs, Address to Association of the United States Army, Army Medical Symposium, San Antonio, Texas, July 22, 2009.

Major Bernard Francis Fisher. Unless otherwise noted, the photographs in this chapter are courtesy of the Fisher Family Collection.

Chapter Eight

MAJOR BERNARD FRANCIS FISHER: THE RESCUE AT CAMP A SHAU

March 1966

The A-1E Skyraider dated from World War II era—an aircraft-carrier-based, single-engine propeller warplane. It was also on fire. Flames and smoke wreathed into the cockpit. The pilot was fighting to control the plane as he quickly considered his options. None was appealing. Could he bail out? No, he was already too low. Could he land the plane? Doubtful. The Skyraider was losing airspeed and altitude fast, the engine fire was spreading, and the only possible landing area in this unforgiving terrain of jungle and mountain was the war-torn and debris-littered dirt strip beneath him in the narrow valley. Under the best of circumstances, it would have been risky; but now it was also "hot"—meaning, under intense enemy fire.

With only a few seconds to decide, the pilot, a U.S. Air Force major who had flown P–38s in the Pacific during World War II, chose the second option: a forced landing on the airstrip. It was a terrible prospect. Just hundreds of yards away, the American A Shau Base Camp was under siege by more than two thousand

North Vietnamese regulars. The most likely result if he survived a crash landing was capture.[1]

Major Dafford ("Jump") Wayne Myers employed all his skill, enduring the heat and ignoring the smoke in the cockpit. He maneuvered the stricken Skyraider into an approach and glide path. He couldn't actually see the approach because of the smoke and flames; but coming over the radio was the reassuring voice of a fellow pilot, directing him down and trimming his directions. Amazingly, the landing was made smoothly under adverse conditions. It was fabulous flying, but the curtain went up immediately on the second act. The Skyraider burst into flames from the gear-up landing when the auxiliary "drop" fuel tank under the fuselage exploded. The Skyraider skidded some 800 feet on the short 2,300-foot dirt and steel-planked runway, scattering a trail of parts and debris. The aircraft, now a fireball, slid off the runway to the right and smashed into a dirt mound with Myers still strapped inside.

The other pilot, also a major, was from Idaho. He made a low-level pass over the burning hulk. There are few experiences more depressing, especially in war, than to see a comrade die. At this point, all that the other pilot knew about Myers was his radio call sign, "Surf 41." The major decided to fly another oval pattern near the triangular-shaped Special Forces camp at A Shau that was under heavy attack. He approached from the high ridge on the east where several enemy antiaircraft positions were pouring murderous fire at the half dozen American planes making gun and bomb runs.

The pilot from Idaho made a pass over the airfield only twenty-five feet off the deck. As he neared the crash site, now an inferno, Myers suddenly jumped up from the weeds where he was hiding to avoid enemy small-arms fire and waved at the speeding Skyraider. The pilot saw Myers, acknowledged and immediately radioed the forward air controller: "We have a downed pilot." He stayed on the radio, arranging a rescue by helicopter.[2]

As the battle raged on the ground, several other Skyraiders continued to strafe the enemy ground troops. The terrain was challenging—a long narrow valley socked-in with a low cloud ceiling. They flew a "loose string" formation, making run after run against hostile forces. Now with a fellow aviator down, they also fought to protect him as best they could by pouring a withering fire into the enemy locations that were within striking distance of the downed major. According to the official reports, the pilots had basically destroyed a reinforced company-size assault force at the south wall of the base camp, accounting for an estimated three hundred dead.[3]

After several minutes that seemed like hours, many radio calls, and delays, the major from Idaho, who was also the senior pilot on station and, by default, the air mission leader, made a dangerous decision. He would land on that awful dirt strip and pick up Jump Myers. The air controller advised against it, but the major knew something had to be done and quickly. It wasn't a tough decision. As he explained later, "I didn't think the pilot could survive until a chopper got there, and I didn't think a chopper had much chance of getting down through that ring of fire and out again." Also, Myers had crashed in a burning plane. How serious were his injuries? How long could he survive without medical attention?[4]

The major from Idaho rolled his Skyraider over and dived toward the "hot" airstrip.

Down in the weeds behind a five-foot dirt embankment, Major "Jump" Myers from Newport, Washington, was not counting on being rescued. It was just a matter of time before he was captured. He would probably be tortured for intelligence. If he survived, then it would be months or even years before he returned home. He tried not to think about it.

Just then Myers saw another Skyraider make an approach to land on the strip. Later, he tried to reconstruct his thoughts:

> I knew a chopper could never survive the ground fire, and it simply never occurred to me that somebody would be crazy enough to put an A–1E down on that strip. It was too short to begin with. The steel planking was all buckled up into spikes by mortar rounds, and it was littered with rocket pods, fifty-five-gallon fuel drums, and the debris from my plane. My only thought right then was to signal the

other A–1E's somehow to get out of there before they all got shot down. When I heard . . . and I saw him circle around and then head into the north end of the runway, all I thought was. *Well, now there are two of us down here.*

The enemy fire was intense from mortars, antiaircraft fire, and hundreds of small arms carried by individual North Vietnamese soldiers. The brave Skyraider descended and touched down on the dirt strip. The other aircraft flew covering patterns to support the crazy rescue attempt, but they were running out of ammunition.

The next ten minutes became an instant legend. As the other pilots circling over the narrow valley watched with horror and wonder, this lone Air Force pilot made a decision, acted "above and beyond" the call of duty, and performed a feat of heroism and skill.

By the end of the day, March 10, 1966, the daring pilot, Major Bernard F. Fisher, a Latter-day Saint from Kuna, Idaho, was in the office of a U.S. Air Force general officer. The general, who had received reports throughout the day about the action at A Shau, was thrilled by the daring rescue. That very day, the recommendation for the Medal of Honor was under consideration. Within twenty-four hours, it would be formally written and submitted.

March 12, two days after the action, Major "Bernie" Fisher called home from Vietnam to share the unbelievable news of his nomination for America's highest award with his wife, Realla, and family. He discovered that she had already learned about the heroic rescue and was in New York City as a guest on the *Ed Sullivan Show*.[5] Honor and fame mushroomed. Within months a feature article would appear in the *Saturday Evening Post* about his exploits and valor. Eventually a U.S. Naval vessel, city parks, highways, artwork, articles in journals and magazines, hundreds of speaking engagements, and monuments memorialized his name and achievement. The A–1E Skyraider he flew that heroic day would be preserved in the U.S. Air Force Museum in Dayton, Ohio.

Of all the LDS Medal of Honor recipients, Colonel Bernard Fisher, a career officer, experienced the most fame and fanfare; he lived a life of a celebrity, but he did so with honor, humility, respect for the decoration, and the utmost professionalism.

* * *

Bernard Francis Fisher was born in San Bernardino, California, on January 11, 1927, and grew up in Clearfield, Utah. His parents, Bruce Leo Fisher and Lydia Lavina Stoddard Fisher, were Latter-day Saints and had Utah roots. From an early age, Bernie loved exciting things that moved fast—cars, trains, and especially airplanes. In the late 1930s, the Army built an airfield on a prominent hill north of Layton and east of their Clearfield home. It was named for Major Ployer Peter Hill from Massachusetts, an earlier Army flyer, who was killed on October 30, 1935, when he crashed in Boeing Aircraft Company's experimental Model 299. This model was the prototype of the famous B–17 Flying Fortress.

Bernard would often visit the airfield by bicycle on his paper route and watch as pilots trained in old biplanes from the Army Air Corps. In high school, he owned an old 1929 Ford convertible. One day as he was driving down Main Street in Layton, suddenly one of the front wheels came off and rolled along for a distance down the street. The wheel-less axle dropped to ground and the Ford skidded to a stop in front of Cowley's Drug Store.[6]

In 1940, Bernie took his first airplane flight. Haven Barlow, a youth leader in Fisher's LDS ward, was a licensed pilot and often flew a single-engine Piper Cub out of the Ogden airport. He gave Bernie and some friends their first airplane ride. It was a thrill for all of them; but from then on, Bernie Fisher knew he wanted to fly.[7]

War came to America in 1941 with the attack on Pearl Harbor while Bernie was still a student at Davis High School. In January 1945 at age eighteen, he qualified for early high school graduation and joined the Navy. He took basic training ("Navy Boot") in Memphis, Tennessee, and then became a mechanic on Navy fighters, especially the gull-winged, F–4U Corsair, one of the great aircraft of World War II. The war ended before Fisher was sent overseas.

While Fisher was in the Navy, his parents moved to Kuna, Idaho, a small farming community south of Boise in the Snake River Valley. From that point on, Bernie Fisher called Kuna home. After his discharge in 1946, he enrolled at Boise State Junior College where he struggled with certain classes. He also joined the Idaho National Guard where one of his duties was to maintain aerial targets towed behind B–26 bombers. It was an interesting and sometimes adventurous job, but it was also a duty associated with flying which he loved. He met a pretty young LDS girl, Realla Johnson, at a Church activity. After a year of dating and courtship, they were married in the Salt Lake LDS Temple. The officiating authority was none other than Ezra Taft Benson, an apostle and future president of the Church.[8]

In 1949, Fisher made the decision to enroll at the University of Utah in Salt Lake City and enter the Air Force Reserve Officer Training Corps program in hopes of gaining one of the slots for flight training. In 1947 the U.S. Army Air Forces became the U.S. Air Force, a separate service from the Army. He eventually achieved his goal, graduated with good grades, and was commissioned in 1951. Among several hundred applicants, he was selected as one of the envied few to have a slot for flight school.

Soon he and Realla were in Marana Air Force Base in Arizona for primary flight training. Lieutenant Fisher soon strapped on one of the finest and most dependable trainer planes in American history, the AT–6 Texan. Bernie seemed to be a natural pilot. He recalled his first solo flight, "I was scared but also thrilled. This was the moment I'd been waiting for," he said. "I made a good, clean takeoff and circled out high over the airfield. . . . On the third approach, I let the aircraft settle in for a good solid landing. I could hardly suppress a grin as I taxied off the runway and onto the tarmac."[9]

Flying, as Fisher would soon learn, has its moments of frustration and failure. After several weeks of training and solo flights, Fisher was ready for his final check-ride for the primary phase of his training. During the evaluation, he performed all the maneuvers to standards until he was given a simulated engine failure. He went by the book and followed the checklist emergency procedures except for one step. He did not lower the landing gear.

Fisher failed the check ride.[10]

There are few things more humiliating and distressing in professional aviation than failing a check ride. But after a few more "dual" training flights with his instructor, he passed the re-check and moved on to advanced training. At this point in the flight training program, the student pilots were screened for selection to various types of aircraft: bombers, transports, or fighters. Fighters meant jets; and Bernie, like most new pilots, craved to fly jet fighters.[11] His dream became reality.

He and Realla next went to Williams Air Force Base, also in Arizona, where Bernie learned to fly the T–33 trainer. It was a version of the F–80 fighter with a side-by-side seat arrangement for the instructor pilot. Flying a jet aircraft in the mid-1950s compared to an AT–6 Texan was like going from a tricycle to a motorcycle. Fisher learned the intense and fast world of near-supersonic flight with G-forces, pressure suits, and ejection seats. Everything in jet flying was based on speed; even decisions were based on time and speed. The training was challenging, and Bernie admitted that it affected his personal life, "I was simply obsessed with being in the top 50 percent of the class. . . . I'd go to sleep at night memorizing procedures and practicing drills over and over in my mind." To relieve his anxiety, Realla would take him golfing some evenings to help him relax. Finally, Bernie Fisher passed all his check rides and graduated from jet fighter training. He said it was one of the greatest moments in his life. Yet he still had gunnery and instrument training ahead of him.[12]

In just over a year, the Fishers were making their third military move, this time to Tyndall Air Force Base near Panama City,

Florida. The Fishers were learning the life of the professional military family and dealing with the joys and challenges of family life.
Eventually they became the parents of six sons. The Fishers bought
a new Buick station wagon and tried to establish a strong family
basis along with the heavy demands of intensive flight training and
classroom instruction.

Instrument training was a difficult challenge for anyone, especially in that era where instruments were still rather primitive
compared to modern digital and satellite systems. Homing bea-
cons and radio navigation systems were state-of-the-art in the
1950s. After instruments, Bernie and his peers went through a demanding weapons school at Tyndall. Bombs, .50 caliber machine
guns, 20mm cannons, and aerial rockets were the main course every day.[13]

Not only was engaging targets on the ground a major part of
the training, but also avoiding enemy antiaircraft guns and radar
systems was essential. Perhaps the most rigorous and also fun
part of the training was "air to air" maneuvers, good old-fashioned
"dog-fights" reminiscent of World War I aces but without scarves
flapping in the air in open-cockpit biplanes. After several more
months, finally the training was finished, marked by the ceremonies of final graduation and Bernie's first operational assignment.

* * *

Bernard Fisher's first unit after nearly two years of flight training was at Chicago, O'Hare Air Force Base, which was really both
a military and commercial airdrome. It was named for William
("Butch") O'Hare, a Navy flyer in World War II, who a decade
earlier had received the Medal of Honor. Fisher joined the 42nd
Fighter Interceptor Squadron, where he would soon learn to fly
one of the most popular, sleek, and lethal jet-fighters in United
States history: the F–86 Sabre Jet.

The mid–1950s was the era when the Cold War matured. This
new type of political war occurred during a time when an inter-

national paranoia gripped nations with mistrust and fear, causing military forces to fight a perplexing game of speed and lethality. The nuclear age with long-range bombers and eventually intercontinental ballistic missiles changed the face of defense and deterrence. One of the missions of the Air Force at this time was the duty of alert crews—airmen, scrambling to their aircraft to launch into the blue to intercept enemy bombers massing on the borders of America or its allied nations. Today it may seem an ineffective way to defend American sovereignty, but it was one of the best and perhaps only solutions at that time. Considering the technology, limitations, and means available then, these measures were vital. For the pilots, aircrews, and ground support crews, it meant many, many long day-and-night duty shifts, sitting alert, and preparing for nuclear Armageddon. The hope was that the "balloon" would never go up—meaning that nuclear war would never occur.[14]

Though the F–86D was a superb aircraft for its day and for the type of missions the Air Force required, compared to today's modern aircraft it was an antiquated relic. The radios were heavy with vacuum tubes, transistors, and resistors; the hydraulics and control systems were simple but also limited; the armament sighting systems required much more human expertise, and the pilot had to be well skilled to be accurate. Lieutenant Fisher faced an unusual training situation at O'Hare. The F–86 had no trainer models with two seats, so Bernie strapped on one aircraft while his instructor flew another jet, and together they flew the required maneuvers for many hours until he was qualified to perform missions alone or as part of a flight or squadron.

During their tour at Chicago, the Fishers were very involved in their LDS ward. Bernie served as elders' quorum president in the Mormon priesthood, and Realla served as the presiding officer in the Relief Society, the women's service organization. These were very important and also time-consuming positions in an all-volunteer or lay religious denomination.[15]

Over the next several years, Fisher had assignments in Japan, then at Malstrom Air Force Base in Great Falls, Montana, where he acted as a ground control officer in a radar-based, weapons interceptor command post. In Japan Bernie Fisher got into trouble with his commanders—twice. First, he taught the Boy Scouts in his LDS troop how to place traps in the forest near the air base. Soon his commander ordered him to remove the traps because Japanese soldiers had been caught in them. Fortunately, no one was hurt. In the second incident, Fisher was called on the carpet for something Realla had done. His wing commander, a colonel, explained how a package addressed home to Idaho by his wife had a hundred small, ball-like firecrackers inside that had accidentally exploded in a mail room and slightly injured a worker. The newly promoted Captain Fisher gulped as his commander announced that an Article 15 would go on his record. This measure is a catch-all provision of the Uniform Code of Military Justice (UCMJ) and a rather light measure, but it was more serious than a personal reprimand. For one year, this action would remain in his local, temporary personnel file but not his permanent official file. During this time he was technically "flagged," meaning that he was ineligible for promotion or even awards until the flag was lifted. But only a few weeks later, an administrations officer came up to Fisher and handed him the original copy of the Article 15. The wing commander had been packing to leave for his next assignment, and the administrations officer saw, on the desk, Bernie's Article 15. The admin handed it over, commenting that he thought the wing commander would never miss it. Bernie was amazed, but he kept the paperwork.[16]

In Montana he did not fly as much because his duty was to serve as pilot liaison officer in the ground control intercept mission. Captain Fisher's duty was to work in a facility of complex radar and communication systems and consoles. He was the pilot on duty to assist the interceptor weapons controllers as they monitored and tracked flights displayed on dozens of consoles. He was not a "line pilot" so he was allowed to fly only four hours a month to maintain his currency. Yet like many pilots in such situations, Bernie volunteered for "ash and trash" missions, meaning that he flew any mission in any aircraft he was qualified to fly during his spare or off-duty time. Some months he would log sixty hours of flight time as a "strap hanger."

That was his life until about 1959. Then Bernie received orders for Homestead Air Force Base near Miami, Florida.[17] The move to the Deep South with its staggering humidity and distinctive culture was a challenge, but what made up for any inconvenience was that Bernie could fly the new, sleek, F–104 Starfighter. This Lockheed fighter-interceptor was one of the fastest, most glamorous, and technologically advanced aircraft in the world at the time. It could cruise faster than most fighters of the day, achieving Mach 2 with little effort. Mach 1 is the speed of sound—approximately 720 miles per hour. The Starfighter was a long, tube-like aircraft with short stubby wings and a "T" tail with its horizontal stabilizer. The forward or leading edge of its short, seven-foot wings was razor sharp; the radius of the leading edge was only .016 inch wide. Ground crew members had to place covers on the forward edges to protect themselves from accidental lacerations of their bare flesh. The F–104, a marvelous aircraft, was a vast improvement over the early American fighters of the 1950s in most ways, with more modern flight control, life support and engine systems, avionics, and electronic advancements.

Captain Fisher and his fellow pilots of the 319th Fighter Interceptor Squadron were standing guard in Florida during the trying days of the Cuban missile crisis of October 1962. The United States and USSR teetered on the brink of war—the moment when the "Cold War" came closest to "total war." Commanders and their aircrews had to be nearly perfect in their planning, orders, briefings, and mission performance.

During his service at Homestead, Bernie had a flight experience that all pilots dread: a "flame out" in an F–104. In a flame-out, the engine fails—a potentially fatal situation that can be caused by a number of mechanical or technical reasons. Bernie, with superb guidance from air traffic controllers and his own finely honed skills, was able to rescue the situation with finesse and skill, landing the powerless jet without damage.[18]

The Cold War droned on as Fisher continued to fly intercept missions and hone the skills and experience that he would certainly need in his next stage of his career. Another war in Southeast Asia was brewing by the mid-1960s. More and more American troops were entering the fray as advisors. Then in 1965, the United States entered the conflict with separate ground combat units. Soon, Air Force and Navy flyers were involved in an air war over Vietnam. And Major Bernard Fisher, age thirty-eight with about twelve years of flight experience, volunteered for duty in Vietnam.[19]

* * *

As major ground units entered combat in Vietnam, a serious internal conflict arose among the separate services over airspace and the operational control of aircraft. The Air Force argued that all aircraft and air missions—whether the aircraft was owned by the Navy, Marines, or the Army—should be commanded and controlled by the Air Force. The wrangling continued for months and was never completely resolved; the services basically performed their own missions.

The newly established 7th Air Force, based in Thailand, was the major command for all of Southeast Asia, thus emphasizing the importance of Air Force control. The commanders stressed the overriding principle of air superiority. Once that major strategic objective of controlling the air space above the battle area was secured, other missions followed, such as air interdiction, strategic bombing, supporting ground troops, transportation, and medical evacuation.[20] American policy in 1965 had not yet determined whether to bomb North Vietnam; but air interdiction—destroying the enemy's ability to move men and matériel into South Vietnam—was essential. Army and Marine commanders were adamant about having quick and responsive Close Air Support (CAS); but since the Korean War, the Air Force had largely moved away from

CAS. Thus, the Forward Air Controller (FAC) role was reintro-
duced to support ground commanders with CAS.[21]

These Forward Air Controllers were perhaps among the least
known and least celebrated heroes of Vietnam. A controller was
usually a pilot on the ground with the combat soldiers. The Air
Force FAC was incredibly important to any ground or maneuver
commander, the unit, and the operation. As the war matured, a
FAC could often bring CAS into the battle area in thirty minutes—an amazingly quick response. FACs lived, served, and died
with their comrades in ground units and suffered all the privations
that infantry and other troops endured. They had to be superbly
trained in map reading, orientation, and radio communications to
function effectively. Most FACs were on the ground, but occasionally some piloted or were aircrew members in small reconnaissance
aircraft such as O–1 Birddogs and OV–10 Broncos. They also ac-
companied more senior-level commanders in aerial command and
control aircraft—the UH-1 Huey helicopters. Not only did FACs
call in CAS missions, but they also helped with artillery support,
air medical evacuation, and rescue missions.[22]

The air space over Vietnam became a busy place. The Army
was pioneering the new doctrine of air mobility with the creation
of the 1st Cavalry Division (Airmobile); the Marines watched and
allowed the Army to contest the Air Force. Finally, the Army gave
its small fleet of fixed-wing aircraft to the Air Force, but the Army
maintained control of its helo-borne fleet. Meanwhile, the Air
Force had to place more emphasis on supporting ground troops
through CAS. The Navy and Marines flew their own missions
from aircraft carriers as they saw fit; and the Marines, like the
Army, had their own airmobile units. Yet given the possibilities
for confrontation and head-butting, the services coordinated and
planned major air operations amazingly well.[23]

The porous Vietnamese-Laotian border included an area in the
far southeast corner of Laos identified as "Tiger Hound." With
the increase of covert activity in this area, Tiger Hound became
a major problem by the end of 1965. Reconnaissance and inter-

diction missions increased to more than a hundred a day. Besides air missions, it was essential to disrupt the enemy logistical movements and insurgency with forces on the ground. Both the North Vietnamese Army (NVA) and the Viet Cong (VC) established an amazingly efficient transport route through Laos and Cambodia called the Ho Chi Minh Trail. One way to disrupt this movement of personnel and equipment was to establish base camps near key enemy supply routes and use local forces as the scouts and reaction forces. The best military units for such missions were Army Special Forces with partisan and indigenous support.[24]

* * *

For six months Fisher trained at Hurlbut Field near Panama City, Florida, where he learned to fly the A–1E Skyraider, a vintage, propeller-driven fighter-bomber. Because Fisher's primary mission would be associated with CAS, he also underwent training for Air Ground Operations Support (AGOS). This training taught him to coordinate air missions with Army and Marine elements, while also understanding their capabilities, tactics, and operations.[25] He had to be very familiar with the types of soldiers and units on the ground, especially ARVN (Army of the Republic of Vietnam), the South Vietnamese militia and irregular forces. Bernie received training also on two enemy elements: first, the regular units of the North Vietnamese Army (NVA), which had the best soldiers, training, and equipment; and second, the merciless and brutal Viet Cong (VC). These were demanding days and the Fisher family stayed at Homestead while Bernie endured long, difficult days and weeks away from home.[26]

In mid-1965 Major Fisher said good-bye to his family and headed for Clark Air Base in the Philippines for more training. In the jungles and tough conditions of the Philippines, he attended counterinsurgency classes and underwent the normal aviator SERE (Survival, Evasion, Resistance, and Escape) training. After training at Clark Air Base near Manila, he departed for Vietnam.

"After living in Florida and training in the Philippines, I still wasn't prepared for the oppressive heat and humidity of the broad Mekong River delta," Major Fisher recalled. As he deplaned at Tan Son Nhut Air Base north of Saigon, "searing wall of heat . . . seemed to suck the air right out of my lungs."[27] He was assigned to an air base at Bien Hoa, north of Saigon near the Mekong Delta where he would train South Vietnamese pilots in their weak, but growing air force.

The "Farm Gate" program initiated in 1965 was to train Vietnamese pilots in counterinsurgency missions with American assistance; but by the end of the year, training missions were overwhelmed by actual combat missions. One of the major training bases for Farm Gate was Bien Hoa. The very day that Major Fisher checked in at Bien Hoa headquarters, he heard an announcement over a helicopter loudspeaker system, "LDS Services at 1900 hours tonight in the base library." That evening Bernie met a dozen other LDS servicemen and gained their fellowship and friendship. The LDS group leader was Captain Ray Young, an Army helicopter pilot, who eventually determined that Church meetings in the base library were unacceptable. He went to the American wing commander and asked for permission to build a small LDS chapel with excess building material. The commander rejected the idea. Captain Young then approached the base commander, a Vietnamese Air Force officer, who not only approved and thought it was a good idea but even furnished some of the material. When one of the American chaplains learned of the building plans, he was furious that the Mormons had their own place of worship. Later this chaplain had to relent because most of the members of the base choir were LDS, and he wanted to keep their support. Eventually, in a few weeks, a small, frame building with the LDS name stood near the base library.[28]

In October 1965 Major Fisher was involved in a daring rescue mission when an F–105 Thunderbolt fighter-bomber went down. Fisher and his wingman covered the rescue by a CH–3 "Jolly Green Giant" medium-lift helicopter with a jungle penetrator—a

Major Bernard Fisher strapping on his A–1E
Skyraider in Vietnam.

seat or cage attached to a cable and a winch. Fisher and his fellow
pilot were awarded the Distinguished Flying Cross later for the
skill and ability demonstrated during that rescue.[29]

Even at a relatively secure military air base with high security,
Viet Cong mortar attacks occurred frequently. Bien Hoa was near
a very dangerous area designated as War Zone D, an area between
Saigon and the Mekong Delta. War Zone D was a very difficult
jungle and river area that was a perfect place for insurgents to infiltrate and conduct covert operations. From time to time, Bernie
and his fellows had sleepless nights in their bunkers as mortars
landed in the base. Eventually, after many frustrating days training
and teaching Vietnamese pilots, Bernie was reassigned to a combat squadron.

In January 1966, several American units were formed into Air
Commando Squadrons (ACS) to support the increasing combat.

Soon Farm Gate A–1Es were formed into the 1st ACS at Pleiku, hundreds of miles north near the Central Highlands, in II Corps Tactical Zone (CTZ). The II CTZ had a large area of operations from the border with Cambodia and Laos east to the South China Sea. Major Fisher was soon on his way to Pleiku.[30]

Major Fisher was now assigned to fly the carrier-based Navy AD–1 dating from World War II and later designated as the A–1 Skyraider. This aircraft, manufactured by Douglas, was a high-performance, propeller-driven, single-engine, single pilot fighter-bomber used in Vietnam mostly in the ground support role. In the early 1960s the Air Force acquired hundreds of the some 3,180 airframes built and redesignated them as A–1 (models D through J) depending on the version. The low and slow-flying Skyraider was very different from the sleek and graceful F–104 Starfighter.

The Skyraider was a workhorse and even looked like one with its old-fashioned, straight-edge wings, not swept back like those of jet fighters. The plane was thirty-eight feet long with a wing-span of fifty feet, so it was nearly square. Its empty weight was 12,000 pounds. With fuel and ordnance the gross take-off weight was double, 25,000 pounds. The Skyraider was powered by a Wright radial engine that delivered 2,700 shaft horse-power and could cruise at 180 knots or about 200 miles per hour. Its top air speed was 220 knots or 240 mph. There were 15 hard-point mounts for ordnance loads, normally 100–, 250–, and 300–pound HE (high explosive) bombs or napalm canisters. The A–1E also carried aux-iliary fuel in "drop" tanks, thus allowing an on-station loiter time of up to eight hours. There were four 20mm cannons—actually, belt-fed machine guns, two in each wing. The total ordnance pay-load was 8,000 lbs. The A–1E was a single-pilot aircraft, unpressurized and with no ejection system, though many had a "side-by-side" cockpit configuration—with or without dual-flight controls.[31]

Though slow, the Skyraider was an extremely dependable, du-rable, and maneuverable airframe with a tight turning radius. As a CAS bird, it had excellent short-field capabilities, besides a strong undercarriage for unimproved fields and runways. The Skyraider was a perfect aircraft for quick, deadly, and very close ground support operations.[32] Bernie Fisher himself admitted that, "after flying the jets," the A–1E was "not much of a thrill," but he went on to praise it as "a real stalwart bird" that "will take a lot of punishment and still keep going."[33] The type of missions he would experience in Vietnam required such a durable aircraft.

* * *

The U.S. military was organized under the Military Assistance Command-Vietnam, commonly called MACV, with its headquarters in Saigon. The Air Force had the responsibility of supporting the ground troops in this unforgiving jungle climate, besides conducting strategic missions—namely bombing targets in North Vietnam.[34]

Many of the missions that Fisher and his comrades of the 1st ACS flew were in direct support of the 1st Cavalry Division (Airmobile) based in An Khe, east of Pleiku, and areas in the north. The 1st CAV was a innovative tactical unit that used helicopters as the primary means of maneuver, especially in and out of battle areas, using LZs, or Landing Zones. The speed and flexibility of these tactics were revolutionary in warfare. Another innovation was that the aviation assets were organic to the division and were controlled by the division commander. The cavalry division had some 15,787 troopers, 428 helicopters in several battalions, and only half the ground vehicles of other combat divisions.

The first major ground battle of American forces in Vietnam was at Ia Drang in November 1965, which demonstrated the capability of the airmobile concept and doctrine. Therefore, the 1st CAV was a special unit that the leaders at MACV wanted to receive timely and particular air support. But Bernie and his fellow Skyraider pilots would also support other units besides the famous Cavalry.[35]

Camp A Shau, as the Army Special Forces soldiers called it, was only two miles from the Laotian border in Thua Thien prov-

North Central Vietnam with Camp A Shau. Cartography
by Hyrum H. Fleek.

ince. The camp lay in a long, narrow valley running north and south
called A Shau-Aloui. This base camp was staffed by a dozen or so
American Green Berets of the 5th Special Forces Group, called an
A Team, Detachment C–1. The camp was augmented by two interesting fighting forces common in this war—some two hundred
Vietnamese Civilian Irregular Defense Group (CIDG) troops,
the equivalent of a local militia force. The second group, was 140

Chinese Nungs, better known as Montagnards, organized into two companies and called "Mike Force." Thus, Camp A Shau in March 1966 had some 450 combatants and a few dozen civilians—cooks, laundresses, and actually some women and children.[36]

In early March 1966, intelligence sources and even a few defectors confirmed that the NVA 325th Division in several separate battalions was planning a major attack on the camp. Camp A Shau was a speed bump in the NVA's ability to move men and matériel into the central highlands. Some 2,000 troops were massing to attack the compound. For weeks patrols had discovered captured documents and prisoners confirming that a major concentration and imminent attack was underway.

The compound was shaped like a triangle with the most defensible positions and bunkers to the north, at the apex of the triangle. To the east was a high mountain ridge on which the NVA installed some twenty antiaircraft positions of 37mm and other guns. The enemy selected this ridge because it could easily cover the unimproved airstrip that lay between the ridge and the compound. The runway was covered with pierced steel planking and was only 2,300 feet long. Between the airstrip and base camp was a small berm or embankment that was about five feet high, rising sometimes to double that height. If American air support was denied the airstrip, then reinforcements and resupply could be disrupted.[37]

At 0350 on March 9, 1966, the NVA's 325th Division began to fire 81mm mortar rounds at Camp A Shau. At 0430 two companies, well over two hundred soldiers, attacked the south perimeter wall. The defenders were able to repel the attack, inflicting some losses on the enemy. Captain Tennis Carter, the Army special forces commander and an expert marksman, killed sixteen of the attackers, "I know I killed that many," he claimed later, "because I seen their heads come apart. After that we all switched to automatic, and nobody kept count."[38] The mortar and small-arms fire continued until about 0900 when a lull fell. There was heavy damage to the supply room and the water supply system. Two

Americans had been killed, and thirty other defenders had been wounded.[39] Most seriously, they had lost communications with the outside higher units and support—fortunately only a temporary circumstance. Soon support was on the way. Because of the early intelligence reports and imminent threat, the commander had prearranged these reinforcements. Bernie and his fellows were part of it, though it was hours before they knew it.[40]

By 1100 CAS was en route, and soon the planes were in tactical holding patterns above the camp area but unable to descend because of the variable ceilings and layers of cloud between 200 to 800 feet—topping out at 8,000 feet above ground level (AGL). Eventually some aircraft were able to penetrate the cloud layers and provide support. At 1300 one of the most unusual aircraft types in the Air Force fleet arrived on station: an AC–47 gunship informally called either "Spooky" or "Puff the Magic Dragon." It was, in fact, a Douglas DC–3, the famous World War II C–47 "Dakota." As the Vietnam War progressed, the Air Force rehabilitated these aging C–47s by mounting three 7.62mm miniguns on the left (port) side of the fuselage. With a cyclic rate of fire of 6,000 rounds per minute, each was a six-barreled "Gatling gun" that rotated at a tremendous rate of speed. One three-second burst would place a round every 2.2 meters across an elliptical area of forty-seven meters. The AC–47 carried 24,000 rounds of ammunition and flares to illuminate the battle area at night. The Spooky was a devastating weapon platform, though it was slow, cumbersome, and a large target.[41]

Almost immediately after the AC–47 penetrated the cloud cover, it began to take enemy fire, especially from the twenty gun positions on the high ridge east of the camp. On Spooky's second pass at tree-top level, the right (starboard) engine mount was torn away by enemy fire, and the lumbering aircraft crashed on a jungle hillside about five kilometers north of Camp A Shau. One enlisted crew member had both legs broken in the crash. Captain Willard Collins, the pilot, and his co-pilot, First Lieutenant Delbert Peterson, called for rescue assistance and were soon receiving hostile fire.[42] Their personal defense was their .38 caliber revolvers.

At this time, about 1430, Major Bernie Fisher and his wingman, Captain Bruce Wallace, were being briefed for a routine mission when they received a note from the squadron operations officer with a new mission, a "divert." Bernie Fisher read the note about A Shau but was not familiar with the location and grid coordinates. Soon Fisher and Wallace climbed aboard Fisher's assigned Skyraider, tail number 32649, manufactured in 1943 and launched with a full "bag of gas," a full complement of bombs, and the controller's instructions about the course, vector, and compass heading. In the seat to Fisher's right was Captain Robert Blood, a newcomer to Vietnam, who was there to observe and learn the mission profiles. Upon arriving at the area, Bernie found what aviators call a "sucker hole" among the clouds and layers. A sucker hole can be dangerous. A pilot may think there is an opening in the clouds but soon realizes there is no clear channel either down to the ground or upward above the layers. The main determination is lighter clouds—thinner layers that pilots can use to maneuver among the covering clouds while not flying under instrument rules.[43]

In this day's action and that on the following day, March 10, Major Fisher had an uncanny ability to find passages through the cloud cover. Several times, he led the fellow pilots on the same mission down safely through the cloud cover and separate layers. Fisher also led helicopters, bombers, and airborne controllers through the dangerous weather conditions several times. On this first attempt with Captain Wallace, Fisher recalled later, "It wasn't exactly a hole, but [it was] a kind of light spot in the clouds." Once he and Wallace broke through and visually oriented themselves, they immediately began strafing the south wall area of the camp. Captain Blood, riding with Fisher, described the maneuvers as "strafing runs in such a tight bank between the ridges, that one wing was in the clouds and the other was almost scraping the ground."[44] It was a harrowing and nerve-wracking business.

In the next few hours, Fisher left the narrow valley and besieged camp to lead other A–1Es down into the fight; then he
led a rescue CH–3 helicopter and, on a separate run, two C–123
Providers, which made low-level air drops to the defenders at A
Shau. Finally he once again flew up through the overcast to lead
two B–57 bombers down into the battle area.[45] There were many
other sorties flown into A Shau that afternoon. A CH–3 evacuated twenty-six wounded; supplies and ammunition were delivered
by Army CV–2 Caribous.

At the Spooky crash site, three of six crewmembers were eventually rescued by the CH–3 that Fisher led to the location. Captain Collins and the severely injured sergeant with two broken legs
were killed when the NVA tried to overrun the position. Even as
the rescue was going on, the enemy swarmed toward the plane,
hoping to salvage equipment from the crashed aircraft. Lieutenant
Delbert Peterson charged toward them and their automatic weapons, armed only with his M–16 and personal firearm, a .38 caliber
revolver. He drove them off, covering the rescue. Tragically as the
battle in the A Shau Valley continued, Lieutenant Peterson was
never seen again and his body was never recovered.[46]

A thankless task that Major Fisher received from the FAC,
relayed from higher headquarters, was to destroy the Spooky's
wreckage so that the enemy could not recover sensitive information such as maps, equipment, and armament. His wingman, Captain Wallace, made a pass over the site and dropped or skipped
several bombs onto the wrecked plane, reducing it to a blazing
fireball.

By now, evening was approaching, and the support crews,
including Bernie, had spent several hours in the A Shau Valley.
The Skyraiders under Fisher's operational control returned to
their respective bases. The defenders were resupplied, most of the
wounded had evacuated, and the enemy attacks had ended. Later,
Captain Wallace was awarded the Distinguished Flying Cross for
his superb airmanship and courageous support of the mission.
The next morning at 0600 Bernie's commanding officer called

him, announcing that he was nominating Fisher for the Silver Star Medal because of his exemplary leadership and heroism as acting air mission commander. All the pilots and others involved were impressed by how Fisher had braved deadly enemy fire and severe weather conditions again and again in the crucial defense of Camp A Shau.[47]

* * *

March 10, 1966, Day of Days

The new day at Camp A Shau was a repeat of March 9. At 0200 mortar rounds began to strike the camp, which years before had been an old French fort and base camp. At 0335 a major ground attack commenced, and the entire compound was under heavy mortar, automatic weapons, and small arms fire. The 430 defenders fought off the savage onslaught for hours, but soon the south wall was in danger of falling to the enemy's advance. Above the cloud cover, Air Force C–123s and AC–47s dropped flares for illumination. After sunrise, the defenders called in artillery support and, as soon as conditions permitted, CAS. By 0705 a Marine Corps A–4 Skyhawk, a jet fighter-bomber, was en route to provide support. It never arrived and was later reported missing. Once again, like the day before, the weather was perilous with low ceilings and shifting layers of cloud cover. Other Marine A–4s were able to penetrate the cover and dropped napalm on the south wall to stop the attack.[48]

At Pleiku, after being awakened by the colonel's congratulatory phone call, Bernie Fisher ate breakfast in the room he shared with five other pilots, and then he wrote Realla a letter. At 1005 he and his wingman for the day, Captain Francisco ("Paco") Vazquez, an ROTC graduate from Puerto Rico, took off on a standard mission. Ten minutes into their flight, they were diverted to A Shau. Other aircrews were also diverted to the besieged camp. By 1100 a dozen or more aircraft were above the cloud cover stacked in traffic patterns by air controllers at 1,000 feet intervals as if they were commercial airlines landing at Los Angeles International.[49]

On the ground, the situation at Camp A Shau was extremely critical. Despite the napalm strikes, the NVA had breached the south wall and were entering the center of the compound. The defenders, led by the Americans, were holed-up in the bunkers at the north end of the fort. As the enemy slowly moved into the camp, Captain Tennis Carter radioed that he estimated they could only hold out only for another hour or so.[50]

For some time the aircraft flew patterns high above the embattled camp. Finally, Bernie Fisher took the initiative to once again fly down through the layers of clouds. His wingman, Paco Vazquez, followed, as did two other A–1E pilots: Major Dafford ("Jump") Myers and his wingman, Captain Hubert King, of the 602nd Fighter Squadron from Qui Nhon. Soon the Skyraiders were in a "loose string" formation (also called a "trail") where they followed one another at tight intervals, strafing and bombing the enemy-held positions at the old fort. During one of the first passes, Captain King took a direct hit in the plexiglas canopy and could not see well enough to continue the gun runs. Using his instruments, he applied power and climbed up out of the overcast.[51]

On the third gun run, Jump Myer, age forty-six, was hit. The enemy from the heavily fortified east ridge was pouring tremendous fire on the American fighters. "It was a good solid hit that shook the whole plane and rattled my teeth," Myers recalled later. "I've been hit before by the fifty-caliber in Vietnam, and this was something a lot bigger, maybe the Chinese thirty-seven millimeter cannon." The aircraft was in serious trouble. "Almost immediately the engine started sputtering and cutting out, and then it conked out for good. The cockpit filled up with smoke."[52]

That morning Jump Myers had received a phone call from his commanding officer informing him that his name had been put on the promotion list for lieutenant colonel. He was also leaving in a day or two for a seven-day leave in Bangkok; it was supposed to be a good day.

Myers's call sign was "Surf 41" and he immediately radioed to Fisher and the others that he had a problem. Myers said, "I've been hit and hit hard." Bernie Fisher ("Hobo 51") replied, "Roge[r], you're on fire and burning clear back to your tail." Myers was at about 800 feet AGL when he was hit and was parallel or abeam the 2,300 foot strip. He was too low to bail out. The A–1E did not have an ejection system, so the pilot would have to crawl out of the cockpit onto the wing and leap from the aircraft.

"Bernie was very cool about it, and that helped," Myers said later, but the smoke was so bad that he had a hard time breathing or seeing. "I held my breath for as long as I could, but then I started eating a lot of smoke." Fisher flew abeam Myers and guided him to establish a final approach, cueing him on when to lower his flaps and landing gear. Then he remembered that Myers still had his bomb load under his wings. He told Jump to jettison them, which Myers did as he approached the north end of the airstrip with only a few hundred feet to spare. The drop tank, filled with fuel, failed to jettison, but neither Myers nor Fisher noticed it. The fighter was just moments from critical touch down.[53]

Fisher continued to guide Myers down: "That looks good, that looks good," until, at the very last moment before Myers touched down, Fisher realized: "You're too hot, you're too hot, get your gear up. You'll have to belly her in." Myers pulled the landing gear handle, retracting his landing gear. He and Bernie both realized that, on wheels, the aircraft would over-shoot the short runway and probably crash at the south end at a high rate of speed. Unfortunately, as Myers hit the runway, the fuel tank exploded into a ball of fire. The Skyraider skidded eight hundred feet down the runaway, then slid off and plowed into the dirt embankment west of the airstrip. It was an amazing feat to have landed in one piece at all, given the runway's terrible condition. It was littered with battle debris and steel planking shards, cratered from mortar hits—and, furthermore, was too short for even the A–1E.[54]

Myers quickly ripped off his survival vest, his pistol, helmet, and other gear. Just as he reached up to slide back the canopy, a

gust of wind lifted the fire and smoke away, giving him a clear view
and a breath of clean air. He jumped from the plane, just as the
flames engulfed it and sprinted to the berm a few meters away. He
dived behind it into the weeds. It was a miracle that he escaped the
inferno with only superficial burns.[55]

From Bernie Fisher's view, the crash and the fire must have
been fatal. He did not know the downed aviator's name—just his
call sign of "Surf 41." Bernie made another pass as Paco Vazquez
made another strafing run against the enemy at the southern end
of the compound. As Bernie flew down the runway at about twenty
feet off the deck, suddenly from behind the berm, Myers jumped
up and waved with both hands.

Major Fisher was stunned and immediately called the airborne
FAC and other controllers. His report of a downed pilot mobilized an immediate rescue mission by helicopter. But it would take
fifteen minutes for the chopper to arrive. The situation for the two
pilots, Fisher and Vazquez, now changed. Their objective was not
only to support the camp but to protect Myers on the ground. As
they did so, they received hits from the deadly ground fire coming
the high east ridge. Vazquez told Fisher that the enemy fire from
the east ridge was increasing.

Fisher called back, "Well, go get them!" And Captain Vazquez
did just that. With ten 100-pound fragmentation and two incendiary bombs or white phosphorus, Vazquez with great skill and
precision dropped his package of ordnance at tree-top level with
devastating effect to the NVA artillery placements.[56]

The time was past 1145 and the Skyraiders had been on station for about an hour. Bernie then learned that another flight of
A–1Es was loitering above the overcast. Captains Jon Lucas and
Dennis Hague from Fisher's 1st Air Commando Squadron, fellow
"Hobo" flyers, soon came down and joined the flight of Skyraiders protecting their downed fellow pilot and Camp A Shau. Two
more Skyraiders also joined the flight.

Enemy troops were on the move, searching for the American pilot. Jump Myers had cleverly hidden in the weeds and also

crawled several hundred meters down along the embankment to position himself for an avenue of escape. The fighting along the camp's perimeter and runway increased. The defenders tried a counterattack against the NVA who held the south wall. The CAS attacks on the enemy were devastating, but the attempts to recover the south wall failed.[57]

At approximately 1215, Major Fisher called the air controller to learn the status of the helicopter rescue mission. The estimated arrival time was at least twenty more minutes. Later Fisher remembered, "They told me the chopper was having trouble finding the hole, and could I go out and bring him [the chopper] in?" The situation was deteriorating and something had to be done. "I couldn't leave the guy down there without any cover and go off looking for a chopper. I told Control that I was going in and get the pilot. They told me they did not advise it, but that I could make the decision myself."[58]

Major Bernard Fisher made the decision.

He called the other Hobo elements in the flight and informed them that he was going in to try and recover "Surf 41." The Hobo flight "rogered" and prepared to provide cover. At this point, the ground fight had a lull.

Amazingly, the radio operator of a C–123 Provider that was stacked above the battle area recorded the radio calls of the rescue. The transcript, first classified as secret, has now been declassified. It gives a literal blow-by-blow of the action. The transcript that follows has not been modified. I have added necessary explanations in brackets. Some names and call signs have not been previously mentioned in the narrative.[59]

> Fisher: He's about 20 feet.
> Lucas: Understand he's 20 feet?
> Fisher: Roger.
> Lucas: Which way you gonna land?
> Fisher: I'm gonna make a 180 degrees, come in to the southeast.
> Lucas: OK. Well, then, we'll come up behind you and strafe parallel to your heading with you.

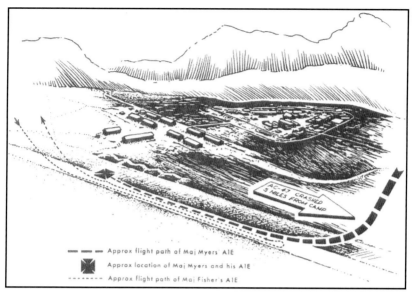

Diagram of A Shau and airstrip depicting Myers's and Fisher's flight paths.

Fisher: OK, I'm rolling in now.

Unknown: Make it slow or you'll lose it.

Lucas: I'm right behind you, Bernie. I took a hit in my pitot system, and I'm smoking a little. [A pitot is the tube on an aircraft where relative wind and ambient air pressure enter the system, allowing the measurement of airspeed and altitude.]

Hague: OK, I'm right back at your six o'clock, Luke. [Luke is Jon Lucas.]

Lucas: OK. Ahh, do you see any smoke?

Hague: Negative. It looks pretty good.

Major Fisher followed the same approach as Myers because the wind was not a major factor, and he intended to land to the south on the airstrip. He had already dropped his last bombs and fuel tanks to be as light as possible for the landing. As he touched down, he immediately realized that he had come in way too fast; but if he stomped on the brakes, the speed and the condition of the runway might cause the aircraft to nose down, damage the propeller, and probably crash. So he made an unplanned "touch and go"—meaning that he added power and became airborne again just as the plane reached the end of the runway.

> Lucas: OK, my air speed's gone to hell, and my hydraulic pressure's fluctuating.
> Hague: All right. You want me to stay with you?
> Lucas: OK. Bernie, you gonna land out of this one?

Whether Fisher replied to Captain Lucas's question is not recorded. But here's what happened next. Fisher made a low-level "tear drop" turn and established another approach to land to the north. This time he planted the aircraft exactly on what pilots call the numbers—the large white number of the runway direction. Of course, A Shau airstrip had no marked runway numbers, but the concept is important to understand. From a comment below in the radio transmission, the runway headings are given as 150° and the reciprocal would be runway 330°. Thus, for Fisher and the other pilots, landing to the south would be runway 15 and to the north would be runway 33. Fisher lined up for a runaway heading of 330°.

> [Unknown] Fighter: Five-Two, Oxford 81, over.
> FAC: Oxford 81, Birddog 52. [A Birddog is a civilian Cessna 152 high-wing aircraft designated as the O–1 Birddog by the military.]
> Fighter: Roger, we're headed your position for time on target of 1240. We're ten minutes late. We have eight 500 GPs retarded and 20 mike-mike. [GP is "general purpose" bombs, or high explosives known also as HE or fragmentation; 20 mike-mike is 20mm cannons.]
> FAC: All right, Sir, hold on high and dry. ["Dry" means weapons on hold.] At the present time we have A–1H's working underneath. There's an aircraft down there at the present time and we're trying to get the pilot out.
> Unknown: (garbled) all aircraft.
> Fighter: This is (Call sign) 07–1. We're still orbiting up here at 20,000.
> FAC: Roger, hold high and dry for now, Sir.

Fighter: Roger.

Fighter: Ahh, 5–1, this is Congo 56 with eight napes and eight bombs and 20 mike mike. ["Napes" are napalm bombs.]

FAC: Roger, stand by. The weather underneath is not too good for napalm at the present time.

Fighter: Roger.

Hague: Bullshit.

Unknown: (Call sign) Bird Dog 52.

Lucas: OK, Paco [Paco Vazquez], you in trail with us now?

Lucas: Hobo 51, Hobo 03.

Unknown: Zero three, uh, Shoeseller 03.

Lucas: Roger. Go ahead, Jim.

Gunter: Roger, which kind of help do you need? We're about three miles up the valley.

Lucas: OK, Jim, do you read me?

Gunter: Roger.

Lucas: OK, Babe, come on down the valley. As you come down the valley you run over that airstrip, pick up a heading of one five zero. And as you run down, you can run the napalm right down the east side of the runway.

Gunter: Understand. 150 down the east side of the runway. OK, got that, Pete?

Houk (Jim's wingman): Roger Dodger, Jim.

Lucas: You'll see quite a bit of smoke.

When Fisher landed, it took the entire length of 2,300 feet to roll out and then stop. In fact, he stopped beyond the PSP in the mud overrun. His wings missed hitting several fifty-five-gallon drums that were lying about. He was also taking ground fire at this time. Fisher turned the aircraft around, then taxied nearly the entire length to reach Myer's location, dodging debris and steel planking shards. He stopped at Myer's burning A–1E with mortar rounds and small-arms fire striking all around him.[60]

Hiding in the weeds, Jump Myers could hardly believe what was happening. At first he thought another pilot had made a forced landing, then he remembered thinking, "Why, that crazy son-of-a-bitch has come to get me out." He began running to Fisher's aircraft. "The gunfire was deafening, the bullets were whining all around," Myers related, "I thought it was all aimed at me. My shoulder blades were really puckering. This was the third time that day I thought I was dead, I can tell you I made that run as fast as any old man of forty-six ever could."[61]

Gunter: OK, I see an aircraft down there to the left. Who's that? You?

Lucas: No, I'm coming down the east side of the runway now. Why don't you come down one time and look it over?

Fighter: OK, this is Hobo 21. We're up here, Luke.

Birddog 52: Hobo 21, Bird Dog 52.

FAC: Roger, 52. We're orbiting the airfield to the north at 6000 feet. [This altitude means these aircraft were above the cloud cover and layers.]

Lucas: OK, let's hit everything, Denny, except the Fort.

Hague: Roger, I gotcha. . . . I'm Winchester. [out of ammo]

Lucas: OK, so am I. Let's keep making passes though. Maybe they don't know it.

Hague: Roger.

Lucas: OK, Jim, the area's smoking pretty badly, and you'll see an aircraft burning on the runway. Bernie's taking off to the north. [Fisher actually took off to the south.]

Once Bernie saw Myers, it took a hundred feet to stop. He lost sight of Myers, and enemy fire was continuing. He quickly unbuckled, set the parking brake, pulled the power lever back to idle, and began to slide over to exit the cockpit from the other seat when he saw, in the rearview mirror, two large, red-rimmed eyes glaring at him. It took some time for Myers to climb up on the trailing edge of the wing and get to the door panel. The prop blast almost blew him off the wing. Myers crawled on all fours to the cockpit where Bernie reached up, grabbed him, and yanked him inside. Myers tumbled, gasping, onto the floor boards.[62]

Enemy rounds were peppering the dirt around the Skyraider and occasionally hit the aircraft with a thud. Later, some nineteen hits were counted on Fisher's Skyraider. From that position far

down the ruined runway, Fisher applied full power. He had calcu-
lated the margin perfectly. Because he carried no bombs and was
low on fuel, he negotiated a perfect short-field take-off as mortars
and machine gun fire whizzed around them. Myers crawled up
into the right-side seat and, in a moment of nerve-induced humor,
exclaimed, "You dumb son-of-a-bitch! Now neither of us will get
out of here!"[63]

> Gunter: OK, understand to the north. OK, I can see him. Is he
> rolling now?
> Hague: Roger. Roger.
> Lucas: OK, get the east side, Denny.
> Hague: Roger. Roger, Babe.
> Gunter: OK, where do you want those trenches strafed, Jon?
> Lucas: OK, you got us in sight? We're breaking off. I'm coming
> left.
> Gunter: OK, where you want the strafe here? Right on the east
> end of the runway?
> Lucas: Yeah, put it all down the east side of the runway, in the
> grass area. Put a couple of bursts in there and then get hold of Barry.
> Gunter: OK. Get a hold of who?
> Lucas: Correction, it'll be Hound Dog 23 if he's still up.
> Gunter: OK, right here, we'll be going right in now.
> Lucas: OK, all the gun fire is over here on the east side in these
> trees.
> Gunter: OK, Luke, you got a chopper comin' in up here to the
> north. Uh, he may be able to get the pilot out.
> Lucas: We already got him out.
> Gunter: Roger.

Fisher then looked at Myers and recognized him. They had
served in the same squadron together earlier in their careers, but
they did not know each other well. Jump Myers had no helmet
or headset to talk to Fisher so he signaled for a cigarette. Fisher
signed back that he did not smoke.[64] Fisher and Myers climbed up
and gained altitude as the furious combat continued below. Cap-

Illustration depicting the rescue, *Saturday Evening Post*, June 4, 1966. Copyright 1966 Curtis Publishing, Independence Square, Philadelphia.

tain Vazquez and the other pilots eventually broke contact and departed, following Fisher through the cloud cover.

* * *

The half-dozen pilots directly involved with the rescue witnessed the entire feat. It was perhaps the most amazing act of bravery they had ever seen. To rescue a fellow pilot in such a way, not using the more accessible and versatile helicopter that can hover and land nearly anywhere, was beyond belief. Several dozen other players and controllers had heard the entire drama by radio. Word spread quickly and the mission became legend within hours.

Yet despite all the bravery, daring, and courage of the ground troops and that of the airmen above who flew dozens of resupply, CAS, medical evacuation and then extraction missions, Camp A Shau was overrun. The daring rescue of Myers was over by 1300 hours or so. By 1500 the situation was hopeless. Marine helicopters were ordered in to evacuate the survivors and wounded. Soon documents, communications instructions, codes, and plans at

Majors Bernie Fisher, left, and Dafford ("Jump") Myers , after rescue, 1966. Courtesy Fisher Family Collection.

Camp A Shau were destroyed. An evacuation plan was quickly arranged and, considering the gravity of the situation, it was executed quite well. Most of the defenders were evacuated that afternoon; the American Special Forces and the Montagnards served as the rear guard as dozens of Vietnamese militia, including dozens of noncombatants, wives, children, and others were extracted. The evacuation lasted through the night and cost the lives of four Marines when a helicopter crashed. On March 11, the 95B Regiment of the NVA 325th Division entered the compound. Of a total of some 434 individuals in Camp A Shau, military and civilians: 186 people were extracted; 101 were wounded; 248 were missing, with

172 of them believed killed. The Americans suffered 100 percent casualties. Of the seventeen Americans at the camp, all were extracted but twelve were wounded and five were dead.[65]

The loss of Camp A Shau was a major defeat early in the war for the American and South Vietnamese effort. The NVA was able to move men and materièl more easily into the central highlands. Even though a major B–52 bomber raid attacked the camp area on March 19, it was two years before the A Shau Valley came under friendly control again.

General William Westmoreland, the MAC-V commander, commended the air support by the Air Force, Army, and Marines for Camp A Shau, calling it "equal to any in aviation history. The repeated heroic deeds of . . . [the] crews and forward controllers, accomplished under extremely adverse conditions, reflects the utmost credit on the crews themselves." Army Special Forces Captain Tennis Carter who fought at the camp said, "Without the air support you provided, we wouldn't have lasted one day."[66]

* * *

Landing at Pleiku, Major Fisher's home base, he and Major Jump Myers were greeted with awe and delight by the ground crew and others that afternoon. The next day, Paco Vazquez, Myers, and Fisher were flown to Tan Son Nhut Air Base near Saigon and were soon interviewed by the press. They met with Major General Gilbert Meyers, deputy commander of the 7th Air Force, and the headquarters protocol officer. The protocol colonel asked, "Bernie, what does this deserve? . . . How would you rate this mission?"

"I don't know, but I know somebody that received a Silver Star," Bernie said to the colonel who smiled. Even as they spoke, the nomination for the Medal of Honor was underway, as the colonel soon informed him. Eventually, Major Dafford Myers and Captain Jon Lucas received the Silver Star Medal. Captain Francisco Vazquez and Dennis Hague received the Distinguished Flying Cross.[67]

Soon Major Fisher was again flying missions, but an operations officer in the squadron read in the Air Force regulations that a recipient or nominee for the Medal of Honor was exempted from combat. By May 1966 Major Fisher received orders that sent him to a post in Germany where he flew jet fighters again. He left Vietnam with the Silver Star Medal, six Air Medals, the Distinguished Flying Cross, and a nomination for the Medal of Honor.

* * *

Returning to his home in Kuna, Idaho, in the summer of 1966, he was met at the Boise airport by the governor, the mayor of Boise, and many well-wishers. At this time his nomination for the Medal of Honor was still not officially approved. Nevertheless, Bernie was a hero. The Fisher family was excited to move to Germany, to Hahn Air Base north of Frankfurt. Bernie served in the 496th Fighter Interceptor Squadron. During a well-deserved leave, while en route to Germany, Major Fisher spoke at a Rotary Club meeting in Salt Lake City, Utah. Afterward he had the rare opportunity to visit with LDS Church President David O. McKay in his office. Bernie realized that he would soon be an ambassador not only for the Air Force but also for the LDS Church.[68]

In Germany in December 1966, Fisher received orders to report to White House for the Medal of Honor ceremony on January 19, 1967. The Fishers flew on the command jet of the Air Force commander of Europe and arrived in Washington, D.C., as a snow storm blasted through the capital. In the Red Room, President Lyndon B. Johnson presented the very first minted Air Force Medal of Honor to Major Bernard F. Fisher. On hand were Realla and their children, Lieutenant Colonel Dafford ("Jump") Myers, and some of the others pilots involved that day. One of the special highlights was the performance of a song especially written about the rescue. Later, the famous folk singer, Tennessee Ernie Ford, recorded it. The next day the Fishers flew to New York City as

Major Fisher's A-1 Skyraider after the rescue. Now restored, it is on display at Wright-Patterson Air Force Base near Dayton, Ohio.

guests on the *Ed Sullivan Show*, where Realla had appeared nearly a year earlier.[69]

The Fishers returned to Germany where Bernie continued to fly a new jet, the F–102 Delta Dart. Soon he was promoted to lieutenant colonel and transferred to the 525th Fighter Interceptor Squadron at Bitburg, a hundred miles to the west near the French border. Six months later he became the squadron commander. During the summer of 1967, N. Eldon Tanner, a counselor in the LDS Church First Presidency, invited him to speak at a large Boy Scout event in the Salt Lake Tabernacle.[70] Also, on August 12, 1967, during the same visit, Clearfield City named the small city park at South Clearfield Elementary School in honor of Bernie Fisher. Among others in attendance were Hugh B. Brown, second counselor in the LDS First Presidency, my father, and me, age eleven. (See Introduction.) This was the first of several memorial roads, parks, and monuments dedicated in Lieutenant Colonel Fisher's name.

Lieutenant Colonel Fisher and his family returned to the United States for duty at Duluth, Minnesota, where he learned to fly F–106 Delta Daggers. It was 1969 and the Vietnam War was still raging. Fisher then competed for a position with the famous Air Force precision and demonstration team, the Thunderbirds. The choice came down to him and another pilot, but Fisher was not selected.[71] For years Bernie had been trying to be assigned to the Idaho Air National Guard as an active duty advisor. He finally received his wish with promotion to colonel, and the Fishers returned to Idaho for their last time. Several years later in 1974, Colonel Fisher retired from active duty after some twenty-seven years of military service with the Navy and Air Force.[72]

As of this writing, Colonel Bernard Fisher is still with us, living on the Fisher farm in Kuna. Realla, his wife of nearly sixty years, passed away in 2008. Honors continued to come his way. Parks in Boise and Kuna are named after him, as is a highway leading to Hill Air Force Base in Utah. In 1999, the U.S. Navy announced that a commercial container ship would be christened the MV *Maj. Bernard F. Fisher*.[73]

BERNARD FRANCIS FISHER

Rank and organization: Major, U.S. Air Force, 1st Air Commandos. Place and date: Bien Hoa and Pleiku, Vietnam, March 10, 1966. Entered service at: Kuna, Idaho. Born: January 11, 1927, San Bernardino, Calif.

Citation

For conspicuous gallantry and intrepidity at the risk of his life above and beyond the call of duty. On that date, the special forces camp at A Shau was under attack by 2,000 North Vietnamese Army regulars. Hostile troops had positioned themselves between the airstrip and the camp. Other hostile troops had surrounded the camp and were continuously raking it with automatic weapons fire from the surrounding hills. The tops of the 1,500-foot hills were obscured by an 800 foot ceiling, limiting aircraft maneuverability and forcing pilots to operate within range of hostile gun positions, which often were able to fire down on the attacking aircraft. During the battle, Maj. Fisher observed a fellow airman crash land on the battle-torn airstrip. In the belief that the downed pilot was seriously injured and in imminent danger of capture, Maj. Fisher announced his intention to land on the airstrip to effect a rescue. Although aware of the extreme danger and likely failure of such an attempt, he elected to continue. Directing his own air cover, he landed his aircraft and taxied almost the full length of the runway, which was littered with battle debris and parts of an exploded aircraft. While effecting a successful rescue of the downed pilot, heavy ground fire was observed, with 19 bullets striking his aircraft. In the face of the withering ground fire, he applied power and gained enough speed to lift-off at the overrun of the airstrip. Maj. Fisher's profound concern for his fellow airman, and at the risk of his life above and beyond the call of duty, are in the highest traditions of the U.S. Air Force and reflect great credit upon himself and the Armed Forces of his country.

Notes

1. Richard Armstrong, "It's Great to Be Alive," 21.
2. Ibid., 24.
3. "After Action Report: The Battle for A Shau," April 30, 1966.
4. Armstrong, "It's Great to Be Alive," 24.
5. Ibid., 26.
6. Bernard Fisher and Jerry Borrowman, *Beyond the Call of Duty: The Story of an American Hero in Vietnam*, 11.
7. Ibid., 8–9.
8. Ibid., 18–19.
9. Ibid., 24–25.
10. Ibid., 25–26.
11. Ibid., 26–27.
12. Ibid., 29–30.
13. Ibid., 35–36.
14. Richard W. Stewart, ed., *The United States Army in a Global Era, 1917–2003*, Vol. 2 in AMERICAN MILITARY HISTORY, 252–54.
15. Fisher and Borrowman, *Beyond the Call of Duty*, 42–43.
16. Ibid., 59.
17. Ibid., 65–68.
18. Ibid., 82–84.
19. Ibid., 96–97.

20. John Schlight, *The War in South Vietnam: The Years of the Offensive, 1965–1968*, 6–7, 10–11.

21. Ibid., 27–28.

22. Ibid., 294–95.

23. Ibid., 26–28.

24. Ibid., 198.

25. Ibid., 97.

26. Schlight, *The War in South Vietnam*, 3, 16, 46, 35, 194, 201.

27. Fisher and Borrowman, *Beyond the Call of Duty*, 102.

28. Ibid., 106–8.

29. Armstrong, "It's Great to Be Alive," 22.

30. Schlight, *The War in South Vietnam*, 4, 17, 113.

31. René J. Francillon, *McDonnell Douglas Aircraft since 1920*, 403–5.

32. Ibid.

33. Armstrong, "It's Great to be Alive," 21.

34. Schlight, *The War in South Vietnam*, 47–49.

35. Stewart, *The United States Army in a Global Era*, 277, 307–9.

36. " After Action Report: The Battle for A Shau," 1.

37. Schlight, *The War in South Vietnam*, 200.

38. Armstrong, "It's Great to Be Alive," 22.

39. Kenneth Sams, "The Fall of A Shau," 1.

40. "After Action Report: The Battle for A Shau," 2.

41. Schlight, *The War in South Vietnam*, 91.

42. Sams, "The Fall of A Shau," 2.

43. Armstrong, "It's Great to Be Alive," 22.

44. Ibid.

45. Sams, "The Fall of A Shau," 3.

46. Schlight, *The War in South Vietnam*, 200.

47. Armstrong, "It's Great to Be Alive," 22.

48. Sams, "The Fall of A Shau," 4.

49. Armstrong, "It's Great to Be Alive," 23.

50. Sams, "The Fall of A Shau," 4.

51. Ibid., 6.

52. Armstrong, "It's Great to Be Alive," 23.

53. Ibid.

54. Ibid.

55. Ibid., 24.

56. Ibid.

57. Sams, "The Fall of A Shau," 6.

58. Armstrong, "It's Great to Be Alive," 26.

59. This transcript was attached to Kenneth Sams, "The Fall of A Shau." When he wrote it in April 1966, the transcript was classified as "Secret." Years later, it was declassified and is available in history offices. I have standardized the names of speakers in upper and lower-case letters (from the original all-caps), removed the bold-face type from the names, and standardized the punctuation.

60. Armstrong, "It's Great to Be Alive," 26.

61. Ibid.

62. Sams, "The Fall of A Shau," 7; Armstrong, "It's Great to Be Alive," 26.

63. Sams, "The Fall of A Shau," 8.

64. Armstrong, "It's Great to Be Alive," 26.

65. "After Action Report: The Battle for A Shau," 6.

66. Sams, "The Fall of A Shau," 9–10.

67. Fisher and Borrowman, *Beyond the Call of Duty*, 162–64.

68. Ibid., 191.

69. Ibid., 196, 199.

70. Ibid., 206.

71. Ibid., 210–13.

72. Ibid., 212–13.

73. Office of Assistant Secretary of Defense (Public Affairs), News Release: No. 465–99, October 5, 1999.

Corporal Larry Leonard Maxam, United States
Marine Corps, about 1965. Unless otherwise
noted, all photos in this chapter are courtesy of the
Maxam Family Collection.

Chapter Nine

CORPORAL LARRY LEONARD MAXAM, THE LIONHEARTED: THE DEFENSE OF CAM LO

February 2, 1968, Republic of South Vietnam

A two-and-a-half-ton transport truck, called a "deuce and a half," bounced along the dusty, rutted road with its cargo of the living and the dead. The dead, mostly American Marines, were stacked like cordwood against the cab, several layers high and deep. In the stack of corpses was a U.S. Army major, the senior officer on station and one of the first killed in the initial attack. A vicious night assault by some 750 troops—two battalions of North Vietnamese Army (NVA) regulars and Viet Cong (VC)—had struck a small compound of fewer than fifty American Marines, soldiers, and South Vietnamese local militia troops. The fight was an awful and maddening ordeal.

Toward the rear of the truck were the wounded, some Marines, and a few Vietnam Communists, or "Charlie" as the Americans called them. One North Vietnamese soldier had been wounded severely in the neck and his bandages had become loose. He was slowly bleeding to death.

Sitting on the floor of the truck, two wounded Marines holding their weapons bounced and swayed with the bumps and ruts. Dirty, grimy, exhausted, alive in the tropical heat, but still numb from the stunning attack during Tet—the Vietnamese annual New Year's holiday—the Marines sat silent, marveling at their survival. A half dozen U.S. Army advisors and an under-strength platoon of Marines had withstood the attack of wave after wave of hundreds of enemy armed with rockets, mortars, machine guns, and small arms during a night that seemed as if it would never end. Finally the blessed dawn, came and reinforcements arrived with armored vehicles. It was a miracle. It was like the Alamo, but with the difference that this time the defenders had survived.

The bleeding Vietnamese soldier groaned as his life slowly ebbed away. The two Marines glanced at him incuriously, then looked away. The medics had patched him up once. Why help him now? It was the North Vietnamese who had asked for a truce and armistice during Tet—and then had attacked. In fact, all over South Vietnam, hundreds of actions took place—violent insurgent fights and also full-scale conventional attacks. The Tet Offensive would be regarded later as the turning point of the American involvement in the war.[1]

Then one of the Marines noticed something, pointed, and said, "Cover Max up." This Marine would later be awarded the Navy Cross, the Navy's second highest decoration for valor. The other Marine, who would receive the Silver Star, crawled past the bleeding "Charlie" to the stack of American dead.[2]

There lay the most honored of the dead from the intense defense of Cam Lo district headquarters. On top was the body of a twenty-year-old Marine corporal from California, joggling up and down from the rhythm of the moving "deuce-and-a-half" serving as an ambulance. He had single-handedly defended nearly half of the perimeter against several determined assaults, taking wound after wound until he finally succumbed. He had killed dozens of the enemy in the dark and surreal battle. A quiet, unassuming Marine with steel nerves, known for his great smile, lay exposed. The green plastic poncho had slipped away from his lifeless face. The surviving Marine covered the "lionhearted warrior" carefully, respectfully—shaken by his comrade's nightmarish wounds. Then he crawled past the bleeding enemy soldier and sat down next to the other survivor. In silence, the two Marines waited numbly as the truck careened along the dusty track, and the wounded North Vietnamese died.[3]

* * *

Corporal Larry Leonard Maxam, United States Marine Corps, was killed on February 2, 1968. He served as a squad leader in the defense of the Cam Lo District Headquarters, a training compound for South Vietnamese local forces. Exactly two weeks later, Captain Richard D. Weede, the commanding officer of D "Delta" Company, 1st Battalion, 4th Marine Regiment ("D/1/4"), submitted AWARD RECOMMENDATION, NAVPERS 1650/3, the standard naval form for awards; it was signed February 15, 1968. In block #16, these words appear: MEDAL OF HONOR. The form was two pages and had the typical bureaucratic blocks and spaces demanding such information as location, weather, dispositions of friendly and enemy forces, and finally, actions justifying the award. Blank 27 instructed: "When Medal of Honor is recommended, append free hand sketch of area." The nominating official also had to write a "continuation page" which gave a summary of the action and reasons why this individual should be awarded the medal. Captain Weede, who had not been in the action that night, wrote: "All those who observed Maxam's sacrifice that night are convinced that his actions, above and beyond the call of duty, salvaged what would have been a disaster."[4]

For the Medal of Honor in all the services, eyewitness accounts are essential for approval. Attached to the basic form are statements that justify the recommendation for America's highest award for valor. Second Lieutenant Michael O. Stick, Corporal

Maxam's platoon commander during the fight at Cam Lo, wrote below the typed portion of his statement, that Maxam had "single-handedly . . . defended almost ½ of the entire perimeter. He insisted on giving his life so that 40 of his fellow Marines might live and triumph." Lieutenant Stick, who would receive the Silver Star for his heroism in this same action, continued, "He had freely chosen loyalty above life; he had acted above, & beyond, the call of duty."[5]

These were statements from others—Larry Maxam's comrades. One had been in the fight, the other had not. Yet one of the true measures of a brave warrior is the regard that his comrades have for him and his actions. Lance Corporal Nathaniel Moss wrote, "Cpl. Maxam's extreme heroism and dedication to duty helped in breaking the backbone of the NVA [North Vietnamese Army] attack."[6]

The recommendation moved up the chain of command: from the company commander to the 1st Battalion commander for concurrence; then to the commanding general, 3rd Marine Division (Reinforced); then to the commanding general, III Marine Amphibious Force; and, finally to the commander U.S. Military Assistance Command-Vietnam (MACV). This position was then held by General William Westmoreland, one of the architects of the Vietnam War. After leaving Vietnam, the recommendation went through five more Marine and Navy commanders before it arrived for review in Washington, D.C. From there the last approving authority prior to the President of the United States was the Secretary of the Navy. The Navy Department Board of Decorations and Medals determined that all of the documents and supporting material were in order. Then it was ready for the review of U.S. President Lyndon Baines Johnson.

This process may seem tedious and boring. Bureaucratic routines are. But the important point is that, at any stage moving through these official channels, any one of these commanders could have "non-concurred" and downgraded the Medal of Honor recommendation to a lesser decoration—and in this case, probably the Navy Cross, or perhaps even the Silver Star. The authority of commanders in the chain of command is awesome. A non-concurrence could have been appealed, but that process was dauntingly complicated. The key question on all awards, but especially the Medal of Honor is: Does this individual truly deserve it? America has high standards of bravery and competence for its fighting men. Were this individual's valor and actions exceptional? truly above and beyond the normal expectations? Commanders, the service secretaries, even the U.S. president, are stewards of this decoration, guarded and protected by procedures of proper review and approval.

Unfortunately, the process is not a perfect one. Some individuals who truly merited the Medal of Honor did not receive it. A few others received it who perhaps should not have.

But Corporal Larry Leonard Maxam, a Marine and also a Latter-day Saint, without any doubt rightfully deserved the Medal of Honor for his incredible courage and selfless service in the face of tremendous odds and extreme danger. His actions were crucial in defending Cam Lo against an overwhelming enemy of superior numbers. Larry Maxam, the most recent LDS serviceman to receive this decoration, presents a compelling story.

* * *

Larry Maxam grew up in sunny California, a fun-loving and adventurous boy. He was at times mischievous but always honest and resourceful. He could be serious when necessary. His parents were Lauren Leonard Maxam and Alice Bernadette Crouse Maxam. Lauren Maxam, a California native, had served in the U.S. Army during World War II and later became an electrician specializing in lighting. Alice grew up in upstate New York and came to California during World War II. Together they had three children, Larry, daughter Linda, and son Robin.[7]

Larry was born at Glendale, California, on January 9, 1948, but the family moved to Burbank, just down the road in the late 1950s. Also about this time, the Maxam family joined the Church of Jesus Christ of Latter-day Saints—a tremendous and life-changing decision for the family. Larry was baptized on October 13, 1956, at the customary age of eight.[8]

Sharing a room with his younger brother Robin, Larry soon developed an interest in outdoor adventures, shooting firearms, and Boy Scouting. He worked diligently on his animal husbandry merit badge to the point of keeping live scorpions, tarantulas, and snakes in his room. Sometimes his specimens escaped and wandered about the Maxam house on Magnolia Boulevard. On one occasion, Larry was stung by a scorpion and became frightfully sick. At that point, Alice laid down the law, and Larry's creepy crawlers were banished to the garage.[9]

Young Larry seemed to have had a mind of his own when it came to medical care and enduring pain. In 1960, at age twelve, he had an appendectomy. The day after he returned from the hospital, Larry was climbing trees in the backyard. He might have gotten away with it; but when he jumped down from a tree, he ripped open his stitches and Alice, fuming, had to take him back to the hospital for treatment. Alice was fuming because of his daring adventurous nature. Besides Boy Scouting, the Maxam men were shooters and joined the National Rifle Association and a marksmanship club nearby. The Maxams were not well off, so these inexpensive recreational opportunities provided fun and family time together. Lauren Maxam worked as a mechanic and handyman for local businesses, small manufacturing firms, and a few entertainment businesses. Times were tough, and money was tight for the Maxams.[10]

As teenagers, the three Maxam youngsters enjoyed the LDS Church's youth program, dances, and sports. At age fourteen, hard-working Larry earned his coveted Eagle Badge, pinned to his shirt by his proud mother as his father looked on. William Flinders was the local LDS Scoutmaster, and his son Steve was one of Larry's best friends. They attended school and church activities together and also advanced in the priesthood, officiating in such Mormon ordinances as blessing and passing the sacrament on Sundays.[11]

In 1962 Alice Maxam pins on Larry's Eagle Badge
as his father, Lauren Maxam, and Scoutmaster
Bill Flinders, left, looks on.

Larry was naturally intelligent, but much of school bored him
and he was lacked the determination to push past his ennui to excel
academically. What enchanted him were the outdoors, shooting,
camping, hiking, and a life of adventure. Girls also by this time
were a fun and exciting aspect for Larry, most of whom he met at
Church meetings and activities.

Then in March 1963, Lauren Maxam died. Fifteen-year-old
Larry, a student at Burbank High School, had to take more responsibility for the family and make mature decisions.[12]

In 1965 as a senior in high school, Larry made a momentous
decision: He would quit school and join the Marine Corps. This
was a terribly troubling proposition for the family, especially for
his mother, who would have to give permission for this underage
enlistment. Robin was shaken at the thought of Larry's absence,
for he was a great role model and protective older brother. Larry

was a slender, dark-haired, and handsome young man. Standing five foot seven, he was not immediately physically imposing; yet his personality, demeanor, and manner soon impressed others. Despite the family's concerns about his decision, he felt ready to leave his family and serve his country. He enlisted with Alice's consent.

* * *

That same year, 1965, the United States was ramping up its first major escalation in Vietnam, adding combat forces to existing advisor and military assistance groups. The year before, the Congress had passed the Tonkin Gulf Resolution approving armed intervention in the civil war that had been raging since the end of World War II in 1945. The first sizable American ground force to enter Vietnam and begin combat operations was a Marine brigade. On March 8, 1965, some 3,500 Marines of the 9th Marine Expeditionary Brigade landed near Da Nang, initially to help the South Vietnamese Army (ARVN) secure U.S. air bases. From this first step would come an armed escalation that would witness, at its height, half a million American service members in the theater of operations. That same day, March 8, thousands of miles to the east in Los Angeles, Larry Maxam of Burbank, California, swore his oath and enlisted as a United States Marine; he was two months past his seventeenth birthday.[13]

On March 9, 1965, Maxam entered Marine boot camp at the Marine Corps Recruit Depot at San Diego, California. He was in 3rd Recruit Training Battalion. He and the other new recruits were not "Marines" yet, as their drill instructors were quick to inform them. They barely qualified as "maggots," "low-lifes," or "ladies," enhanced by various adjectives, colorful metaphors, and expletives. Marine basic training was designed as an intensely difficult and challenging experience that shaped future "leather-necks." No matter what they were later classified or trained to be, a Marine was a rifleman first, last, and always. After some fifteen weeks, Larry graduated from boot camp and then took Individual Combat Training at Camp Pendleton, California, for four weeks. Maxam was assigned to Company A, 2nd Infantry Training Regiment. In August 1965, he attended Marine aviation training at Naval Air Technical Training Center, Jacksonville, Florida. He was now on the other side of the continent from his family in California. It is not clear why he was at an aviation training school as a rifleman for several months, his status that of a student, according to his official records. In February 1966, he joined Company H, 2d Battalion, 8th Marine Regiment of the 2d Marine Division, Fleet Marine Force (FMF) at Camp Lejeune, North Carolina.[14]

* * *

The United States Marine Corps is one of the most versatile, disciplined, lethal, and effective military forces in history. Though a separate branch of the U.S. Armed Forces, the Marine Corps is actually a component of the Department of the Navy. The Marines have it all: fighter aircraft, infantry divisions, tanks, artillery, amphibious landing craft, and a cockiness that is well deserved. What the Marines do not possess is a large logistical and administrative tail. The Marines rely on the Navy for most of their logistical support, including medical and administration. Marines get their courses in armored vehicles, tanks, and airborne training from the Army. This arrangement lets the corps devote most of its men and assets to combat training and combined arms units. Thus, they have developed an incredible sense of pride and unit *esprit de corps.*

For the next fifteen months, Private Maxam served in various duties and locations such as Marine Corps Base, Quantico, Virginia, and then in Puerto Rico at Camp Garcia on Viequas Island. His unit, the 8th Marines (a regiment of ten companies), also deployed for a four-month Caribbean "cruise" that has nothing to do with the romance and exoticism suggested by the name. A Navy cruise is normally a six-month-long deployment, a very challenging and stressful training exercise traveling to far lands and ports, but always focused on readiness training.[15]

Maxam trained in routine Marine amphibious and tactical exercises as a rifleman and was promoted to private first class in April 1966. After twenty-two months in the Marine Corps, he was promoted to lance corporal. In a letter home in April 1967, he mentioned a field training exercise where his unit, Company F, 2nd Battalion, 8th Marines, was to be "helo-lifted from the ship to the landing zone which is in the northern end of the island. Then we are to make a tactical forced march" to the other end of the island. There, he griped, "my company as usual gets the lousy end of the deal. We get to secure and hold the swampy marshland."[16]

Maxam's mention of being "helo-lifted" was not particularly excited, but both the Marine Corps and U.S. Army were perfecting a new tactical doctrine of "airmobile" operations that had been introduced in Vietnam by the Army's 1st Cavalry Division (Air Mobile) in 1965. Helicopters, "hot ZLs" (landing zones), door gunners, and the sound of "Hueys" (UH–1) and their distinctive flapping rotor blades would be the defining image and feature of the Vietnam War.

Then about April 1967, Maxam received orders for duty in Vietnam. He visited his family in June and July 1967 before he shipped out. At this time in the war, both the Army and the Marines were using the individual replacement system to rotate men in and out of the combat zone. This system, though easier and cheaper to manage, would prove to be one of the terrible policy decisions that affected morale and unit cohesion in Vietnam. The art of war since the dawn of time has derived its strength, discipline, and *esprit de corps* from the team—a group, a unit concept. From Greek phalanxes to Roman legions and cohorts, to Zulu *impis*, and Cromwell's "new model army," the fighting organization is the entity that gives the unity of command and sense of teamwork to soldiers.

Unfortunately, Vietnam-era policymakers violated this critical military principle. A soldier or Marine entered a unit as a "newbie," a "cherry," or the more obscene "FNG," only to encounter "short-timers" who were near the end of their tours. Combat units in Vietnam were plagued by this system, since men had shifting loyalties depending on how much time they had to remain in-country. Short-timers were naturally extremely reluctant to take chances or volunteer for certain missions. Some did whatever they could to avoid combat and dangerous missions. This situation often destroyed unit cohesiveness, loyalty, and team-work.[17]

Larry Maxam, like millions of other Americans, entered Vietnam with individual orders; he had a thirteen-month tour with an "R&R" (rest and recreation) at the mid-point. On July 25 1967, Maxam arrived in Vietnam, never to leave.

* * *

Lance Corporal Larry Maxam was assigned to the 1st Battalion of the 4th Marine Regiment in Quang Tri, the northernmost province in the Republic of South Vietnam. Quang Tri bordered the De-Militarized Zone (DMZ), a buffer zone that both the North and South accepted after the defeat and withdrawal of the French in 1954. The agreement was that neither nation could militarize this strip: no units deployed, no encroachment, no bunkers, mines, or any active military. Since Quang Tri was closest to Communist North Vietnam, it seems logical that most of the infiltration, especially by NVA regulars, would use the DMZ; but this was hardly the case. For years the NVA and Viet Cong used the Ho Chi Minh Trail from North Vietnam through Laos and Cambodia to move men, equipment, and supplies south out of the reach of the South Vietnamese and Americans.

Yet there was enough infiltration across the DMZ that the Americans began to build the "McNamara Line," a defense belt of electronic surveillance devices, patrols, and some bunkers and base camps. They also conducted routine air reconnaissance, although it never materialized to its full capacity as planned. It was not until 1971 that American and ARVN forces crossed into Laos and

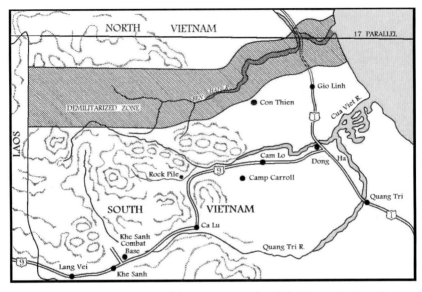

Northern area of Quang Tri province, the DMZ, and Cam Lo on
Route 9. Cartography by Hyrum H. Fleek.

Cambodia to interdict the Ho Chi Minh Trail. The combat and
amount of insurgency varied across the seven-hundred-mile long
and very narrow country.[18]

The 3rd Marine Division had been one of the main combat
units in the I Corps area, or Corps Tactical Zone 1 (1 CTZ), since
its arrival in October 1966. The two Marine divisions were part of
the 3rd Marine Amphibious Force (III MAF), besides the Ameri-
cal (sic) Division, an U.S. Army division, and support units. The I
CTZ covered the two northernmost provinces of South Vietnam:
Thua Thien and Quang Tri. There were also small U.S. Army de-
tachments, mostly advisors, district staff personnel, and trainers
for South Vietnamese units, serving in the provinces and CTZ.
The 4th Marine Regiment was deployed into battalion sectors,
commanded by a lieutenant colonel; it had four rifle companies,
and a headquarters and service company commanded by captains.
A rifle company had the Table of Organization for six officers and
210 Marines, divided into four platoons, led by a lieutenant called
the "platoon commander." Three of these platoons of about forty

Larry Maxam, left, in Vietnam, 1967.

men each were rifle platoons of three squads each. The fourth was the weapons platoon—about sixty Marines with a mortar section, a section of three M–60 (7.62mm) machine guns, and an anti-tank section of six, 3.5–inch rocket launchers or 90mm recoilless rifles. Recoilless rifles, like World War II bazookas, fired an anti-tank round with the back-blast blowing out from the rear of the weapon tube. Thus, it caused no recoil, in contrast to heavy weapons with breech-blocks that did recoil.[19]

The rifle squad was one of the basic tactical units of the time with fourteen Marines: nine riflemen, and one M–79 (40mm) grenade launcher, led by a sergeant. The squad also had three corporals who each led a fire-team of three other riflemen. The M–79 fired a huge "bullet-appearing" projectile from a single-shot weapon with a wood stock that broke at the breech like a double-barreled shotgun to eject and reload. At this time in the summer of 1967, the Marines in Vietnam were exchanging the heavier but dependable M–14 rifle of 7.62mm for the smaller, untested, M–16 rifle of 5.56mm caliber. These were the weapons Maxam had at hand as he went into his first experiences of patrolling, limited engagements, and firefights.

At this time in the war, the tactics and missions that infantry units employed, both Army and Marine, had several components. The Vietnam War was known for "search and destroy" missions and was a "war of attrition," where body counts were more important than defeating the enemy. Though to a degree both of these qualities are true, some standard missions contributed to operational and strategic levels of war. American ground units were to find, fix, and destroy the enemy whenever possible; they also protected key military and civilian sites and conducted route and area security missions. Americans also assisted in "pacification" programs to help the local inhabitants with road and building construction, provide clean water, and sustain education, health, and other programs that tried to provide security, better living conditions, and economic opportunities for the local populace. Though special civil affairs teams were responsible for many of these programs, the "grunt" was there, helping and defending.

Most of the time, small units, companies, or reinforced larger combined units were established in static base camps called Forward Support Bases. Some camps, called "fire bases," were mostly artillery and mortar outposts. Patrols of platoons or less ranged through the countryside or built-up populated areas, providing a modicum of security in the area. If intelligence was accurate and timely, they conducted meeting engagements or ambushes against VNA or Viet Cong forces.

Counter-insurgency warfare throughout history has been a tough military and political proposition. Larry Maxam entered this world of long, dangerous days on patrol in an unmerciful tropical climate, dealing with a less than cooperative local populace, in a bloody guerilla war where, at times, larger units clashed in deadly conventional combat.

In August 1967, Larry wrote home about some of his first combat patrols in Quang Tri province. "Well, here I am," he wrote after, "a 6 day recon patrol, well as it turned out it was over 10 days."[20] He continued, "The operation was called squeak, kind of a funny name for a 7-man patrol . . . and now that we're done with it. I can really say that we were up in the Ashaw Valley (Happy Valley)." The A Shau Valley had been an essential area of operations for both the insurgent NVA and the defending ARVN and American forces. (See Chapter 8.) A Shau was in tough terrain marked by narrow valleys between steep, thickly vegetated hills. It was a terrible location for conventional fighting. In March 1966, the NVA had overrun a U.S. Army special forces base called Camp A Shau. The narrow valley bordered Laos and was directly west of Da Nang.

Maxam had experienced his first armed combat during this mission: "All we did was a little snooping and pooping, Entill [sic] the sixth day when we were supposed to get extracted. Then all kinds of shit happened, Ol' Charles [Viet Cong] was there waiting for the chopper along with us as she started to sit down they fired up at her, and us both."[21]

Maxam explained that they had warned the helicopter off, then "beat feet" out of the "AO" (area of operations). Soon they stopped, set up a hasty ambush, and hit the enemy who were hot on their heels. Then they established a second ambush with the results that the Marines killed nine NVA, captured seven, and confiscated small arms and two RPGs (rocket propelled grenades).[22]

Even with this success, other NVA elements were still in pursuit. "Then yesterday morning we were finally sure that we had lost them," Larry wrote, "so we called up the chopper and were helo-lifted back to Cumberland" (the name of their Fire Support Base). He also mentioned with a warrior's nonchalance: "Oh, by the way, nothing to [sic] serious, just a scratch, I got my first purple heart, got a piece of shrapnel in the right thigh." He continued: "Funny thing. I was so shook in our first fire fight with the N.V.A. I guess that I didn't even realize that I was hit untill [sic] it was all over."[23]

Two months later on October 1, 1967, Larry Maxam was promoted from lance corporal to corporal.

Vietnam had a terrible climate for fighting a war. Tropic heat and mugginess drained energy in the summers. The relentless, cold monsoon rains of winter spoiled roads and turned villages into soggy masses. The flat valleys of rice paddies, bogs, marshes, and causeways were idea places for ambushes and firefights. Huge insects, deadly centipedes several inches long, and lethal species of snakes slithered into clothing and gear. Ant hills the size of automobiles hosted millions of nasty, stinging creatures. Vietnam was like being on another planet for the Americans who served, fought, and died there.

*　*　*

But one of the enduring qualities of men in wartime is the brotherhood of soldiers, the bond between them of shared respect and trust that is one of the great sociological mysteries of warfare. In late November 1967, Private Harold Posner arrived in Vietnam and was assigned as a rifleman in Maxam's fire-team of three Marines. Posner after two and half years in the Marine Corps was still a private (E–1) when he should have been at least a lance corporal or perhaps even a corporal. His rank bespoke a tumultuous career thus far. In "boot camp," he slugged a commissioned officer—a very serious crime in the uniformed service and a capital offense during war. He should have been court-martialed and dishonorably discharged; but his superiors allowed him to remain in the service after serving thirty days in the brig. Eventually he arrived in Vietnam.

According to Posner, Maxam took him under his wing and changed his life. "He treated me like a Marine and the others like me he really cared about us." To this day Harold Posner accords his newfound discipline, combat skills, and loyalty to Maxam.[24]

Arriving at a rear base camp, Posner boarded a helicopter that would take him to his forward assignment. He was carrying some bread in a bag to drop off at the landing area. When he stepped off the chopper at his destination, he heard shouts of "Incoming!"

an alarm that meant they were coming under artillery fire. Posner was momentarily uncertain what to do with his gear and bread; but another Marine yelled from a foxhole for him to come and take cover. Posner jumped into the foxhole, and there, under fire, met Corporal Maxam.[25]

Along with Private Posner, Maxam made enduring friends with many Marines in Delta Company. Comrades such as Larry Herwig, Tim Russell, Bill Flannery, Larry Clinesmith, Don Jakovac, Richard Brandon, and even their platoon commander, Lieutenant Mike Stick, were close. There were other friends as well in their large rifle company numbering more than two hundred men.

The Marines gravitated to Maxam because he was quiet, respectful, and loved other people. He often led his men in prayers, sometimes in a group and sometimes individually with his friends. He and fellow Mormon, Dick Wall from Salt Lake City, also held their own LDS-type devotionals together. Often when either man prayed with the others, they used the King James language common in LDS prayer: "thee," "thou," and "thine." Some of these Marines at first thought Wall and Maxam were Quakers because of these archaic pronouns. Dick Wall often preached Mormonism to the others, which they tolerated, while Maxam was more of a quiet example of LDS doctrine and standards.[26]

Delta Company was attacked nearly every day and night by NVA or Viet Cong mortars and/or small-arms fire. But this did not deter Maxam from making his rounds or "trooping the line" to ensure that his men were alert and performing their duty. "He always checked the squad before every mission and patrol for gear and equipment and [to ensure] that the men understood their mission and task," Posner recorded some forty years later. "It was rare that Maxam got excited. . . . He calmly explained and taught." Maxam instilled many techniques and tricks of a seasoned warrior into his men. For instance, when conducting a night patrol, Corporal Maxam would perform a head count before and after missions to ensure that no enemy had stealthily joined the patrol in the dark and infiltrated the base camp—a trick often employed by insurgent "Charlie."[27]

Posner wrote that Maxam "was a special person and would have been that way as a Marine or anything else he did.... His eyes spoke too." Maxam did not bark or scream his orders. He spoke clearly, but his low-key manner meant that he "was not a typical Marine in Vietnam nor was he a 'John Wayne' type of Marine yelling.... New guys to Vietnam were treated as FNGs, but not to Maxam; he cared and he took time to show it.... He was a rock and fearless.... He would never have put his Marines in more harm's way than we already had to be. Never!"

Posner left Vietnam as a sergeant (E–5) after two tours of duty, thus gaining four promotions. Posner attended college eventually, graduated with honors, and has created and managed several successful businesses since his return from Vietnam in 1969.[28]

Posner was not the only Marine who felt this way about Corporal Maxam. Private First Class Don Jakovac from Pennsylvania arrived in Vietnam in December 1967 and joined D Company 1/4 Marines. Maxam was then acting squad leader because the squad leader was on a "Rest & Recreation" trip out of country. "I could see he knew what he was doing," Jakovac recalled years later. "He was the kind of person people wanted to be around."[29]

In January 1968, Larry Maxam penned a letter home—his last. "Just got back off a five day sweep [patrol]," Maxam wrote. "Not too much new besides that I'm doing real fine and am in good health." He then expressed the thoughts common to most men in combat about the future. "Haven't heard any more about the language school. I guess that they just don't want NCO to go to it," he wrote. The language school was probably the Defense Language Institute at Monterey, California. He then mentioned taking his mid-tour R&R, which would be coming up soon to Hong Kong, Japan, or Australia, "because I'm definitely going to get a few suits and some clothes."[30] There are no premonitions here. He was looking forward to the future and the ordinary pleasures of shopping for new clothes.

* * *

What Corporal Maxam and a half-million Americans in Vietnam did not know in mid-January 1968 is that one of the largest series of battles in that strange war was looming. What is now called the Tet Offensive was about to erupt across the entire length and width of South Vietnam. Many historians consider Tet as the turning point, the shift leading toward the final outcome of the war that began as a revolution against the French in the 1950s. By the 1960s, the conflict turned into a civil war between North and South Vietnam. The American intervention caused the civil war to become a major conflict. Tet is the Vietnamese New Year period and a celebrated holiday. In January a temporary armistice was agreed upon, beginning January 27 and lasting through February 3, 1968, the period of Tet. Yet by the last few days of January, American and ARVN intelligence learned that massive concentrations of Viet Cong and NVA regulars were deploying across the country.[31] Caches of arms were found, many prisoners interrogated, and captured maps and documents confirmed that a major offensive was just days away.

There was not much time to act. General William Westmoreland, commander of Military Assistance Command-Vietnam (MACV), and his staff quickly issued orders to all four of the Corps Tactical Zones and their hundreds of units—divisions, brigades, Air Force, and separate tactical units, to prepare for a major attack.[32]

Along the DMZ, incidents and rumors among villagers reinforced intelligence gathered by local American leaders that a serious threat was developing. On January 27, the first day of the intended armistice, a major firefight occurred in the area called "Mike's Hill" where some 150 enemy and twenty-one Marines were killed. Patrols detected and explored an unusual number of mines along Route 9. More insurgents were crossing the DMZ.[33]

The massive offensive began during the early morning hours of January 31, when NVA and Viet Cong launched attacks, first

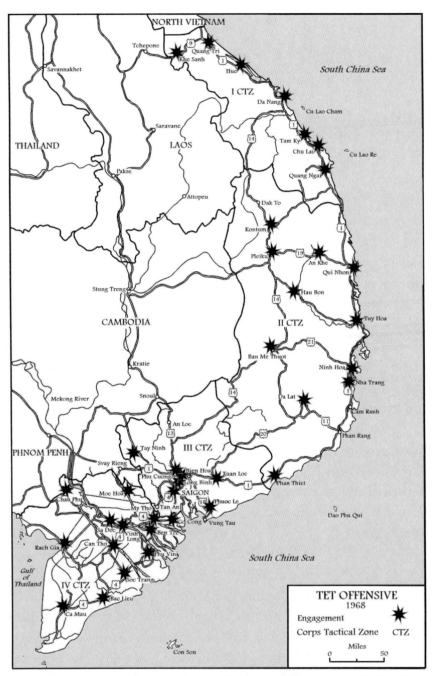

Tet Offensive and major attack sites, January– February 1968. For Cam Lo's location, see p. 332. Cartography by Hyrum H. Fleek.

against the cities of Hue and Da Nang and ultimately against 100 towns and cities, including thirty-six of forty-four provincial capitals, and the national capital of Saigon. This uprising was countrywide and well coordinated, involving more than 80,000 Communist troops.

Though not a total surprise tactically, the shock of Tet was the scope and breadth of the offensive and sheer audacity and treachery of the North in launching such a major effort after asking for—and agreeing to—a truce. Historically, Tet remains an amazing operational and logistical feat, manifesting a remarkable ability to move in so many men and so much equipment and to coordinate and execute such an aggressive and complex insurgent campaign.[34]

Way up north on the DMZ, intelligence of the pending attack alerted American forces, especially those assigned as advisors and trainers of the local area militia called Popular Forces (PF). U.S. Army advisors under the command of Major James C. Payne were garrisoned at Cam Lo District headquarters when intelligence reports arrived with startling news of unusual enemy activity and build up. On January 27, Major Payne requested reinforcements from the nearby Marine base camp of the 2nd Battalion, 9th Marines. Reinforcements were on the way to Cam Lo that very day.

There have been many sieges in the history of war, but in relative size, character, numbers, and ferocity, there are interesting parallels between the battle of Cam Lo in February 1968 and the defense of the farmstead at Rorke's Drift in South Africa in 1879. There about 120 British soldiers withstood as many as three or four thousand Zulu warriors during a battle that lasted for a day and a night. At Rorke's Drift, as at Cam Lo, overwhelming firepower and remarkable courage prevailed in both instances. Eleven soldiers received the Victoria Cross, the British equivalent to the Medal of Honor.[35] It holds the record for the most awards presented in one regiment during a single action in British history. At Cam Lo, nearly every survivor received a decoration for valor: two dozen Bronze Stars, eight Silver Stars, three Navy Crosses, and one Medal of Honor—Corporal Larry Maxam's.[36]

* * *

The Americans had their own nicknames for Cam Lo. They called the town "Tin City" and "Camp Low." It was near the Cam Lo River, fourteen kilometers south of the DMZ. In May 1967, "Operation Hickory" had removed most of the local population from the DMZ, resettling them near Cam Lo. A few miles from Cam Lo were three Marine fire-support bases: C–2, C–3, and Con Thien. The area became known as "Leatherneck Square." Various fire-support bases were stocked with artillery and heavy 4.2-inch mortars. Maxam's company, Delta, 1/4 Marines was attached to another battalion at this time, 2/9 Marines, at FSB C–3—the same unit from which Major Payne had requested reinforcements for Cam Lo. Nearby at Dong Ha was an U.S. Army artillery battery of 155mm howitzers that would provide crucial artillery support during the Cam Lo fight.

The small compound near Cam Lo consisted of nine old French buildings, a stone tower, and several bunkers made of sandbags and lumber. Though there was a chest-high parapet of dirt and three strands of concertina wire surrounding the compound, it was hardly sufficient to withstand a determined assault. Its location was another problem. The compound straddled Route 9 near the DMZ, one of the few "highways" in the area, a generous term for an awful dirt road of barely passable ruts that connected Dong Ha and Khe Sanh, two larger towns with much larger American military bases.[37] (Some weeks later, the Marines at Khe Sanh would attract national attention as they endured a desperate siege of several weeks, saved by American firepower and airpower.)

Along with the Marine reinforcements were several pieces of heavy military hardware that would give the defenders an advantage. There were two "gypsy" antiaircraft guns, "quad-50s," or four .50 caliber machine guns mounted on the bed of a 2.5-ton truck.

One truck was positioned at Cam Lo's entrance to Route 9, the other at the exit.[38]

In the compound was a squad of Marines from a specially trained unit, part of the Combined Action Program (CAP). The CAP program provided military advisors and training to local militia organizations to promote pacification among the local inhabitants with education, civil works projects, and local governance. Also, some Marines from an engineer unit happened to be in the area doing much-needed roadwork when the alert of the pending attack arrived. Thus, the compound had several Army personnel, two squads of Marines from Delta Company, one squad from E Company, 2/9 Marines, a dozen or more additional Marines from separate units, and PF militia. Cam Lo thus numbered some 120 defenders.[39]

The task-organized platoon from two battalions was under the command of Lieutenant Stick, a reserve Marine officer on active duty, and Staff Sergeant Donald Sellers, the ranking Marine NCO, who was acting platoon sergeant.[40] Action reports and intelligence estimates placed the number of enemy forces at 750: two regular battalions of the 320th NVA Division, and an unknown number of Viet Cong troops.[41] The NVA and VC expected to easily overrun the compound and wipe out the few American soldiers and PF defenders. They did not know that Marines had arrived in the afternoon of February 1 to bolster the defense.

The Marines labored to prepare Cam Lo for the imminent attack. They improved the defenses, placed ammunition and crew-served weapons at key positions on the perimeter, filled sandbags, and installed claymore mines among the concertina wire as part of the final protective line (FPL). D Company's Marines under Lieutenant Stick manned the northern and northwestern sector of the perimeter, while the Combined Action Marines manned the southwest sector of the FPL. The South Vietnamese PF guarded the eastern and southern perimeter along with the Army attachments who were not in the command bunker.[42]

Before midnight, Marines with infrared "starlight" scopes guarding the Cam Lo Bridge spotted saboteurs trying to install demolitions. They killed two enemy soldiers. Two hours later, a general attack erupted. Fortunately, the area around the compound for several hundred yards had been cleared of trees and vegetation making clear fields of fire for the defenders.

* * *

February 2, 1968, Day of Days

At 0215 the anticipated attack began with dozens of mortar rounds, RPGs, and heavy small-arms fire—well-placed and accurate. The NVA had done their homework, and it showed. Major Payne was on the radio, calling in reports and requesting artillery support when a RPG made a direct hit on the Command Operations Center bunker. Payne was mortally wounded and died within a short time. Others in the bunker were killed outright. The next in rank was Captain William McMaken, U.S. Army, who assumed command. He was a proven and seasoned officer with eleven years prior service as an enlisted soldier, including time as an NCO. He had attended Officer Candidate School in 1965; for his actions and bravery that night he received the Silver Star Medal.[43]

As soon as the attack commenced, RPGs and mortars destroyed the two gypsy gun-trucks. The "quad .50s" were blown up before they fired a single shot. The screams of at least one man caught in a burning Army vehicle were heard above the battle noise. Captain McMaken and others ran toward the burning vehicle, but the small-arms fire was so intense that they could not reach it. The agonized screams continued until flames engulfed the vehicle, then stopped.[44]

The PF Vietnamese stood up to some of the heavy initial fire, but eventually most of them fled during the opening barrages of mortars and rockets. They either tried to escape from the compound altogether or tried to hide, shaking with fear, in the old

French buildings. Only a few stuck with the American defenders at the perimeter. The chaos of battle erupted across the fortress compound. Flares streaked overhead, illuminating the ground below with eerie shadows as hundreds of NVA and VC moved stealthily toward attack positions while their comrades directed a heavy stream of small-arms fire at the defensive lines. The entire perimeter was under attack, but the greatest volume of fire was along the northern perimeter and its corners, where the enemy intended to attack. The Marines manned their positions and returned fire on the deploying horde.[45]

Night combat is a terrifying scene of flares and tracers, muzzle blasts that explode light in an instant that ruins night vision. Tracers—usually the sixth round in a belt-fed weapon—not only allowed the gunner to observe his hits and correct his aim but also led back to the gunner so that the enemy could pinpoint and engage him. Night fighting is a hellacious affair—distances, perspective, and visual acuity are severely affected, adding to fear and confusion. The din of battle with its thunderous racket, concussive effects, and the smell of choking, grimy gunpowder permeate even the open air. These effects worsen at night because they limit the ability to see what is happening. Night fighting is one of the most dreadful ways to experience war.

The sudden and deadly first strike caused confusion and alarm among the defenders, but they quickly appraised the situation and took action. One of the survivors in the COC bunker was U.S. Foreign Service Officer John Cleary, who immediately manned the radio and was able to communicate throughout the battle. He assisted in transmitting and receiving radio traffic for artillery support and calling in reinforcements.[46]

When the attack came, Private First Class Don Jakovac was asleep in a bunker, awakened by the first crack of gunfire. He jumped up and ran to his position. He was wounded almost immediately; but as soon as another Marine bandaged his arm with a discarded cotton ammunition bandolier, Jakovac resumed his position in the line.[47]

By 0300 some 200 enemy assault troops had massed outside the northwest perimeter preparing to attack. A few, acting as sappers, went forward with Bangalore torpedoes to blow up the concertina wire around the parapet. These devices were long steel tubes filled with explosives and were effective in clearing gaps in the wire. Covering fire from the line of jungle several hundred meters away continued with mortars, RPGs, 12.7mm heavy machine guns, and recoilless rifles. Other attackers were close enough to throw satchel charges to clear the wire obstacles.

Then the assault came.

In the dark between flashes, flares, and gun bursts the enemy moved forward, carefully and deliberately.[48]

The Marines opened fire with everything they had against the shadowy enemy.

Several dynamic acts of bravery and sheer luck marked that night. Marine Private First Class Marlin Resinger of D Company stationed himself in the stone tower near the north perimeter and fired perhaps hundreds of 40mm grenades from an M–79 grenade launcher. Also with Resinger was Lt. Stick, the only Marine officer at Cam Lo. He used this elevated position as a type of command post from which he could observe the battle and direct the actions of the three squads under his immediate command, shouting instructions to the men below. The NCOs also ran from position to position, delivering instructions in the teeth of withering fire. That is why three of them received the Navy Cross for their courage that night. The tower was a fiendishly dangerous location—providing an overlook but also exposed to shattering fire. The NVA constantly fired on the tower. Its stone walls were solid enough to repel much of the fire, thus providing some cover. Several Marines climbed up the rickety ladder during the fight to bring ammunition to Resinger and also receive orders and relay messages to Lt. Stick. Bill Flannery and Corporal Russell each made several trips to the tower. On one such climb, Russell was hit three times by enemy rounds of shrapnel: one ricocheted off his steel "pot" helmet; another glanced off his flak jacket; and the third penetrated his fatigue trousers near his crotch without touching him at all.[49]

One Marine, Private Lawrence Eads, proved the Marine slogan: "Every Marine a rifleman first." Eads was a company clerk with the combined action company. He manned the perimeter when the PF militia deserted and positioned himself forward on the parapet with a .30 caliber machine gun. As the enemy charged, he blasted back. One witness marveled, "I thought sure he'd be hit. He was silhouetted against a burning building. He stood right out there in the open and stacked the enemy on the wires." Eads eventually fired some 3,500 rounds—that's how intense the fighting was. He was later awarded the Navy Cross.[50]

The battle raged across Cam Lo compound with the disorder and clamor of combat. The rockets and noise was deafening. Mortars and small arms roared through the night. Several Marines, a couple of them NCOs, took the initiative and intuitively knew what to do—through training, experience, or just sheer luck. Corporal Maxam, whose story comes later, was one of them. Corporal Timothy Russell, Maxam's counterpart as the other squad leader, was seriously wounded early on; but despite his wounds, he led his squad of a dozen Marines in fighting off several determined attacks on the eastern wall of the compound where enemy soldiers had actually crossed through the wire obstacles and were approaching the parapet. Russell refused medical treatment when offered and "led his men in a tenacious counterattack that forced the NVA to withdraw." For his great courage, daring, and leadership that night at Cam Lo, he was awarded the Navy Cross.[51]

The first major attack was repulsed with heavy enemy losses. Despite the chaos of the fierce battle, Captain McMaken and John Cleary were able to coordinate reinforcements from nearby FSBs and other elements. At about 0430, Colonel R. B. Smith, commander of the 9th Marines, organized and dispatched a relief column from C–3 of two platoons of F Company, 2/9 supported by two M–50 "Ontos" (self-propelled, light-armored antitank vehicles) which had six 106 mm recoilless rifles mounted topside.

In addition, three tanks, probably M–48 Patton tanks that were already near Cam Lo village, began to converge on the Cam Lo district HQ. Then a third element, A Company of the besieged Marines' own 1/4 Marines at their base of C–2, formed up and began a rapid dismounted march of several kilometers to rescue their comrades.[52]

The fire and battle raged so ferociously across the compound fort that it seems miraculous that anyone at all survived the fight. PFC Bill Flannery from Pennsylvania, the squad Radio Telephone Operator (RTO), moved to various positions along the perimeter wall carrying the squad radio on his back. The PRC–25 radio was a solid, flat device the size of a small backpack with its ungainly antenna, bouncing and bobbing about, providing direct communication with the COC. As Flannery moved, a round struck the radio, spinning him around. Just then, a second round hit the radio in nearly the same place, spinning him, just in time for a third round to smash into the radio. By now, he had spun completely around. He would not really understand what happened until he examined the radio later; but he instantly discarded the ruined equipment and continued to fight.[53]

* * *

As these examples show, there were many acts of valor, great initiative, and superior leadership at the small compound of Cam Lo during a hellacious five-hour battle. The most significant, daring, and reckless but also the most effective act of heroism and valor that night was performed by Corporal Maxam.

Maxam was initially in the northwest corner with his squad when the main attack commenced. Shortly after as the attack intensified, the PF scattered, leaving much of the northeast corner and perimeter wall undefended.[54]

Corporal Maxam saw a second major attack forming near the abandoned northeast corner by some two hundred enemy; this was the final and main attack that night that could overwhelm the weakened northeast perimeter. His official award nomination stated: "Corporal Maxam took stock of the situation and realized that it was extremely desperate. He then unhesitatingly turned his fire team over to his automatic rifleman, picked up his own rifle, and began sprinting across the back of his line, over to the abandoned section of the perimeter. From the moment he exposed himself and started his run, he became the target of every enemy soldier." He was hit by shrapnel fragments from grenades and RGPs, but dodged past the tower from which Resinger was firing his grenade launcher and reached the abandoned machine-gun position. Maxam manned a World War II-era Browning, belt-fed, air-cooled, .30 caliber machine gun; the position was ideally situated at the corner of the two perimeter lines, where it had fields of fire for both the north and east FPL, exactly where the enemy was preparing to attack.[55]

The human wave of NVA and VC came on.

"Realizing that he was their only remaining threat on the otherwise completely abandoned line," the official citation stated, "the advancing NVA poured all of their fire into his position." A well-placed RPG round made a direct hit against his sandbag wall. He was thrown back by the blast and severely wounded. Witnesses said that Maxam recovered after a few moments but was holding his face; later, it was noted that his right eye had been basically torn from its socket by the blast.[56]

Maxam returned to the Browning and continued his devastating fire as the enemy regrouped and attacked again. Maxam fired belt after belt of ammunition. At times, he had to stop and reload. By this time, his protective wall was in shambles, and he was exposed to the enemy. The flares, tracers, and night bursts outlined and silhouetted both Maxam and the attackers.[57]

"Very soon he was hit again, this time by small arms fire. He hunched himself up over his [machine] gun and continued to fire," a witness later explained. In great pain from his several wounds, dazed and weakened by the loss of blood, Maxam fired, reloaded, and fired again, holding back the North Vietnamese regulars who at times were only yards from him. "From a nearby woodline RPGs and recoilless fire was directed at him in a frantic effort to silence his devastating [machine] gun." Twice more Maxam was hit; now with five or more wounds, and "too weak to reload [the machine gun], he managed to pick up his rifle and slide off the machine gun into a prone position, from which he continued to fire his M–16."[58]

Dawn came that morning around 0550. Corporal Maxam, who had sustained several severe wounds, was literally propped up by his rifle and sight mount. Finally, he "fell to the ground and very shortly thereafter he succumbed to his wounds." The Medal of Honor recommendation stated: "No less than forty-five enemy bodies were piled up in front of his position, and numerous others were lying in the wire down the length of his FPL." His comrades in the light of day saw the marks of perhaps dozens of other wounded or dead who had been dragged back to the jungle line.[59] The relief element columns began to arrive as the impetus of the enemy attack wavered. Then the NVA began to withdraw, their hope of overrun Cam Lo gone.

The final testimony of the valor of Larry Maxam came from his commanding officer who stated, "All of those who observed Corporal Maxam's sacrifice that night are convinced that his actions, above and beyond the call of duty, salvaged what would have otherwise been disaster."[61]

* * *

The battle at Cam Lo was a grisly affair. The official records state that some 144 enemy were confirmed killed; 100 enemy wounded were taken prisoner and many weapons recovered. The American forces lost seven killed and fourteen wounded.[62] Not only were many individuals cited for bravery, but the Presidential Unit Citation was awarded to the Marine units involved.[63]

During the action, Bill Flannery killed an enemy NVA soldier and later found a flag that the NVA had intended to hoist over

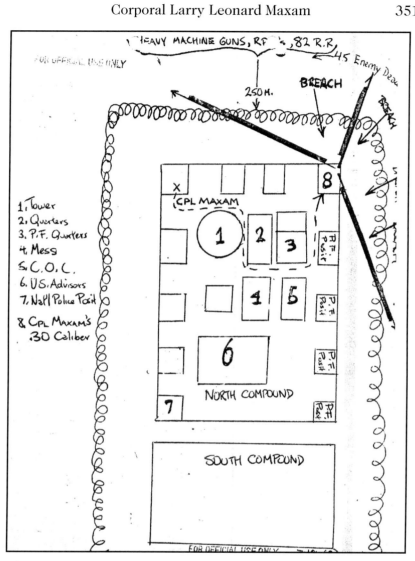

Sketch included in the Medal of Honor nomination packet of the action at Cam Lo, depicting the second attack at about 0315, and Maxam's actions.[60]

Cam Lo once it fell. Bill and others took a photo holding the flag as a grim trophy of war. Years later, Bill Flannery had the hand-written Vietnamese inscriptions on the flag translated. They recorded the locations and time when the 320th Division acquired goods, ammunition, and provisions along the Ho Chi Minh Trail.

Bill Flannery owns the flag to this day.[64] Two wounded Marines, Corporal Tim Russell and Lance Corporal Don Jakovac, rode the deuce and a-half truck that carried the wounded and dead to the field hospital. It was Tim who asked Don to crawl past the dying enemy soldier to cover Maxam with his poncho. Jakovac returned a moment later and sat back down with Russell. As they bounced along the dirt road, the enemy soldier died near them.[65]

The American and South Vietnamese forces thoroughly repelled the Tet Offensive, killing thousands and regaining all the cities, hamlets, and strongholds. Yet Tet was a political defeat exacerbated by media and other commentators who had lost their will and were convinced that the war was not winnable. Their position turned out to be persuasive on the national and world scene. Four years later in 1972, the combined forces of the local Viet Cong and NVA attempted another large-scale operation called the Easter Offensive. It, too, was defeated with overwhelming loses inflicted on the Communist troops. This final failure and the continued bombing of North Vietnam finally convinced the Communist regime to seek a negotiated peace, which occurred in January 1973. American forces had all but pulled out by then.

Two years later in 1975 after the U.S. Congress had failed to support the Republic of South Vietnam as promised, the weak and inferior ARVN crumbled under a major onslaught by NVA and Viet Cong forces. In April 1975, Saigon fell and tens of thousands of Vietnamese tried to flee. Some succeeded, most did not.

* * *

Corporal Larry Maxam's remains were buried in the National Military Cemetery of the Pacific, commonly called the "Punch Bowl," in Hawaii. In 1968, Alice Maxam and her two surviving children, Robin and Linda, moved to Australia. Alice was not about to allow another son die in Vietnam, so they moved as far away from the United States as possible. The family returned to the United States in 1969 for the ceremony awarding her heroic son the Medal of Honor. Alice passed away in September 2008.[66]

Perhaps one of the finest epitaphs for Corporal Larry Maxam came from his younger brother Robin Maxam, some forty years later: "Although Larry was lionhearted, he was neither tall nor imposing on the outside. His imposing nature (and worth) only became apparent when you got to know him—particularly if the going had got tough."[67]

More than forty years after Corporal Maxam died and was awarded the Medal of Honor, his home town of Burbank, California, named one of its city parks in his honor. On April 17, 2010, several hundred people gathered, including Linda and Robin Maxam from Australia and Marines from Camp Pendleton. The Marine Corps Air Ground Combat Center Band played martial music and rendered a formal salute. Several members of Delta Company, older Marines now, also gathered. Their presence was one the highlights of the day.

LARRY LEONARD MAXAM

Rank and organization: Corporal, U.S. Marine Corps, Company D, 1st Battalion, 4th Marines, 3d Marine Division (Rein), FMF. Place and Date: Cam Lo District, Quang Tri province, Republic of Vietnam, February 2, 1968. Entered service at: Los Angeles, Calif. Born: January 9, 1948, Glendale, Calif. Died: February 2, 1968, Vietnam.

Citation

For conspicuous gallantry and intrepidity at the risk of his life above and beyond the call of duty while serving as a fire team leader with Company D. The Cam Lo District Headquarters came under extremely heavy rocket, artillery, mortar, and recoilless rifle fire from a numerically superior enemy force, destroying a portion of the defensive perimeter. Cpl. Maxam, observing the enemy massing for an assault into the compound across the remaining defensive wire, instructed his assistant fire team leader to take charge of the fire team, and unhesitatingly proceeded to the weakened section of the perimeter. Completely exposed to the concentrated enemy fire, he sustained multiple fragmentation wounds from exploding grenades as he ran to an abandoned machine-gun position. Reaching the emplacement, he grasped the machine gun and commenced to deliver effective fire on the advancing enemy. As the enemy directed maximum firepower against the determined

Marine, Cpl. Maxam's position received a direct hit from a rocket-propelled grenade, knocking him backwards and inflicting severe fragmentation wounds to his face and right eye. Although momentarily stunned and in intense pain, Cpl. Maxam courageously resumed his firing position and subsequently was struck again by small-arms fire. With resolute determination, he gallantly continued to deliver intense machine gun fire, causing the enemy to retreat through the defensive wire to positions of cover. In a desperate attempt to silence his weapon, the North Vietnamese threw hand grenades and directed recoilless rifle fire against him, inflicting two additional wounds. Too weak to reload his machine gun, Cpl. Maxam fell to a prone position and valiantly continued to deliver effective fire with his rifle. After 1 & 1/2 hours, during which he was hit repeatedly by fragments from exploding grenades and concentrated small-arms fire, he succumbed to his wounds, having successfully defended nearly half of the perimeter single-handedly. Cpl. Maxam's aggressive fighting spirit, inspiring valor and selfless devotion to duty reflected great credit upon himself and the Marine Corps and upheld the highest traditions of the U.S. Naval Service. He gallantly gave his life for his country.

Notes

1. Phillip B. Davidson, *Vietnam at War: The History, 1946–1975*, 483–88.
2. Donald Jakovac, "Personal Account of the Battle at Cam Lo," 2.
3. Ibid.
4. Larry L. Maxam, "AWARD RECOMMENDATION, NAVPERS 1650/3," Official Records, National Personnel Records Medals Section, St. Louis, Mo; hereafter Maxam Official Records.
5. Michael O. Stick, Statement, attached to "AWARD RECOMMENDATION, NAVPERS 1650/3," Maxam Official Records.

6. Nathaniel Moss, Statement, attached to "AWARD RECOM-MENDATION, NAVPERS 1650/3," Maxam Official Records.

7. Robin Maxam, email to Sherman Fleek, August 29, 2009.

8. Larry L. Maxam, LDS Church Records, file number 537476, photocopy in my possession.

9. Robin Maxam, Letter to Sherman Fleek, July 25, 2009.

10. Ibid.

11. Steve Flinders, email to Sherman Fleek, August 17, 2009; Paul Winn, emailto Sherman Fleek, April 22, 2010.

12. Robin Maxam, Letter to Sherman Fleek, July 25, 2009.

13. Biographical Data, n.d. Maxam Official Records.

14. Ibid.

15. Larry Maxam, Letter to Bessie Maxam, April 5, 1967; Maxam Family Collection.

16. Ibid.

17. Richard W. Stewart, ed., *The United States Army in a Global Era, 1917–2003*, Vol. 2 of AMERICAN MILITARY HISTORY, 305–6.

18. Ibid., 327.

19. USMC Rifle Company, U.S. Marine Corps, website based in the United Kingdom, http://www.eleven-bravo.co.uk/the-war/organisation/usmc-rifle-cpy.php (accessed September 13, 2009).

20. Larry Maxam, Letter to Alice Maxam, August 23, 1967, Maxam Family Collection.

21. Ibid.

22. Ibid.

23. Larry Maxam, Letter to Alice Maxam, August 23, 1967, Maxam Family Collection. If Maxam received a Purple Heart for this action in August 1967, his official records do not note it. He was, however, officially awarded the Purple Heart for the same action on February 2, 1968.

24. Harold Posner, email to Sherman Fleek, July 3, 2009.

25. Ibid.

26. Sherman L. Fleek, Notes, April 17, 2010, Maxam Park Dedication, Burbank, California.

27. Harold Posner to Sherman Fleek, email letter, July 3, 2009; copy on file.

28. Ibid.

29. Donald Jakovac, telephone interview, July 2, 2009, by Sherman Fleek; notes in my possession.

30. Larry Maxam, Letter to Alice Maxam, January 1968, Maxam Family Collection.

31. James P. Coan, "Tet Attack at Cam Lo," *Vietnam*, February 2004, 34.

32. Davidson, *Vietnam at War*, 474.

33. Coan, "Tet Attack at Cam Lo," 36.

34. Millet and Maslowski, *For the Common Defense: A Military History of the United States of the America*, 588.

35. Edward M. Spiers, *The Scottish Soldier and Empire, 1854–1902*, 41.

36. "Others Recommended for the Same Action," Maxam Official Records.

37. Coan, "Tet Attack at Cam Lo," 34.

38. Ibid.

39. Ibid., 40.

40. Ibid., 36.

41. Ibid., 35. The 320th Division was the principal Vietnamese unit that had defeated the French at Dien Bein Phu in 1954. This defeat forced France to leave Vietnam.

42. Ibid., 36–37.

43. Ibid., 40.

44. Ibid., 38.

45. Enclosure 1, Medal of Honor Recommendation, February 15, 1968, Maxam Official Records.

46. Coan, "Tet Attack at Cam Lo," 37.

47. Jakovac, "Personal Account of the Battle at Cam Lo," 2.

48. Coan, "Tet Attack at Cam Lo," 38.

49. Fleek, Notes, April 17, 2010, Maxam Park Dedication.

50. Coan, "Tet Attack at Cam Lo," 40.

51. Ibid.

52. Ibid., 39.

53. Fleek, Notes, April 17, 2010, Maxam Park Dedication.

54. Enclosure 1, Medal of Honor Recommendation, February 15, 1968, Maxam Official Records.

55. Ibid.

56. Ibid.

57. Ibid.

58. Ibid.

59. Ibid.

60. Ibid.

61. Ibid.

62. Ibid.

63. Coan, "Tet Attack at Cam Lo," 40.

64. Fleek, Notes, April 17, 2010, Maxam Park Dedication.

65. Jakovac, telephone interview, July 2, 2009, by Fleek; Jakovac, "Personal Account of the Battle at Cam Lo," 2.

66. Robin Maxam, email to Sherman Fleek, September 27, 2009.

67. Ibid.

Glossary

ACS   Air Command Squadron: An U.S. Army Air Forces unit that acts as a headquarters for larger units.

AEF   American Expeditionary Force.

AGL   Above Ground Level: altitude above the ground.

AGOS   Air Ground Operation Support: non-aircrew support units or missions.

AOR   Area of Responsibility: usually a geographical area, or a task, for which a commander and unit are responsible.

ARVN   Army of the Republic of Vietnam (South Vietnamese Army).

Battalion   An organization of several companies in the Army or Marine Corps commanded normally by a lieutenant colonel (a major during World War I) of some 800–1,200 men.

Brigade   A large ground unit consisting of two or more regiments, commanded by a brigadier general (one star), especially during World War I.

CAP   Combined Action Program: A U.S. Marine program in Vietnam that provided civil affairs and civil works projects and programs.
— Combat Air Patrol.

CAS   Close Air Support: fighters or bombers which fly in support of ground units.

Charlie   A term for the enemy during the Vietnam War, applied to both Vietcong and North Vietnam regulars.

CIDG   Civilian Irregular Defense Group: A designation of paramilitary or civilian defense forces.

Company   An Army or Marine unit of some 150–200 commanded by a captain depending on type and also the war.

Corps   A larger tactical unit above division, commanded by a lieutenant general.

CTZ   Corps Tactical Zone: the area of responsibility at the corps level, the tactical unit above a division.

Division   An large Army or Marine organization commanded by a major general (two star) that could have as many as 25,000 men depending on the era and theater of war. It is a numbered tactical unit of either draftee, regular, or National Guard soldiers and origin.

             A large aviation unit comprised of wings, groups, and squadrons during World War II commanded by a general.

DMZ   De-Militarized Zone: a buffer zone that both North and South Vietnam accepted after the defeat and withdrawal of the French in 1954.

ESB   Engineer Special Brigade: A special engineer unit, trained and equipped for seaborne and shore support, building docks, harbors, and marshalling landing craft.

ETO   European Theater of Operation: The area of operations for Europe.

FAC   Forward Air Controller: An Air Force officer, either airborne or on the ground, who coordinates close air in support of ground units.

FEBA   Forward Edge of the Battle Area: The area where opposing
           forces meet on the battlefield.

Flak   German antiaircraft fire, short for *Flugzeugabwehrkanone*.

FNG   A slang term used during the Vietnam War for new soldiers
           or Marines who join a unit: "f- - - - - new guy."

FPF   Final protective fire.

FPL   Final protective line.

FSB   Forward Support Base: An outpost during the Vietnam
           War that supported tactical bases in the forward areas.

Group   An air unit commanded by a colonel of three or four squad-
           rons, consisting of some forty or fifty aircraft.

HE   High Explosive

Jägdflieger   German pursuit or fighter pilot.

KIA   Killed in Action.

LCI   Landing Craft Infantry.

LCVP   Landing Craft Vehicle Personnel, or "Higgins boat."

LD   Line of Departure: The control measure on a map and
           boundary related to position and time where a tactical unit
           crosses in order to attack or conduct an offensive operation.

LST   Landing Ship Tank: A large landing ship designed to carry
           heavy equipment, especially tanks and a large number of
           troops.

LZ   Landing Zone: A tactical area where airborne troops land.

M.A.S.H.   Mobile Army Surgical Hospital.

MACV   Military Assistance Command Vietnam: The United States
           armed forces command that oversaw the tactical and opera-
           tional command of all American forces in Vietnam.

MIA	Missing in Action
MSL	Mean Sea Level: altitude measured from sea level.
NCO	Noncommissioned officer, corporal, or sergeant.
NCOIC	Noncommissioned officer-in-charge.
NVA	North Vietnamese Army.
PF	Popular Forces: A para-military or Vietnamese reserve structure consisting of local volunteers who are not part of the national army.
PFC	Private First Class.
PSP	Pierced Steel Planking.
RAF	Royal Air Force.
ROK	Republic of Korea (South Korea).
RPG	Rocket-propelled grenade.
SERE	Survival, Evasion, Resistance, Escape.
Snafu	A slang expression created by American service-members during World War II; "Situation normal: all f----- up."
Squadron	An air unit of bombers or fighters, normally commanded by a major or captain with some twelve aircraft and ground support personnel.
UCMJ	Uniform Code of Military Justice.
VAC	V Amphibious Corps.
VC	Viet Cong: Well organized and trained Communist guerillas who are not part of the North Vietnamese Army; those Communist forces usually found in the central and southern part of Vietnam.
WIA	Wounded in Action.

Bibliography

Archives

Perry Special Collections. L. Tom Perry Special Collections and Manuscripts Division, Harold B. Lee Library, Brigham Young University, Provo, Utah.

Utah Historical Society. Salt Lake City, Utah.

Idaho Military Museum, Boise, Idaho.

Idaho State Historical Society, Boise, Idaho.

Sources Cited

"After Action Report: The Battle for A Shau." Extract from Enclosure 15, Section 2, Operational Report on Lessons Learned. Headquarters, 5th Special Forces Group, April 30, 1966.

Ambrose, Stephen E. *D-Day, June 6, 1944: The Climactic Battle of World War II.* New York: Touchstone Books, 1994.

Anderson, Charles R. *Leyte.* Washington, D.C.: U.S. Army Center of Military History, 1992.

Armstrong, Richard. "It's Great to Be Alive." *Saturday Evening Post*, June 6, 1966, 21.

"Army Medical Aidman from Idaho Awarded Medal of Honor." Press release No. 595-53, June 1953. Department of Defense, Office of Public Information.

"Army Honors ANL-W Retiree for Gallantry." *Argonne Week*, May 1, 1995. Newspaper clipping, Bleak Collection.

Arrington, Leonard J. "Launching Idaho's Sugar Beet Industry." *Idaho's Yesterdays*, Fall 1965, 17–28.

Bamford, Hal. "Last Mission for the Bertie Lee." *The Airman*, May 1960, 19–20.

Bennion Family Papers, 1842–1960. Utah State Historical Society, Salt Lake City.

Bennion, Howard S. "Mervyn Sharp Bennion, One of the Lord's Noblemen." n.d. Perry Special Collections.

Bennion, Mervyn Sharp. Official Files. Biographical Summary. Utah State Historical Society.

Bleak, David Bruce. Collection, Idaho Military Museum, Boise.

Bleak, David. LDS baptism and membership ordinance record. LDS Family History Library, Salt Lake City, Utah.

Bleak, David. Oral History, August 26, 2005. Interviewed by Ronald Still, U.S. Army Medical Command History Office, Fort Sam Houston, Texas. Photocopy in my possession.

Boot, Max. *War Made New: Weapons, Warriors, and the Making of the Modern World*. New York: Penguin, 2006.

Bottcher, Walter R. United Press. "Idaho's World War Hero, Eking Out Existence on WPA, Returns Congressional Medal of Honor to Congress," April 10, 1939. Photocopy in my possession.

Bowman, Martin. *B–17 Flying Fortress Units of the Eighth Air Force (Part 1)*. New York: Osprey Publishing, 2000.

Brittle, Andrew J. *Years of Stalemate: July 1951–July 1953*. Washington D.C.: U.S. Army Center of Military History, 2000.

Brostrom, PFC Leonard Carl. Memorial Program. November 29, 1945. Special Collections, David O. McKay Library, Brigham Young University-Idaho, Rexburg, Idaho.

Brostom, Leonard C., Private. Website of the Department of the Navy, Naval Historical Center. www.history.navy.mil/danfs/p12/private_leonard_c_brostrom. htm (accessed January 1, 2010).

Cannon, H. Hamlin. *Leyte: The Return to the Philippines*. THE U.S. ARMY IN WORLD WAR II. 1954; rpt., Washington, D.C.: U.S. Army Center of Military History, 1987.

Clarke, Jeffrey J. *Southern France*. Washington D.C.: U.S. Army Center of Military History, 2000.

Coakley, Robert W., and Richard M. Leighton, *Global Logistics and Strategy, 1943–1945: United States Army in World War I*. Washington D.C.: Office of the Chief of Military History, 1968.

Coan, James P. "Tet Attack at Cam Lo." *Vietnam*, February 2004, 34–40.

Collier, Peter. *Medal of Honor: Portraits of Valor beyond the Call of Duty*. New York: Artisan, 2006.

Cooke, James J. *The Rainbow Division in the Great War*. London, Conn.: Praeger, 1994.

Davidson, Phillip B. *Vietnam at War: The History, 1946–1975*. New York: Oxford University Press, 1988.

Davis, Colonel E. G., Office of the Chief of Staff, Department of War. Letter to J. C. Neibaur, November 20, 1918. Copy at Idaho State Historical Society, Boise.

Davis, Richard G. *Bombing the European Axis Powers: A Historical Digest of the Combined Bomber Offensive 1939–1945*. Maxwell Air Force Base, Ala.: Air University Press, 2006.

Doubler, Michael. *I Am the Guard: A History of the Army National Guard, 1636–2000*. Washington, D.C.: Government Printing Office, 2001.

Drea, Edward J. *New Guinea: The U.S. Army Campaigns of World War II*. Washington D.C.: US Army Center of Military History, 1993.

Eisenhower, John S. D. *Intervention: The United States and the Mexican Revolution, 1913–1917*. New York: W. W. Norton, 1993.

Eisenhower, John S. D. *Yanks: The Epic Story of the American Army in World War I*. New York: Free Press, 2001.

Fehrenbach, T. R. *This Kind of War*. 1964; rpt., Leavenworth, Kans.: U.S. Army Command and General Staff College, 1994.

Fisher, Bernard, and Jerry Borrowman, *Beyond the Call of Duty: The Story of an American Hero in Vietnam*. Salt Lake City: Shadow Mountain Press, an imprint of Deseret Book, 2004.

Fisher, Vardis. "Roses, Roses all the Way," *[Boise] Idaho Statesman*, January 4, 1943.

Fleek, Sherman L. Notes, April 17, 2010. Maxam Park Dedication, Burbank, California.

Fleek, Sherman L. *Place the Headstones Where They Belong: Thomas Neibaur, WWI Soldier*. Logan: Utah State University Press, 2008.

Francillon, René J. *McDonnell Douglas Aircraft since 1920*. London: Putnam, 1979.

Freeman, Robert C., and Dennis A. Wright. *Saints at War: Experiences of Latter-day Saints in World War II*. American Fork, Utah: Covenant Communications, 2001.

Freeman, Roger A. *The Mighty Eighth: Units, Men and Machines*. New York: Doubleday, 1970.

Freeman, Roger A. *The Mighty Eighth War Diary*. New York: Doubleday, 1981.

Frisbee, John L. "Gauntlet of Fire." *Air Force Magazine* 69, no. 9 (September 1985).

Gailey, Harry A. *MacArthur's Victory: The War in New Guinea, 1943–1944*. New York: Presidio Books, 1944.

Garand, George W., and Truman R. Strobridge. *History of the U.S. Marine Corps Operations in World War II: Western Pacific Operations, Vol. 4*. Washington D.C.: Government Printing Office, 1970.

Gates, Susa Young. "Alexander Neibaur." *Utah Genealogical and Historical Magazine* 91 (April 1914): 52–62.

Gilbert, Martin. *The First World War*. New York: Henry Holt and Company, 1994.

Godfrey, Matthew C. "Charles W. Nibley, 1907–1925." *Presiding Bishops*. Compiled by Michael W. Winder. Salt Lake City: Eborn, 2003.

Gunston, Bill. *Aircraft of World War 2*. New York: Crescent Books, 1992.

Hegeth, Dana. "Medal of Honor Is Bittersweet, Soldier Says." *Washington Post*, September 16, 2010, A–4.

Hill, Jim Dan. *The Minute Man at War and Peace: A History of the National Guard*. Harrisburg, Pa.: Stackpole Books, 1964.

Hogg, Ian V. *Antiaircraft Artillery*. New York: Crowood Press, 2002.

Hogg, Ian V. *German Artillery of World War Two*. Mechanicsville, Pa.: Stackpole Books, 1997.

Hopper, James. *Medals of Honor*. New York: John Day, 1929.

"Idaho Hero Comes from Fighting Family." *Salt Lake Tribune*, July 3, 1953, 6.

"J. Reuben Clark Jr. and Limited Government." Sutherland Institute, December 13, 2007. http://www.sutherlandinstitute.org/uploads/reubenclark.pdf (accessed December 4, 2009).

Johnsen, Frederick A. *B–17 Flying Fortress: The Symbol of Second World War Air Power*. New York: McGraw Hill, 2004.

Jakovac, Donald. "Personal Account of the Battle at Cam Lo." Email to Sherman L. Fleek, August 2009. Printout in my possession.

Jakovac, Donald. Telephone interview by Sherman Fleek, July 2, 2009. Notes in my possession.

Keegan, John. *The First World War*. New York: Alfred A. Knopf, 1999.

Keegan, John. *The Second World War*. New York: Viking, 1990.

Koscino, Arthur. Interviewed by Sherman Fleek, July 14, 2009. Notes in my possession.

LDS General Conference Report, April 1946.

Livesey, Anthony. *The Historical Atlas of World War I*. New York: Henry Holt, 1994.

Lowe, Julian C., and Florian H. Thayn. "History of the Mormons of the Greater Washington Area." 1991. Unpublished manuscript.

MacArthur, Douglas. *Reminiscences: General of the Army Douglas MacArthur*. New York: McGraw Hill, 1964.

"MacArthur's Amphibs." *The Military Engineer* 36, no. 223 (May 1944): 142–50.

MacGarrigle, George L. *Aleutian Islands*, Washington, D.C.: U.S. Army Center of Military History, 1992.

Malkasian, Carter. *The Korean War: 1950–1953*. New York: Osprey Publishing, 2001.

Manchester, William. *American Caesar: Douglas MacArthur 1880–1964*. New York: Random House, 1978.

Marshall, S. L. A. *World War I*. Boston: Houghton Mifflin, 1964.

Maxam, Larry L. Maxam Family Collection. Photocopies in my possession.

—Larry Maxam, Letters to Alice Maxam, August 23, 1967, January 1968.

—Larry Maxam. Letter to Bessie Maxam, April 5, 1967.

Maxam, Larry L. Maxam Official Records. National Personnel Records Medals Section. St. Louis, Mo.

—"AWARD RECOMMENDATION, NAVPERS 1650/3," February 2–3, 1968.

—Biographical Data, n.d.

—Nathaniel   Moss,   Statement,   attached   to   "AWARD RECOMMENDATION, NAVPERS 1650/3," February 2–3, 1968.

"Others Recommended for the Same Action," February 2–3, 1968.

—Michael   O.   Stick,   Statement,   attached   to   "AWARD RECOMMENDATION, NAVPERS 1650/3," February 2–3, 1968.

McLeod, John. "Bravery and Death on Scarlet Beach," *Yank Magazine: The Army Weekly*, December 31, 1943, 1-2.

Michael, Edward. "A Tale of Two Missions." Typescript, n.d. Louise Michael Collection.

Michael, Edward. "Lt. Michael's Own Story." Typescript, n.d. Louise Michael Collection.

Michael, Louise. Telephone interview by Sherman Fleek, September 19, 2009. Notes in my possession.

Michael, Louise Collection. Personal records. Official Military Records of Edward Michael. Photocopies in my possession courtesy Louise Michael.

Miller, John. *Cartwheel: The Reduction of Rabaul*. In THE UNITED STATES ARMY IN WORLD WAR II. Washington, D.C.: Chief of Military History, 1959.

Millet, Alan R., and Peter Maslowski. *For the Common Defense: A Military History of the United States of America*. New York: Free Press, 1995.

Morton, Louis. *The War in the Pacific, Strategy and Command: The First Two Years*. The United States Army in World War II. Washington D.C.: Office of Chief of Military History, 1960.

Naval Historical Center. USS *St. Louis*, 1906. www.history.navy.mil/danfs/s17/st_louis-iv.htm (accessed December 10, 2009).

Neibaur, Alexander. Journal, February 5, 1841–March 20, 1848. Perry Special Collections.

"Neibaur Day Was a Big Success." *Rexburg [Idaho] Journal*, May 30, 1919.

Neibaur Family Genealogical Records. LDS Family History Library, Salt Lake City, Utah.

Neibaur, Thomas C. "How Private Neibaur Won the Congressional [sic] Medal of Honor." *Improvement Era*, July 1919, 782–90.

Neibaur, Thomas C. Letters and Papers. McKay Library Archives. Brigham Young University-Idaho, Rexburg, Idaho.

Newcomb, Robert F. *Iwo Jima*. New York: Holt, Rinehart and Winston, 1965.

Office of Assistant Secretary of Defense (Public Affairs). News Release: No. 465–99, October 5, 1999. Photocopy in my possession, courtesy of the Bernard Fisher family.

Parrish, Thomas, ed. *The Simon and Schuster Encyclopedia of World War II.* New York: Simon and Schuster, 1978.

Prange, Gordon W. *At Dawn We Slept: The Untold Story of Pearl Harbor.* New York: Penguin Books, 1981.

Prinalgin, [no first name]. Associated Press. "Korean War Medal of Honor Winner David Bleak," April 1995. Bleak Collection.

Quinn, D. Michael. *Elder Statesman: A Biography of J. Reuben Clark.* Salt Lake City: Signature Book, 2002.

Register of Graduates and Former Cadets, United States Military Academy. West Point, N.Y.: Association of Graduates, 2008.

Reilly, Henry J. *Americans All: The Rainbow at War, The Official History of the 42nd Division in the World War.* 2nd ed. Columbus, Ohio: F. J. Heer, 1936.

Report of the First Army, American Expeditionary Force: Organization and Operations. Fort Leavenworth, Kans.: General Service Schools Press, 1923.

Reports of General MacArthur: Japanese Operations in the Southwest Pacific Area. Publication 13–1, Vol. 2, Part 1, 1966. Rpt., Washington, D.C.: U.S. Army Center of Military History. 1994.

Rottman, Gordon. *US Marine Corps Pacific Theater of Operations 1944–45.* New York: Osprey Publishing, 2004.

Sams, Kenneth. "The Fall of A Shau." HQ Pacific Air Force, Contemporary Historical Examination of Current Operations (CHECO) History Project, April 18, 1966. Office of Air Force History, Maxwell Air Force Base, Montgomery, Alabama. Photocopy in my possession courtesy of the Fisher family.

Schlight, John. *The War in South Vietnam: The Years of the Offensive, 1965–1968.* Washington, D.C.: Office of the Air Force History, 1988.

Shawell, Julia. "Army Engineers Go to Sea," *Philadelphia Daily News,* May 19, 1944. Van Noy Family Collection.

Shinseki, Eric K., Secretary of Veterans Affairs. Address to Association of the United States Army, Army Medical Symposium, San Antonio, Texas, July 22, 2009. Photocopy in my possession.

Spiers, Edward M. *The Scottish Soldier and Empire, 1854–1902.* Edinburgh, Scotland: Edinburgh University Press, 2006.

Stewart, Richard W., ed. *The United States Army in a Global Era, 1917–2003*. Vol. 2 of American Military History. Washington, D.C.: U.S. Army Center of Military History, 2004.

Target: Germany. The Army Air Forces' Official Story of the VIII Bomber Command's First Year over Europe. New York: Simon and Schuster, 1943.

Toyn, Gary W. *The Quiet Hero: The Untold Medal of Honor Story of George E. Wahlen at the Battle of Iwo Jima*. Clearfield, Utah: American Legacy Media, 2006.

2006 Church Almanac. Salt Lake City: Deseret News Corp., 2005.

The United States Army in the World War 1917–1919: Military Operations of the American Expeditionary Forces, 17 vols. Washington, D.C.: Historical Division, Department of the Army, 1948.

United States Pacific Fleet and Pacific Ocean Areas. "Operation Detachment (Iwo Jima)," October 7, 1944, U.S. War Plans, 1939–1945. Malabar, Fla.: Krieger Publishing, 1972.

[Untitled article about David Bruce Bleak. No byline.] *Pass in Review: Idaho Military History Quarterly*, June 2007, 6–8.

[Untitled article about Leonard Bostrom. No byline.] *Pass in Review: Idaho Military History Quarterly*, June 2006, 6–8.

USMC Rifle Company. U.S. Marine Corps. Website based in the United Kingdom, http://www.eleven-bravo.co.uk/the-war/organisation/usmc-rifle-cpy.php (accessed September 13, 2009).

Vandiver, Frank E. *Black Jack: The Life and Times of John J. Pershing*. 2 vols. College Station: Texas A & M University Press, 1977.

Van Noy Family Collection. Special Collections, David O. McKay Library, Brigham Young University-Idaho, Rexburg, Idaho; Idaho State Military Museum in Boise, and the Saints at War Project. Perry Special Collections.

Wahlen, George. Oral History, October 30, 1996. Interviewed by Jan Herman. U.S. Navy Medical Corps History Office, Washington, D.C.

Wallin, Homer N., VADM USN. *Pearl Harbor: Why, How, Fleet Salvage and Final Appraisal*. Washington, D.C.: U.S. Government Printing Office, 1968.

Westberg, Lt. Franklin. Statement, June 5, 1944, Medal of Honor Nomination. In Edward Michael, Official Military Records.

Wheeler, Richard. *Iwo*. New York: Lippincott & Crowell, 1980.

Woods, Fred E. "The Life of Alexander Neibaur." *Mormon Historical Studies* 7, nos. 1–2 (Spring-Fall 2006): 23–36.

INDEX

Note: Makes and models of weapons are not indexed. For military units, see the individual country.

A

371

D

E

F

J

K

About the Author

Sherman L. Fleek is a retired US Army lieutenant colonel and serves as the Command Historian at the United States Military Academy at West Point, New York. He has several books and dozens of articles published on military, frontier army, Civil War, Mexican War, and Mormon military history including two historical novels based on the Mormon Battalion and the Army of the West. He previously served as command historian for Walter Reed Army Medical Center in Washington D.C, and his last assignment on active duty was Chief Historian, National Guard Bureau in Arlington, Virginia. His son, Hyrum H. Fleek, is a budding graphic artist who designed the awards and decorations for this book and also most of the maps.

Other Books by Sherman L. Fleek

History May be Searched in Vain:
A Military History of the Mormon Battalion, 2006

Place the Headstones where they Belong:
Thomas Neibaur, WWI Soldier, 2008

Called to War:
Dawn of the Mormon Battalion, 2010

War in the Far West:
The March of the Mormon Battalion, 2011

DECORATIONS OF MORMON MEDAL OF HONOR RECIPIENTS

PRIVATE
THOMAS C. NEIBAUR
U.S. ARMY

Medal of Honor

Purple Heart

WW1 Victory Medal

Légion d'honnuer
(France)

Croix de Guerre
(France)

Cross of War
"Merit of War"
(Italy)

Medal of Military
Bravery
(Montenegro)

CAPTAIN
MERVYN SHARP BENNION
U.S. NAVY

Medal of Honor   Purple Heart   Mexican Service Medal WW1 Victory Medal Nicaraguan Campaign Medal

American Defense Medal   American Campaign Medal   Asiatic-Pacific Campaign Medal   World War II Victory Medal

PRIVATE
NATHAN ("JUNIOR") K. VAN NOY
U.S. ARMY

Medal of Honor

Purple Heart

Good Conduct Medal

American Defense
Medal

American Campaign
Medal

Asiatic-Pacific
Campaign Medal

World War II Victory
Medal

LIEUTENANT COLONEL
EDWARD S. MICHAEL
U.S. ARMY / USAF

Medal of Honor Distinguished Purple Heart Air Medal Air Force
            Flying Cross   Commendation
                                                            Medal

Air Force
Outstanding Unit
Award

Good Conduct American Defense American Asiatic-Pacific
   Medal   Medal   Campaign Medal Campaign Medal

Command Pilot Badge
(US Air Force)

European-Africa- World War II National Defense
Mediterranean Victory Medal Service Medal
Campaign Medal

PRIVATE FIRST CLASS
LEONARD C. BROSTROM
U.S. ARMY

Medal of Honor

Purple Heart

American Defense
Medal

American Campaign
Medal

Asiatic-Pacific
Campaign Medal

World War II Victory
Medal

Major
George E. Wahlen
U.S. Navy / U.S. Army

| Medal of Honor | Purple Heart | Meritorious Service Medal | Good Conduct Medal | American Defense Medal |

| American Campaign Medal | Asiatic-Pacific Campaign Medal | World War II Victory Medal | National Defense Service Medal | Vietnam Service Medal |

Republic
of Vietnam
Campaign Medal
(Vietnamese)

Sergeant
David Bruce Bleak
U.S. Army

Medal of Honor

Purple Heart

Good Conduct Medal

National Defense
Service Medal

Korean Service Medal

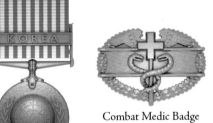

United Nations Korea
Service Medal

Combat Medic Badge

COLONEL
BERNARD FRANCIS FISHER
USAF

| Medal of Honor | Silver Star | Distinguished Flying Cross | Meritorious Service Medal | Air Medal |

| Air Force Commendation Medal | Air Force Combat Readiness Medal | American Defense Medal | American Campaign Medal | World War II Victory Medal |

| National Defense Service Medal | Armed Forces Expeditionary Medal | Vietnam Service Medal | Gallantry Cross (Vietnamese) | Republic of Vietnam Campaign Medal (Vietnamese) |

Command Pilot Badge
(US Air Force)

CORPORAL
LARRY LEONARD MAXAM,
USMC

Medal of Honor

Purple Heart

National Defense
Service Medal

Presidential Unit
Citation (Navy)

Vietnam Service Medal

Gallantry Cross
(Vietnamese)

Military Merit
(Vietnamese)

Republic of Vietnam
Campaign Medal
(Vietnamese)